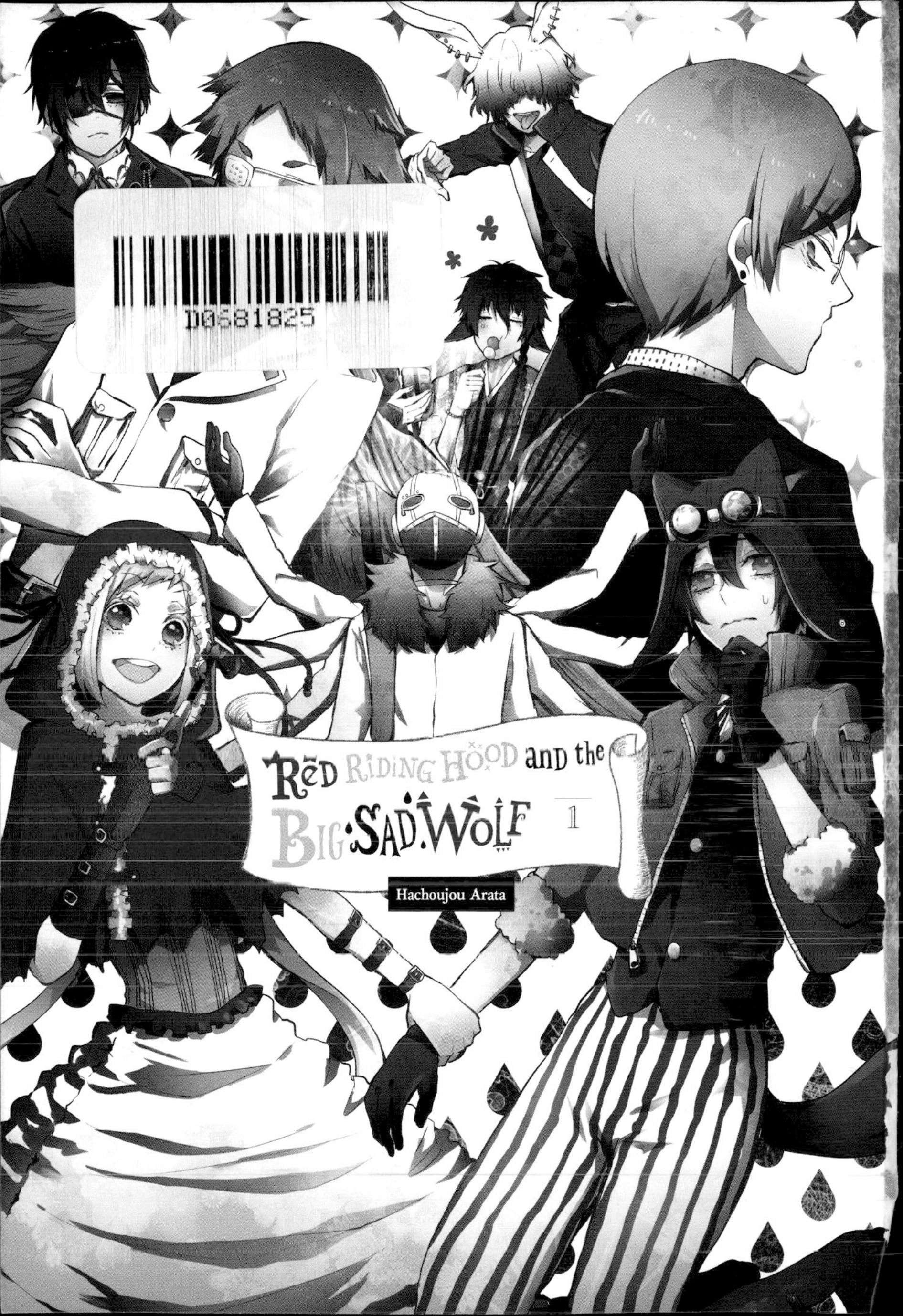
Red Riding Hood and the
Big Sad Wolf
1
Hachoujou Arata

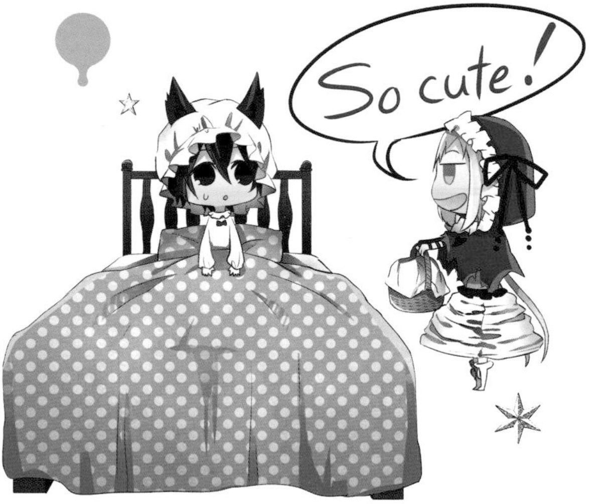
So cute!

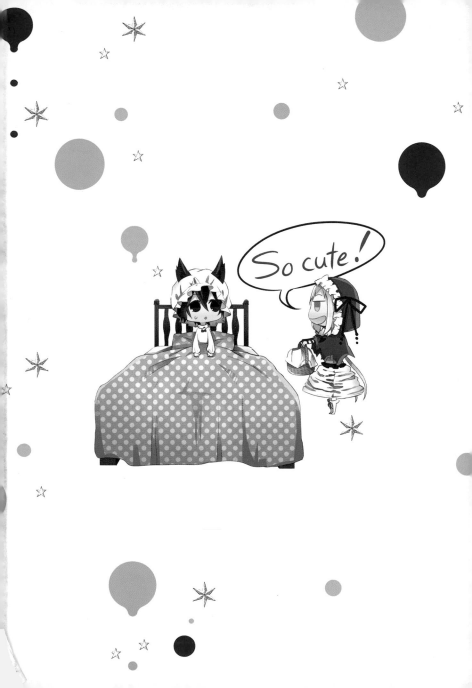

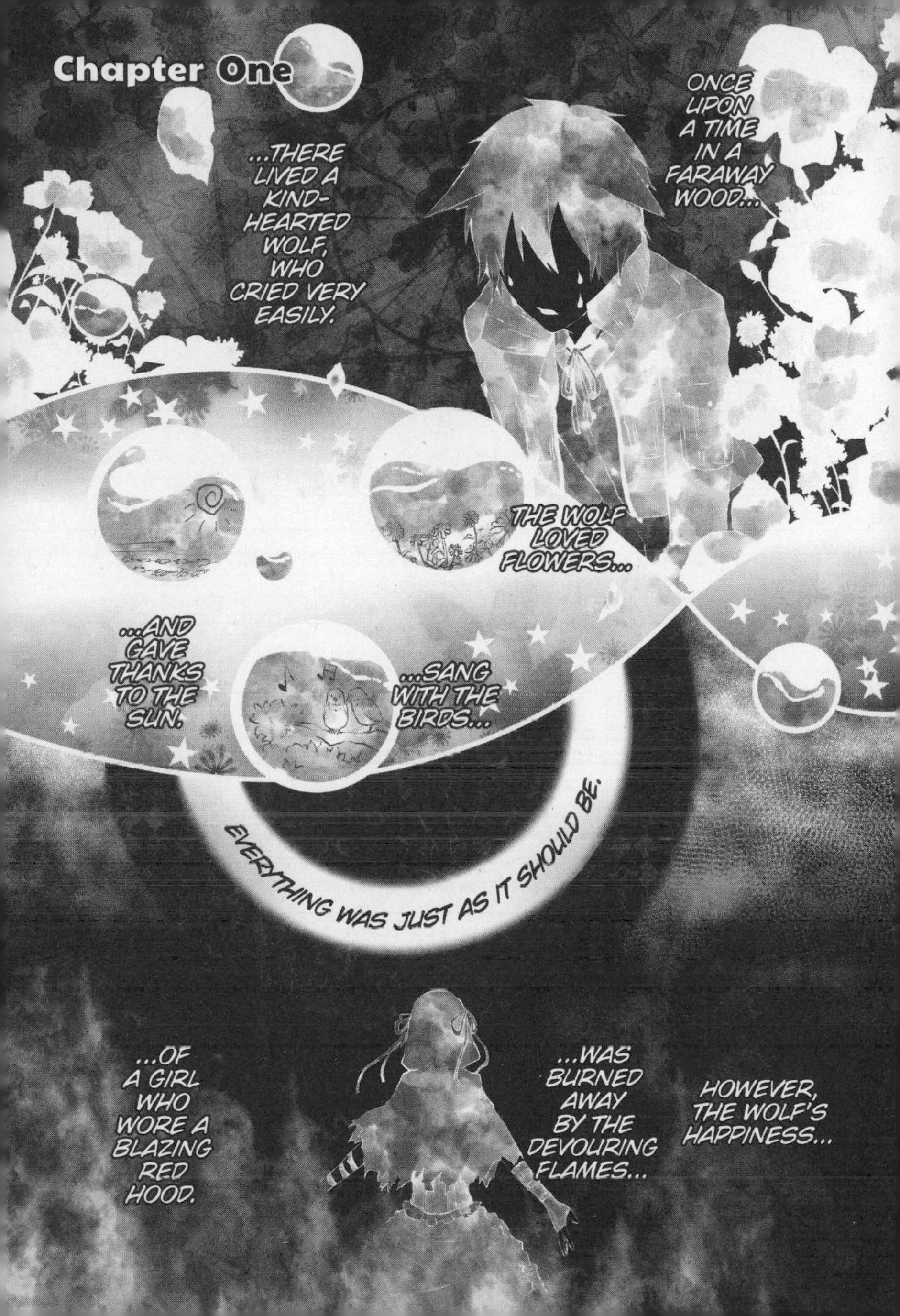
Chapter One
ONCE UPON A TIME IN A FARAWAY WOOD...
...THERE LIVED A KIND-HEARTED WOLF, WHO CRIED VERY EASILY.
THE WOLF LOVED FLOWERS...
...SANG WITH THE BIRDS...
...AND GAVE THANKS TO THE SUN.
EVERYTHING WAS JUST AS IT SHOULD BE.
HOWEVER, THE WOLF'S HAPPINESS...
...WAS BURNED AWAY BY THE DEVOURING FLAMES...
...OF A GIRL WHO WORE A BLAZING RED HOOD.

RED RIDING HOOD and the BIG SAD WOLF

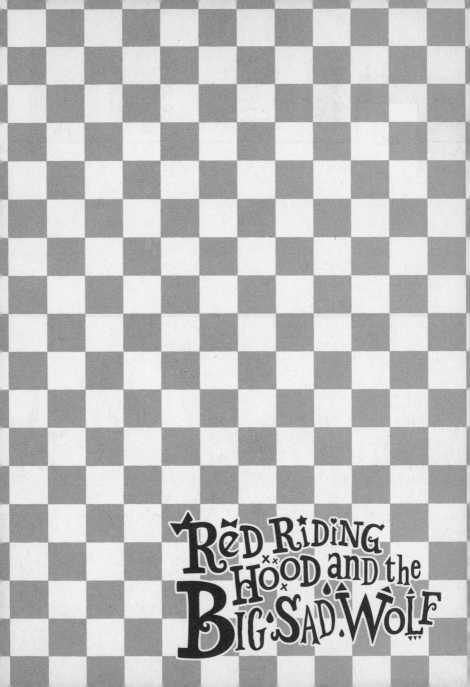

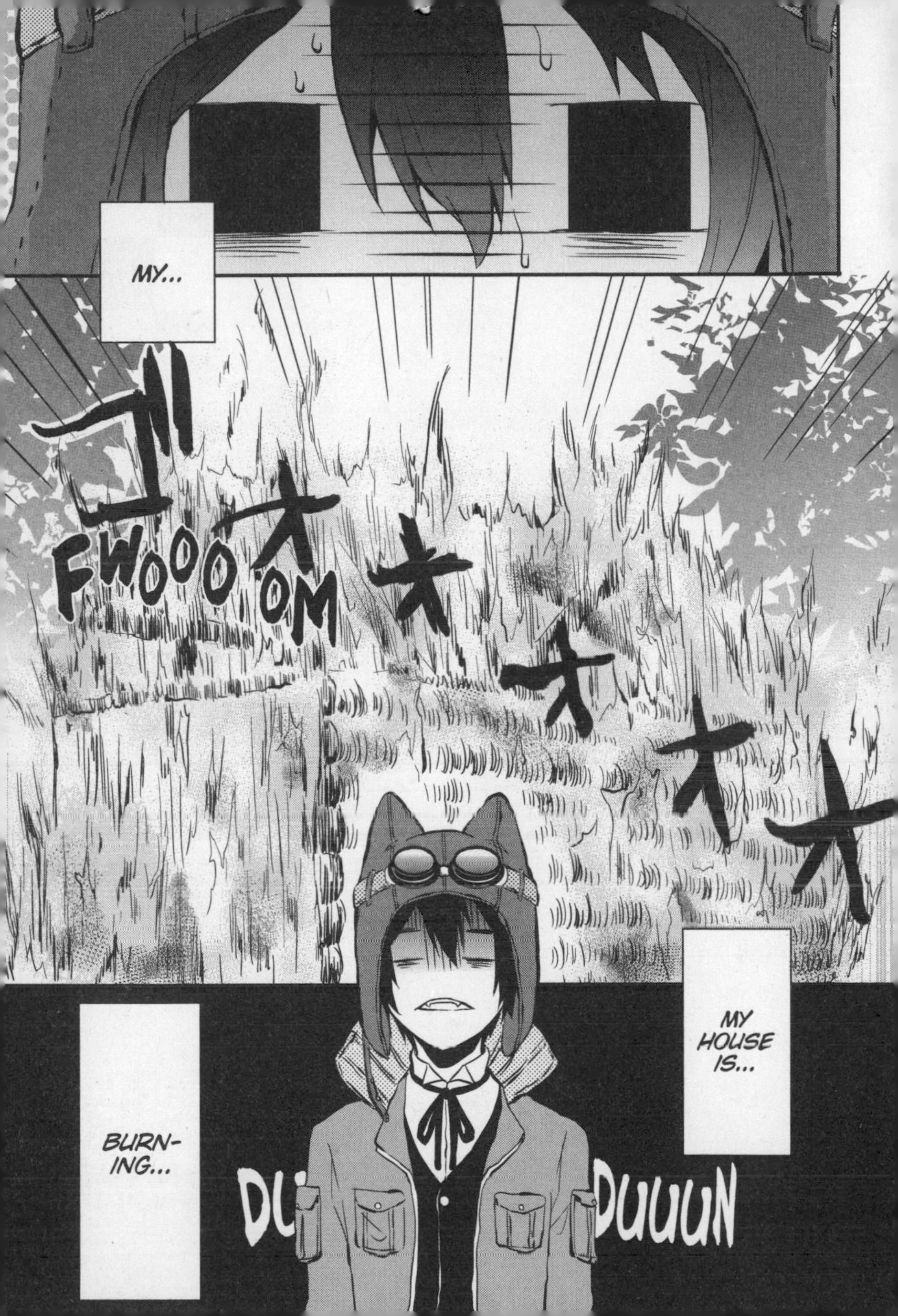
MY...
FWOOOOM
MY HOUSE IS...
BURN-ING...
DU DUUUN

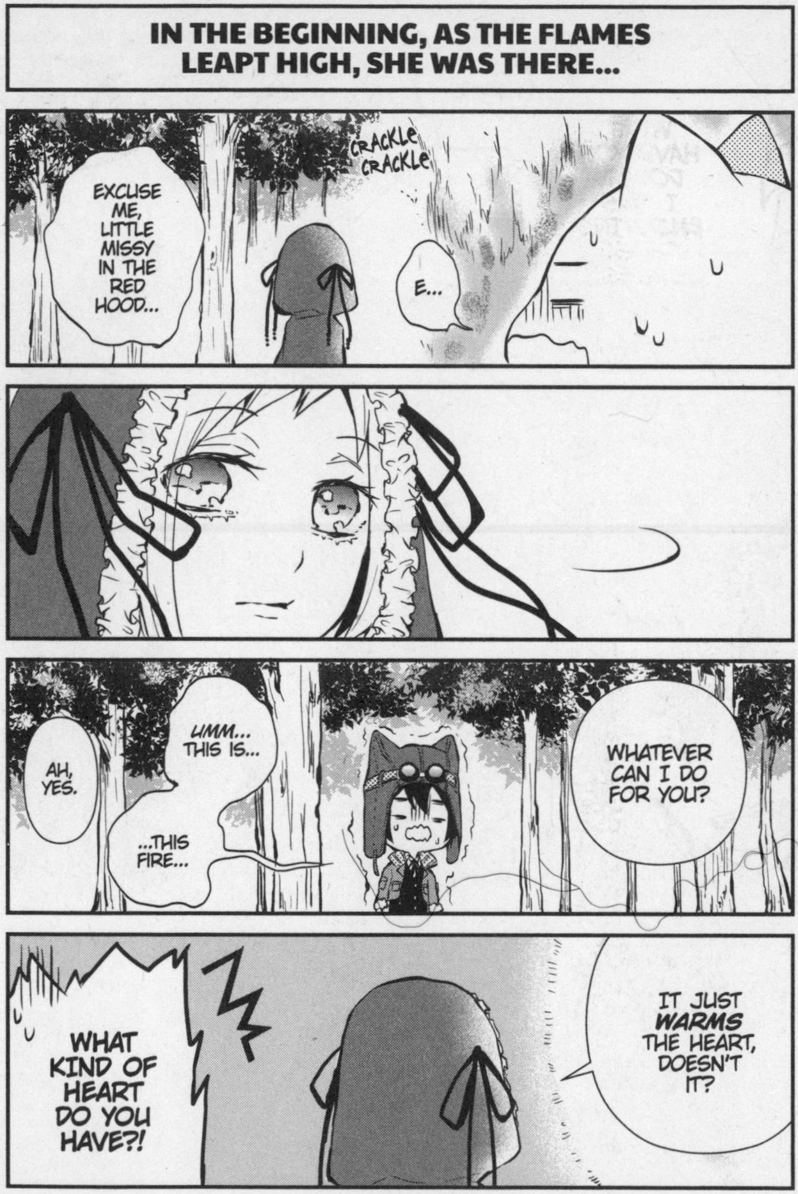
IN THE BEGINNING, AS THE FLAMES LEAPT HIGH, SHE WAS THERE...
CRACKLE CRACKLE
E...
EXCUSE ME, LITTLE MISSY IN THE RED HOOD...
WHATEVER CAN I DO FOR YOU?
UMM... THIS IS...
...THIS FIRE...
AH, YES.
IT JUST WARMS THE HEART, DOESN'T IT?
WHAT KIND OF HEART DO YOU HAVE?!

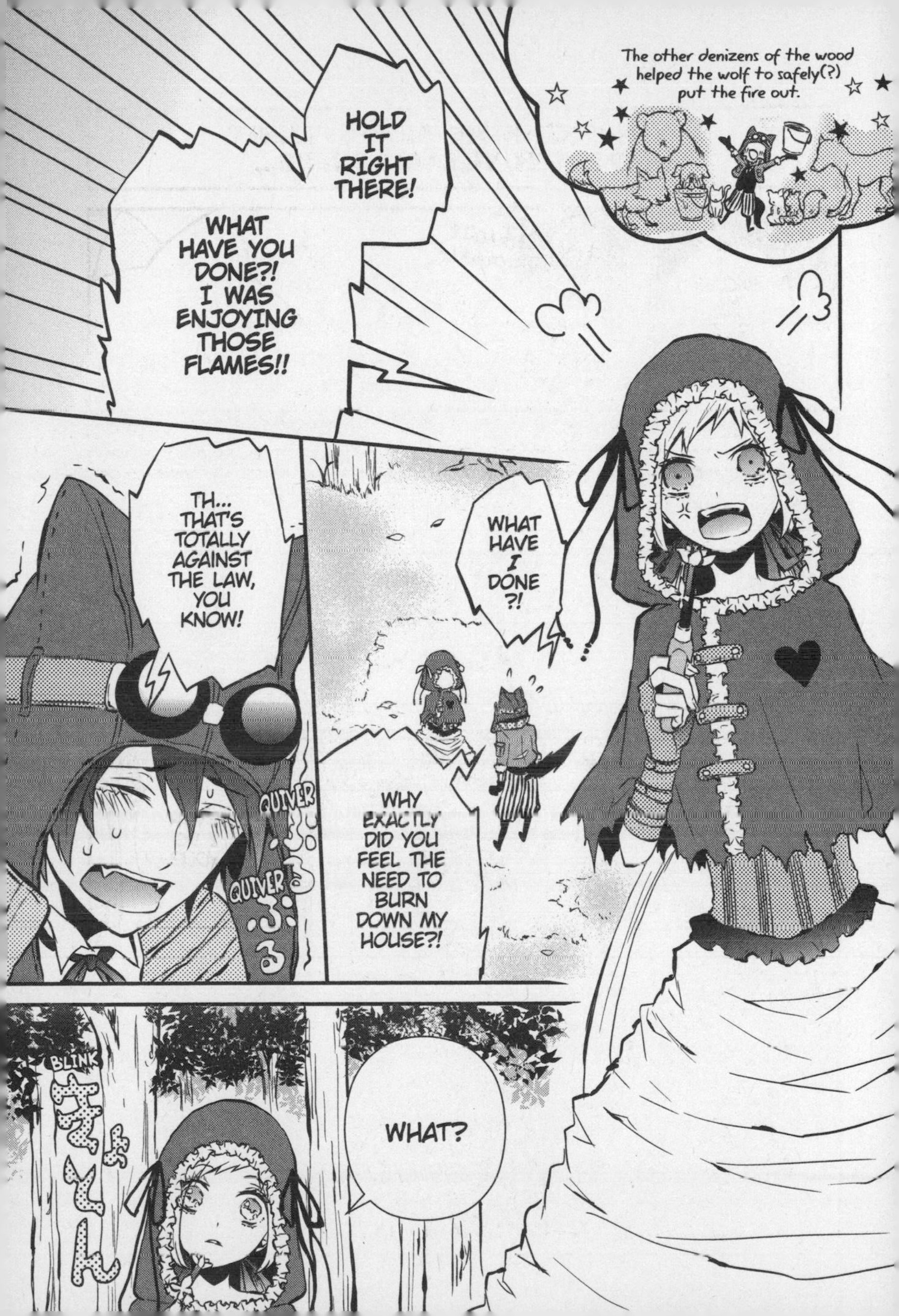
The other denizens of the wood helped the wolf to safely(?) put the fire out.
HOLD IT RIGHT THERE!
WHAT HAVE YOU DONE?! I WAS ENJOYING THOSE FLAMES!!
WHAT HAVE I DONE?!
WHY EXACTLY DID YOU FEEL THE NEED TO BURN DOWN MY HOUSE?!
TH... THAT'S TOTALLY AGAINST THE LAW, YOU KNOW!
QUIVER
QUIVER
BLINK
WHAT?

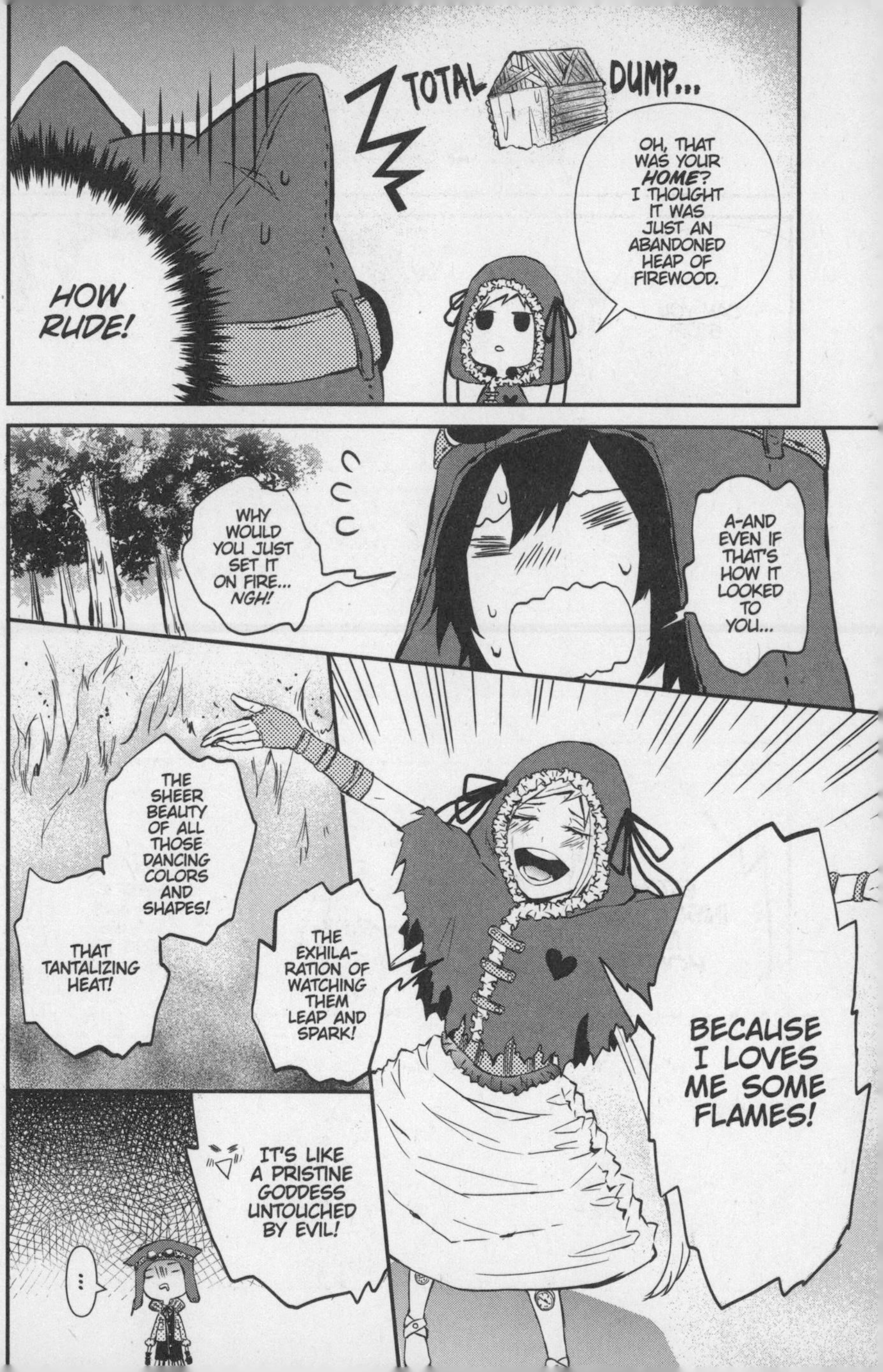
TOTAL DUMP...
OH, THAT WAS YOUR *HOME*? I THOUGHT IT WAS JUST AN ABANDONED HEAP OF FIREWOOD.
HOW RUDE!
A-AND EVEN IF THAT'S HOW IT LOOKED TO YOU...
WHY WOULD YOU JUST SET IT ON FIRE... NGH!
BECAUSE I LOVES ME SOME FLAMES!
THE SHEER BEAUTY OF ALL THOSE DANCING COLORS AND SHAPES!
THE EXHILA-RATION OF WATCHING THEM LEAP AND SPARK!
THAT TANTALIZING HEAT!
IT'S LIKE A PRISTINE GODDESS UNTOUCHED BY EVIL!
...

BEHOLD THE CRIMINAL

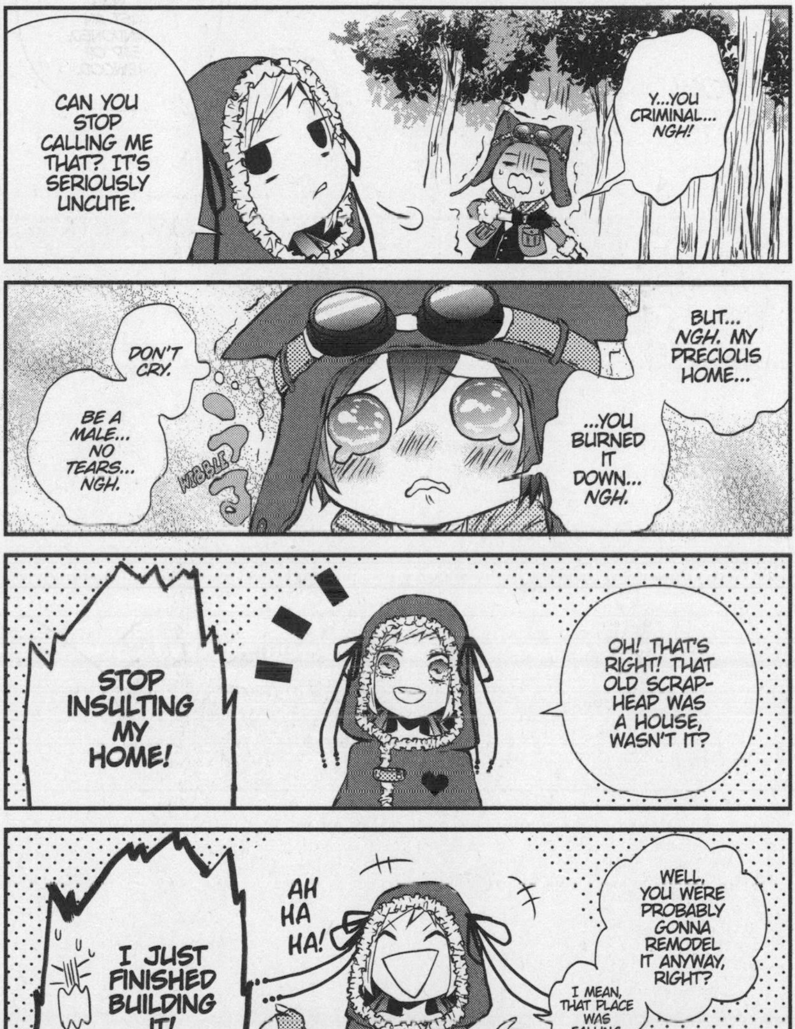
Y...YOU CRIMINAL... NGH!
CAN YOU STOP CALLING ME THAT? IT'S SERIOUSLY UNCUTE.
BUT... NGH. MY PRECIOUS HOME...
...YOU BURNED IT DOWN... NGH.
DON'T CRY.
BE A MALE... NO TEARS... NGH.
WIBBLE
OH! THAT'S RIGHT! THAT OLD SCRAP-HEAP WAS A HOUSE, WASN'T IT?
STOP INSULTING MY HOME!
WELL, YOU WERE PROBABLY GONNA REMODEL IT ANYWAY, RIGHT?
I MEAN, THAT PLACE WAS FALLING APART!
AH HA HA!
I JUST FINISHED BUILDING IT!

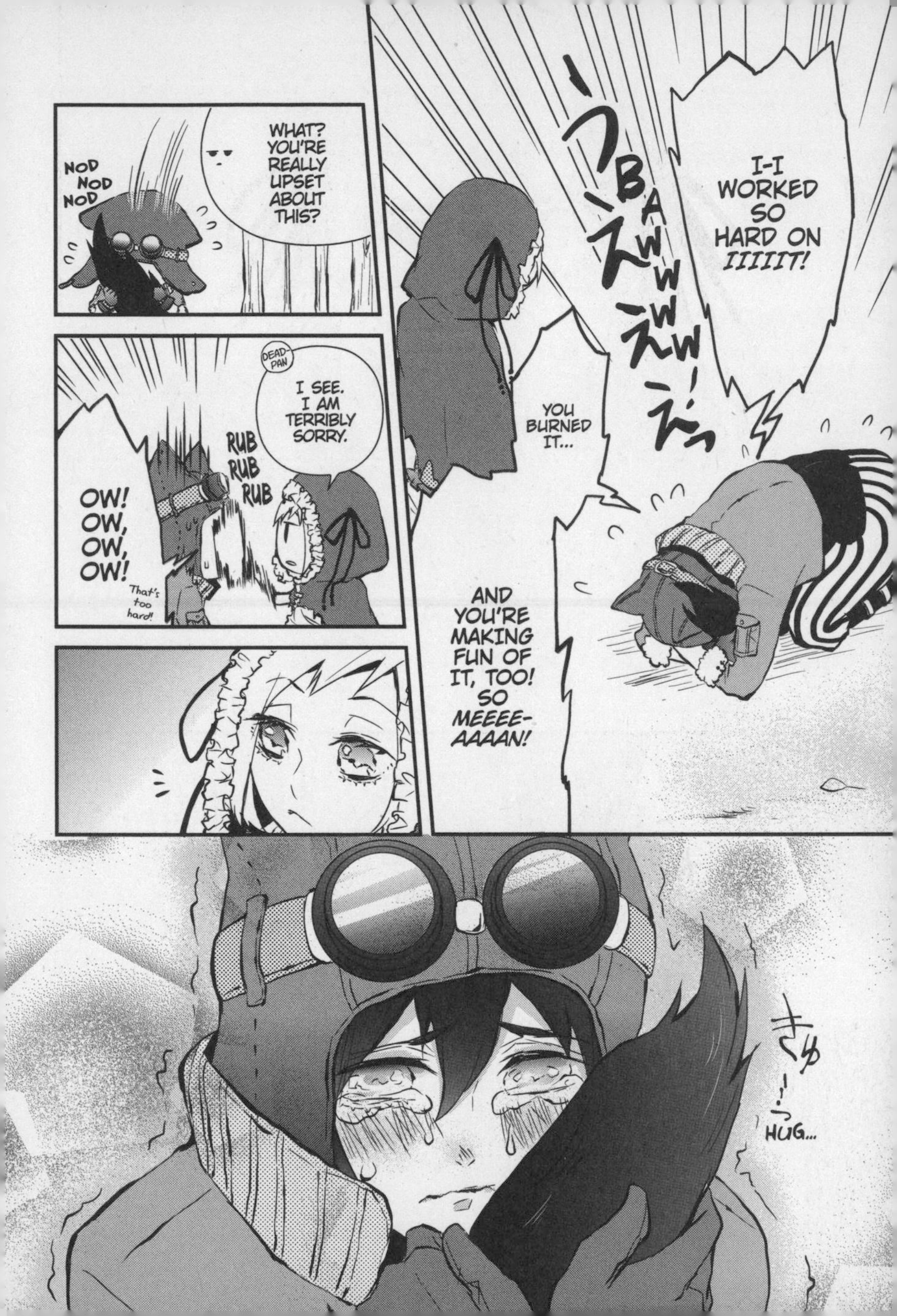

I-I WORKED SO HARD ON IIIIIT!
BAWWWWW
YOU BURNED IT...
AND YOU'RE MAKING FUN OF IT, TOO! SO MEEEE-AAAAN!
WHAT? YOU'RE REALLY UPSET ABOUT THIS?
NOD NOD NOD
DEAD-PAN
I SEE. I AM TERRIBLY SORRY.
RUB RUB RUB
OW! OW, OW, OW!
That's too hard!
HUG...

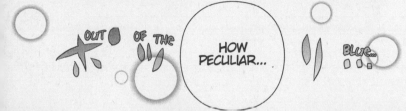

OUT OF THE HOW PECULIAR... BLUE...

FLAMES HAVE ALWAYS BEEN MY PASSION...

BUT NOW, SOMEHOW, I FIND MY HEART BURNS FOR YOU, TOO.

SHFFF...

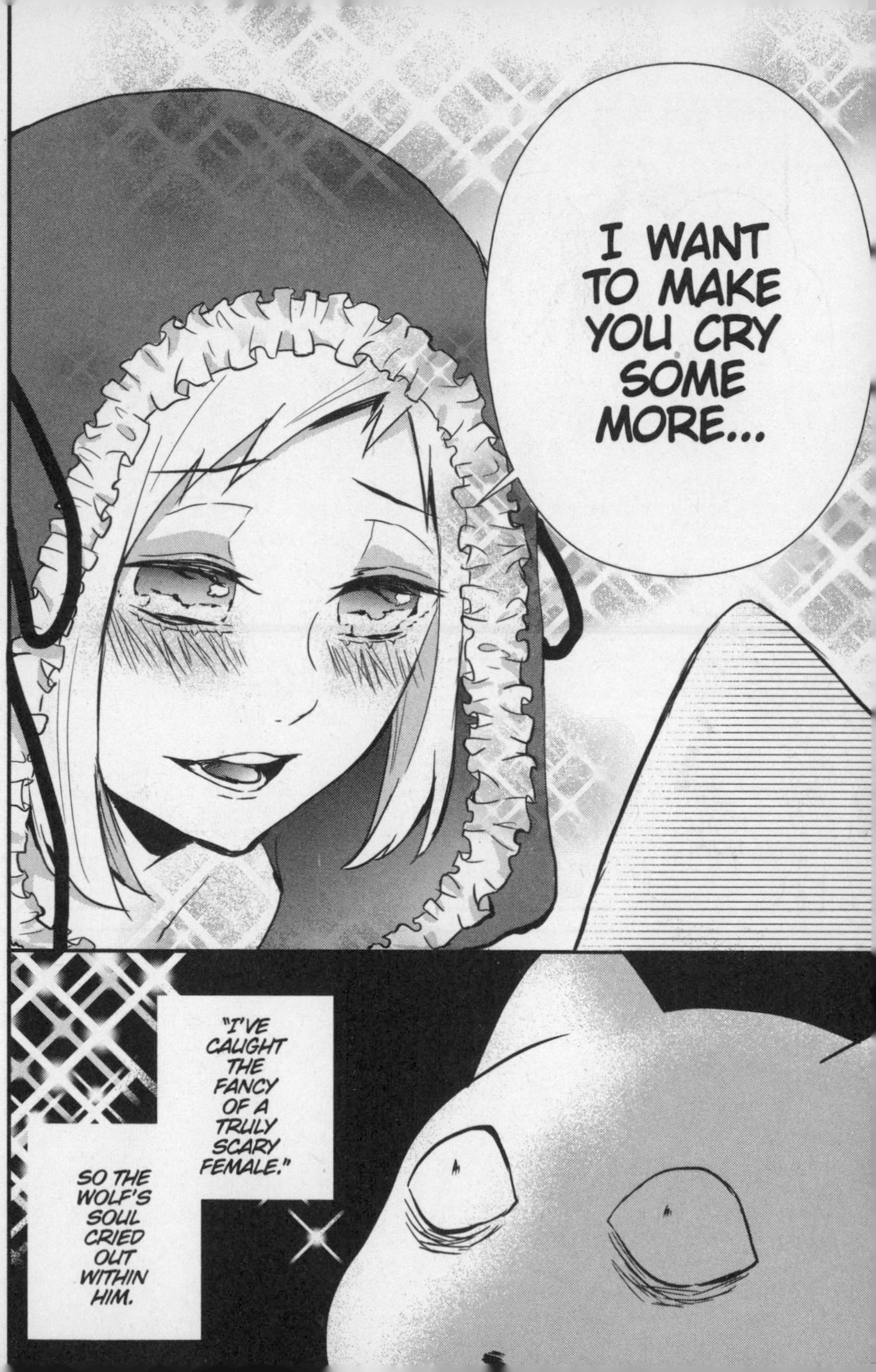
I WANT TO MAKE YOU CRY SOME MORE...
"I'VE CAUGHT THE FANCY OF A TRULY SCARY FEMALE."
SO THE WOLF'S SOUL CRIED OUT WITHIN HIM.

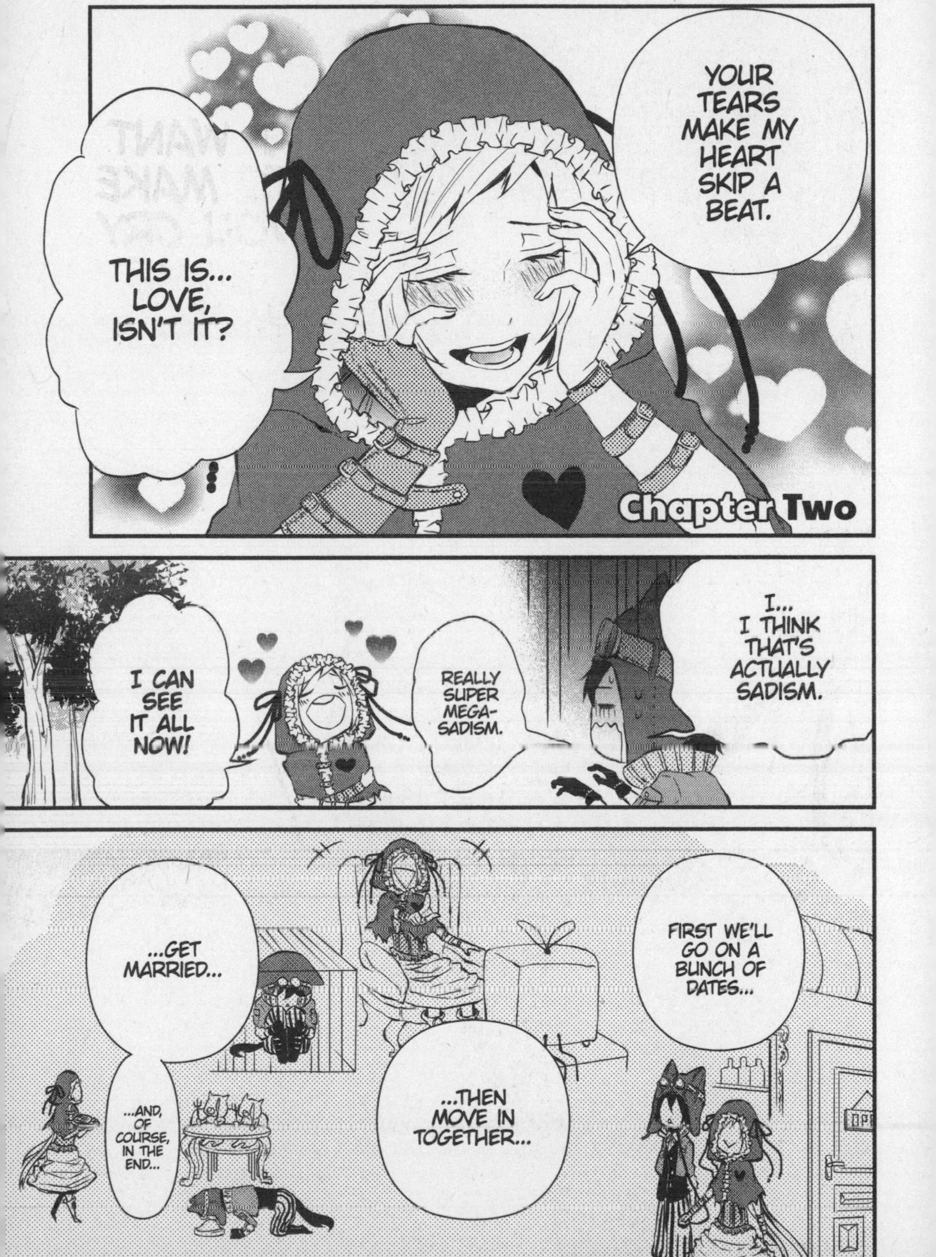
YOUR TEARS MAKE MY HEART SKIP A BEAT.
THIS IS... LOVE, ISN'T IT?
Chapter Two
I... I THINK THAT'S ACTUALLY SADISM.
REALLY SUPER MEGA-SADISM.
I CAN SEE IT ALL NOW!
FIRST WE'LL GO ON A BUNCH OF DATES...
...GET MARRIED...
...THEN MOVE IN TOGETHER...
...AND, OF COURSE, IN THE END...

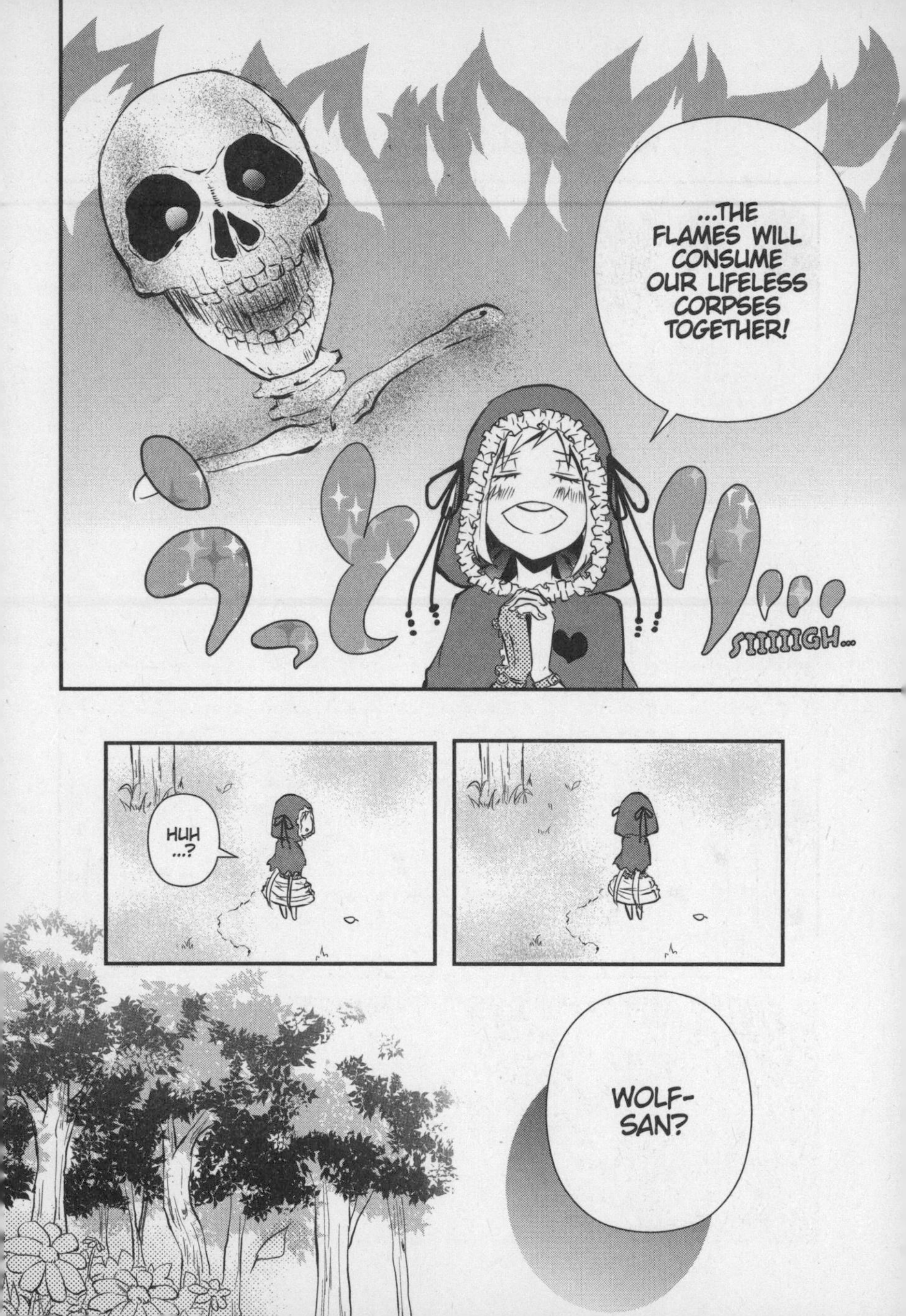
...THE FLAMES WILL CONSUME OUR LIFELESS CORPSES TOGETHER!
SIIIIIGH...
HUH ...?
WOLF-SAN?

WHAT HE FOUND AFTER HE RAN

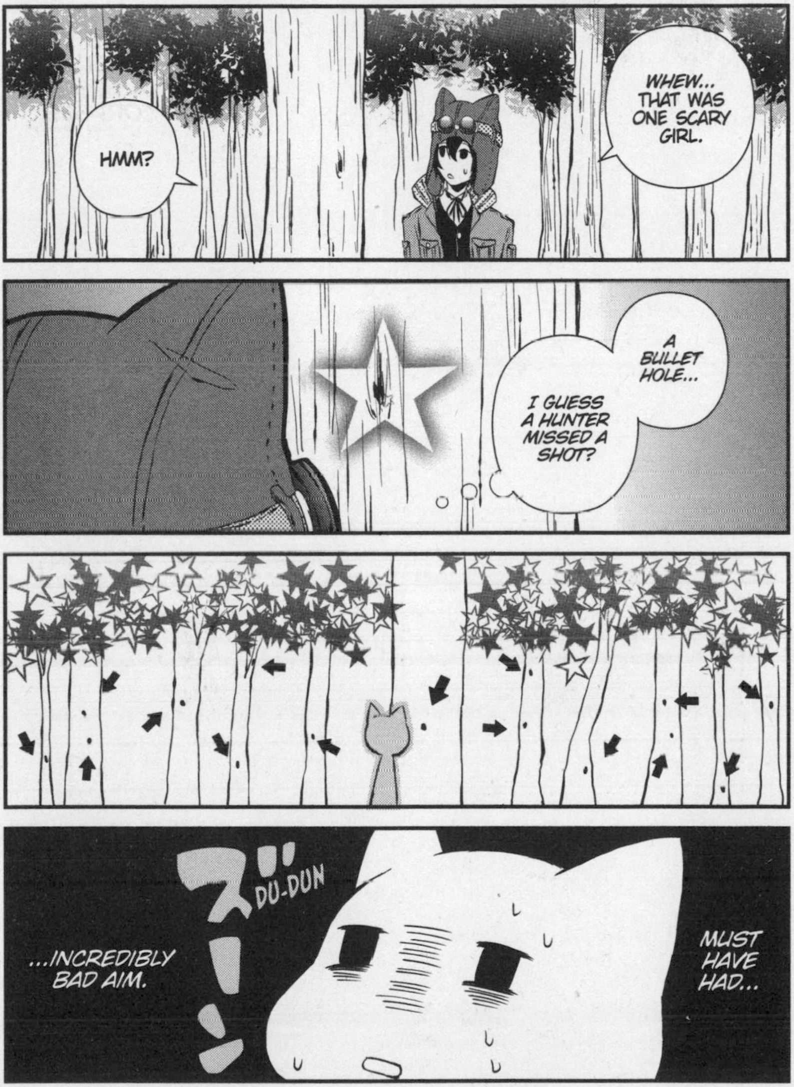
WHEW... THAT WAS ONE SCARY GIRL.
HMM?
A BULLET HOLE...
I GUESS A HUNTER MISSED A SHOT?
MUST HAVE HAD...
DU-DUN
...INCREDIBLY BAD AIM.

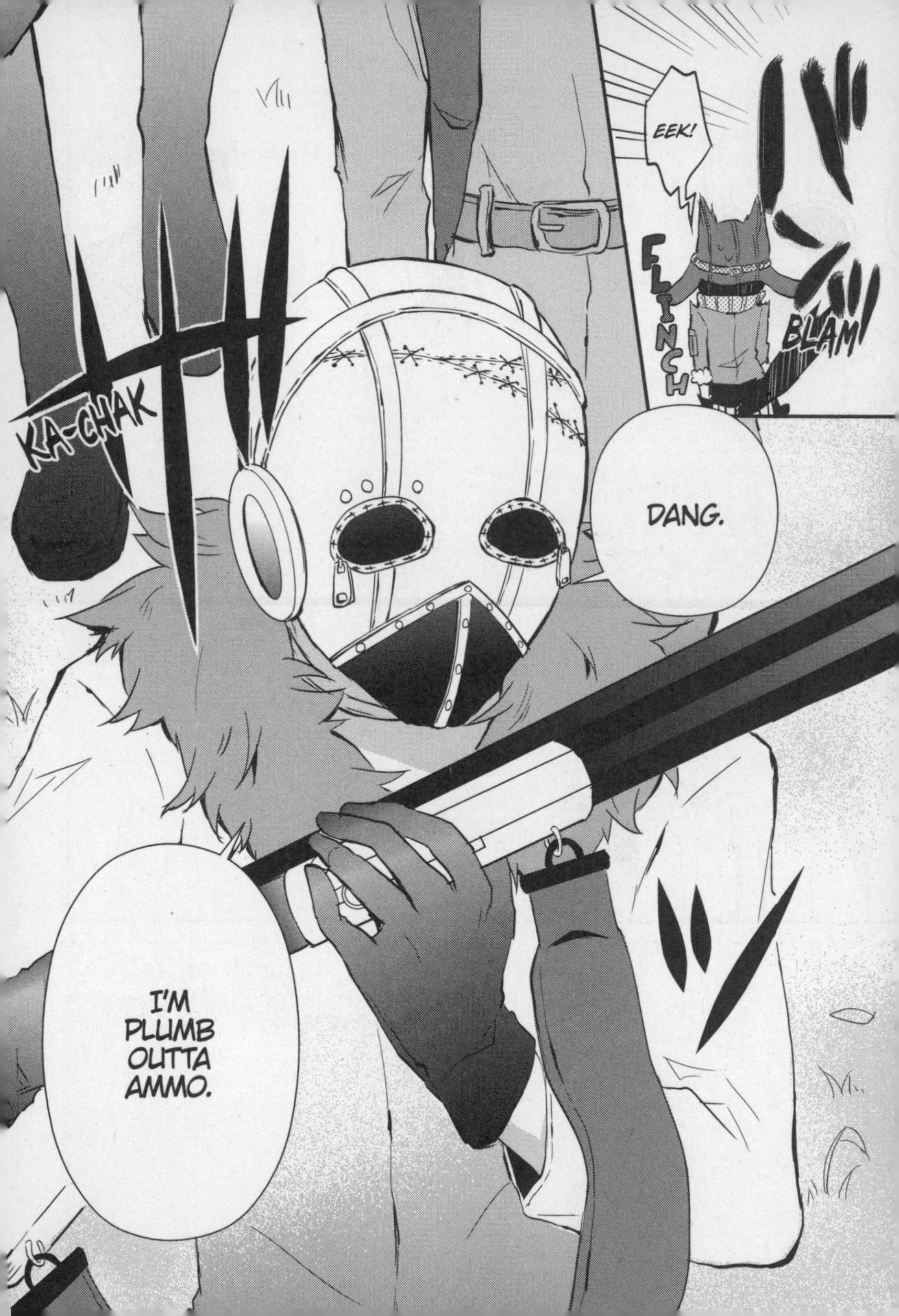
EEK!
BLAM
FLINCH
KA-CHAK
DANG.
I'M PLUMB OUTTA AMMO.

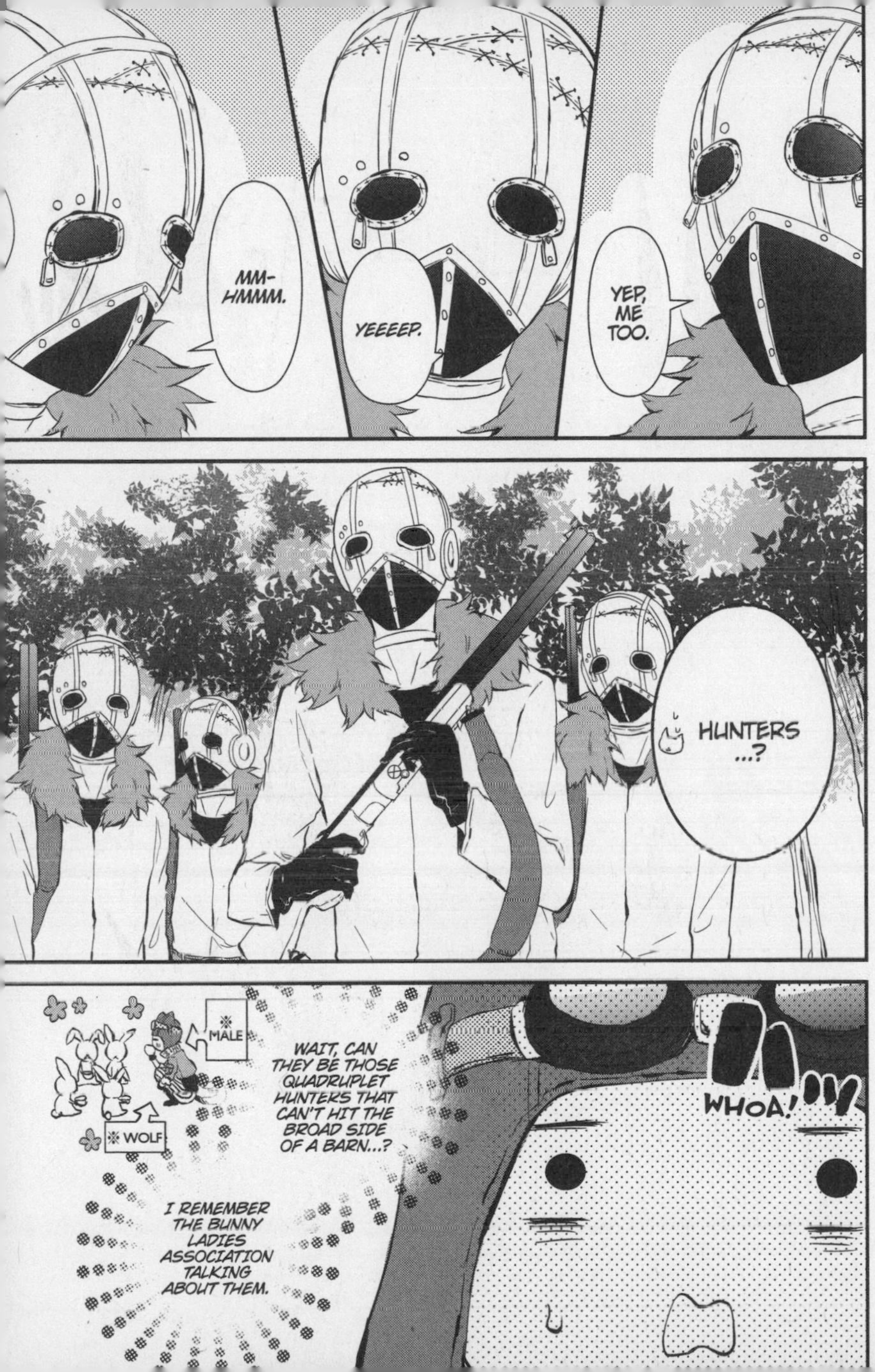
YEP, ME TOO.
YEEEEP.
MM-HMMM.
HUNTERS ...?
WHOA!
WAIT, CAN THEY BE THOSE QUADRUPLET HUNTERS THAT CAN'T HIT THE BROAD SIDE OF A BARN...?
※ MALE
※ WOLF
I REMEMBER THE BUNNY LADIES ASSOCIATION TALKING ABOUT THEM.

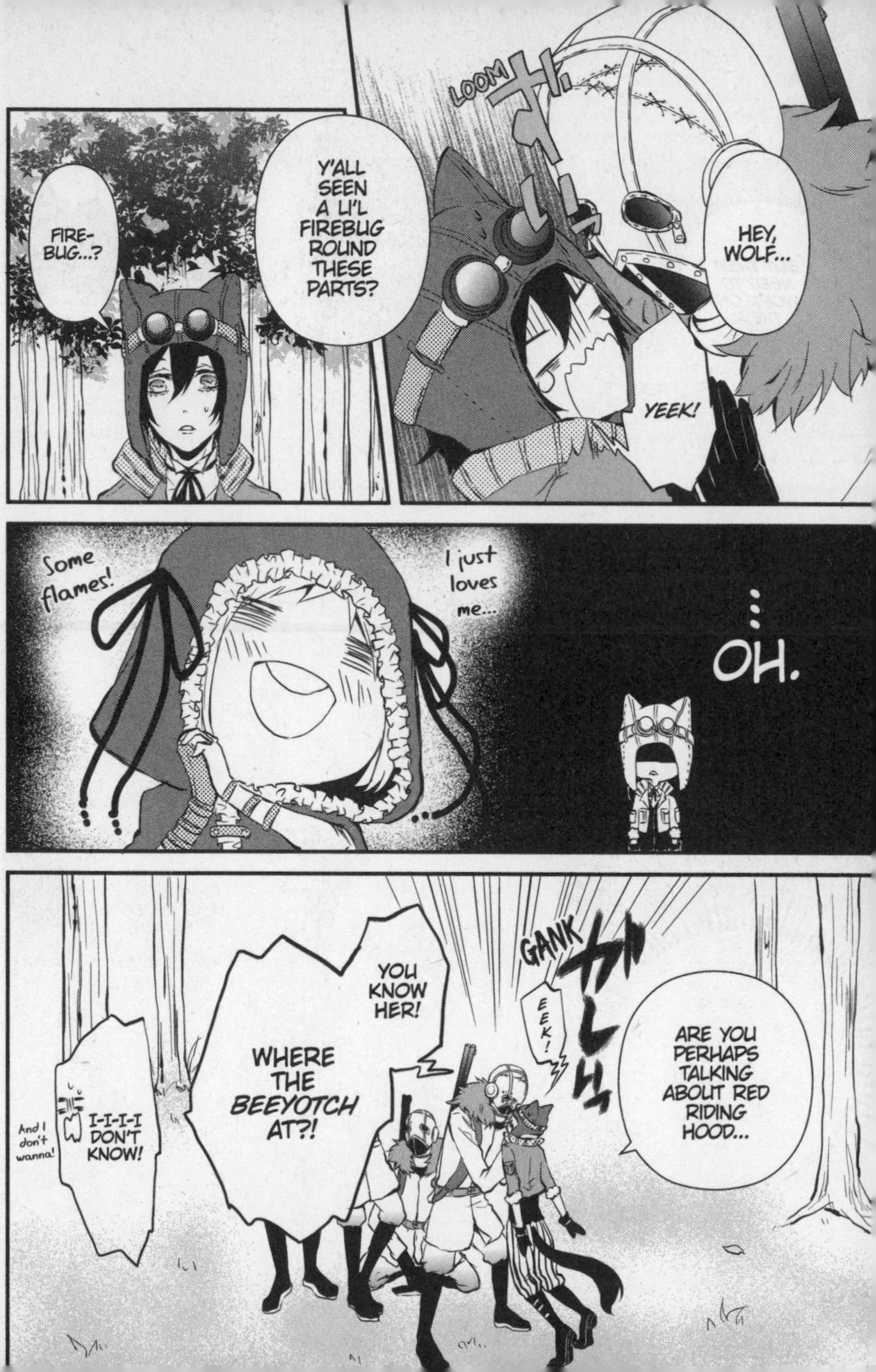
LOOM
HEY, WOLF...
Y'ALL SEEN A LI'L FIREBUG ROUND THESE PARTS?
YEEK!
FIRE-BUG...?
...
OH.
I just loves me...
Some flames!
GANK
ARE YOU PERHAPS TALKING ABOUT RED RIDING HOOD...
EEK!
YOU KNOW HER!
WHERE THE BEEYOTCH AT?!
I-I-I-I DON'T KNOW!
And I don't wanna!

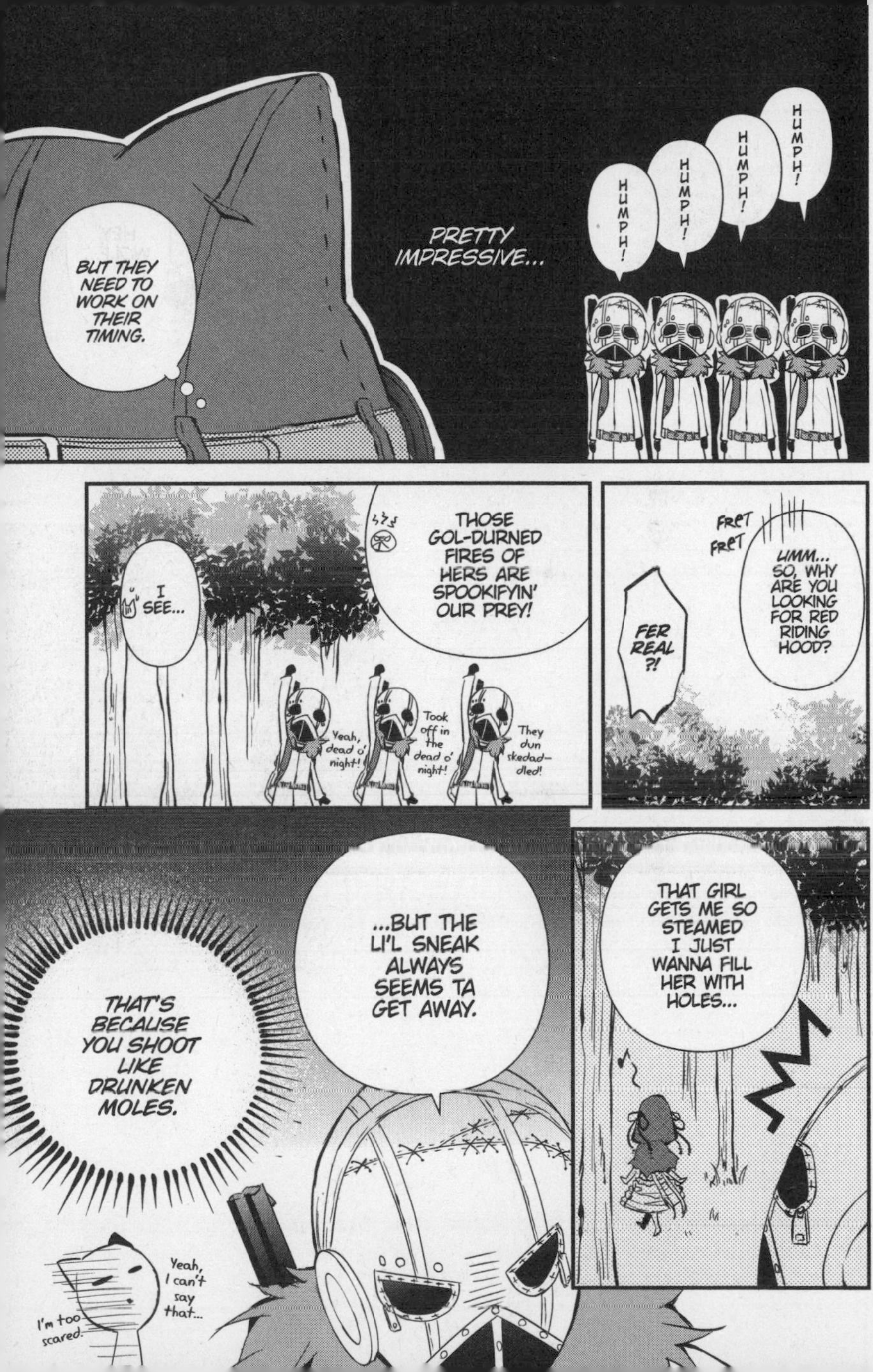
HUMPH!
HUMPH!
HUMPH!
HUMPH!
PRETTY IMPRESSIVE...
BUT THEY NEED TO WORK ON THEIR TIMING.
FRET FRET
UMM... SO, WHY ARE YOU LOOKING FOR RED RIDING HOOD?
FER REAL?!
THOSE GOL-DURNED FIRES OF HERS ARE SPOOKIFYIN' OUR PREY!
They dun skedad-dled!
Took off in the dead o' night!
Yeah, dead o' night!
I SEE...
THAT GIRL GETS ME SO STEAMED I JUST WANNA FILL HER WITH HOLES...
...BUT THE LI'L SNEAK ALWAYS SEEMS TA GET AWAY.
THAT'S BECAUSE YOU SHOOT LIKE DRUNKEN MOLES.
Yeah, I can't say that...
I'm too scared.

GRASPING AT STRAWS

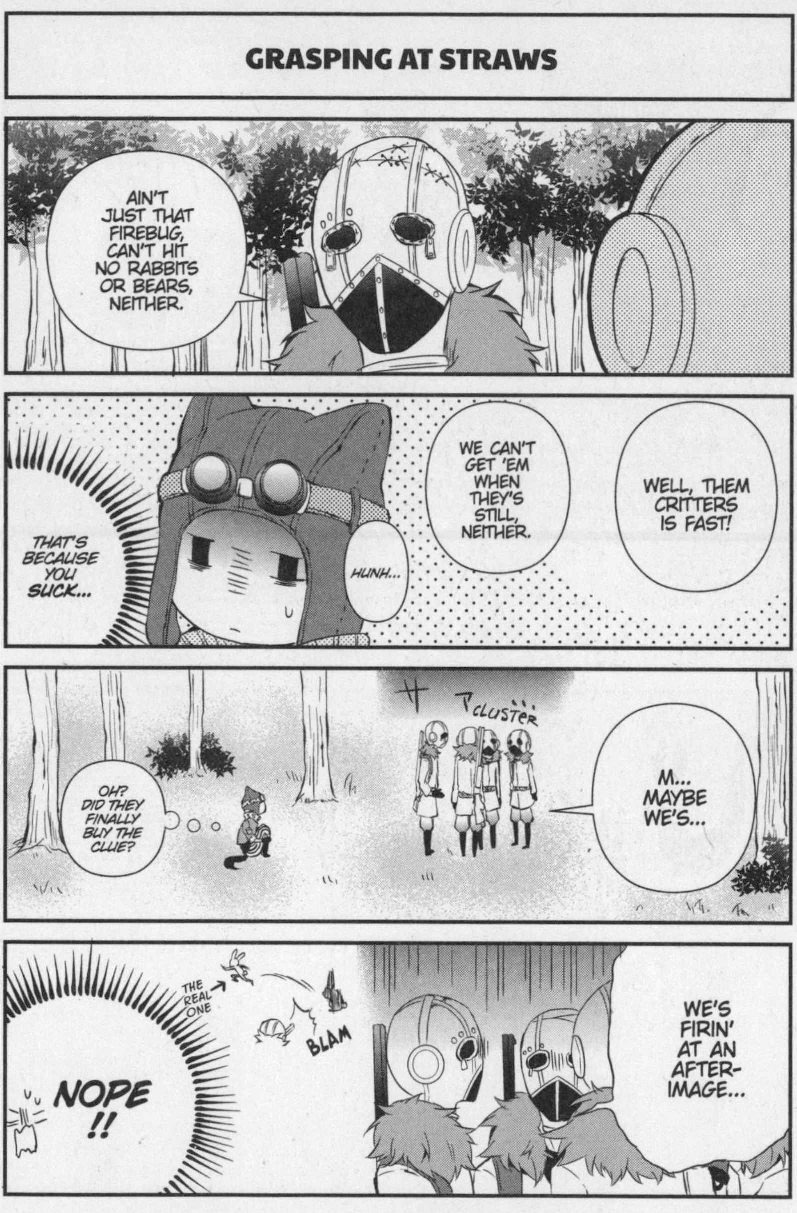
AIN'T JUST THAT FIREBUG, CAN'T HIT NO RABBITS OR BEARS, NEITHER.
WELL, THEM CRITTERS IS FAST!
WE CAN'T GET 'EM WHEN THEY'S STILL, NEITHER.
HUNH...
THAT'S BECAUSE YOU SUCK...
CLUSTER
M... MAYBE WE'S...
OH? DID THEY FINALLY BUY THE CLUE?
WE'S FIRIN' AT AN AFTER-IMAGE...
BLAM
THE REAL ONE
NOPE!!

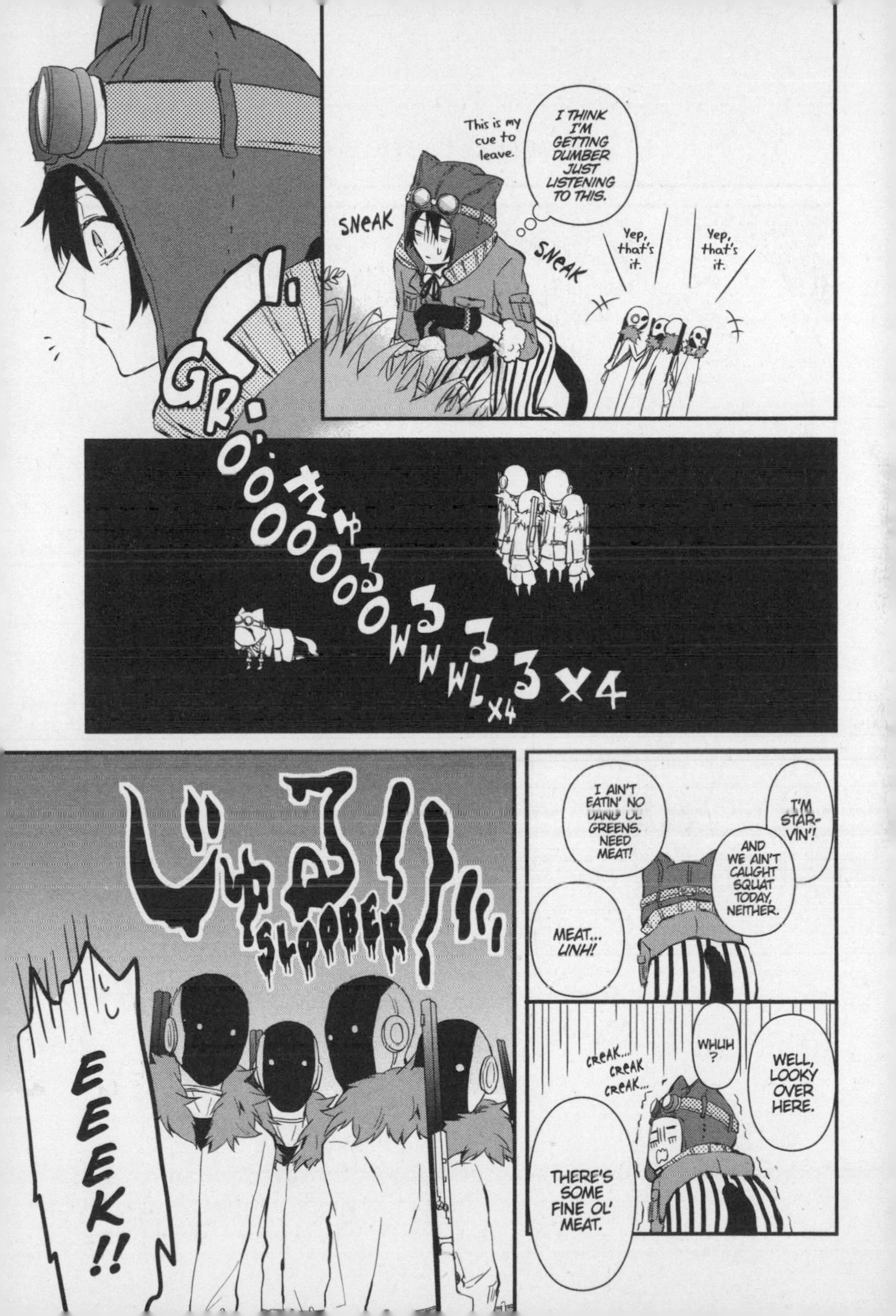

I THINK I'M GETTING DUMBER JUST LISTENING TO THIS.
This is my cue to leave.
SNEAK
SNEAK
Yep, that's it.
Yep, that's it.
GROOOOOOOWWWL×4
きゅるるる×4
I'M STAR-VIN'!
AND WE AIN'T CAUGHT SQUAT TODAY, NEITHER.
I AIN'T EATIN' NO DANG OL' GREENS. NEED MEAT!
MEAT... UNH!
WELL, LOOKY OVER HERE.
WHUH?
CREAK... CREAK CREAK...
THERE'S SOME FINE OL' MEAT.
じゅるり
SLOBBER
EEEK!!

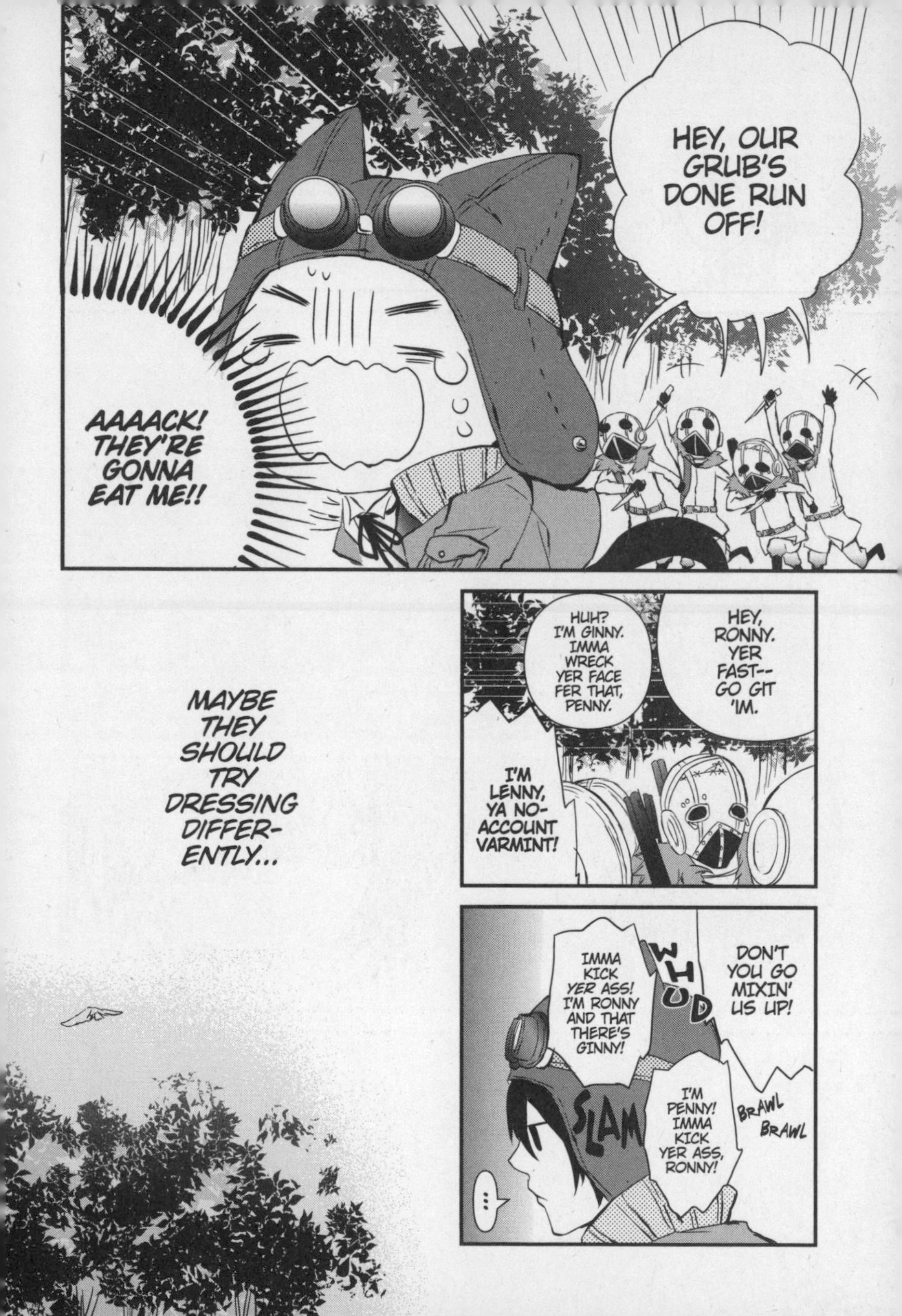
HEY, OUR GRUB'S DONE RUN OFF!
AAAACK! THEY'RE GONNA EAT ME!!
HEY, RONNY. YER FAST-- GO GIT 'IM.
HUH? I'M GINNY. IMMA WRECK YER FACE FER THAT, PENNY.
I'M LENNY, YA NO-ACCOUNT VARMINT!
DON'T YOU GO MIXIN' US UP!
WHUD
IMMA KICK YER ASS! I'M RONNY AND THAT THERE'S GINNY!
SLAM
BRAWL BRAWL
I'M PENNY! IMMA KICK YER ASS, RONNY!
...
MAYBE THEY SHOULD TRY DRESSING DIFFER-ENTLY...

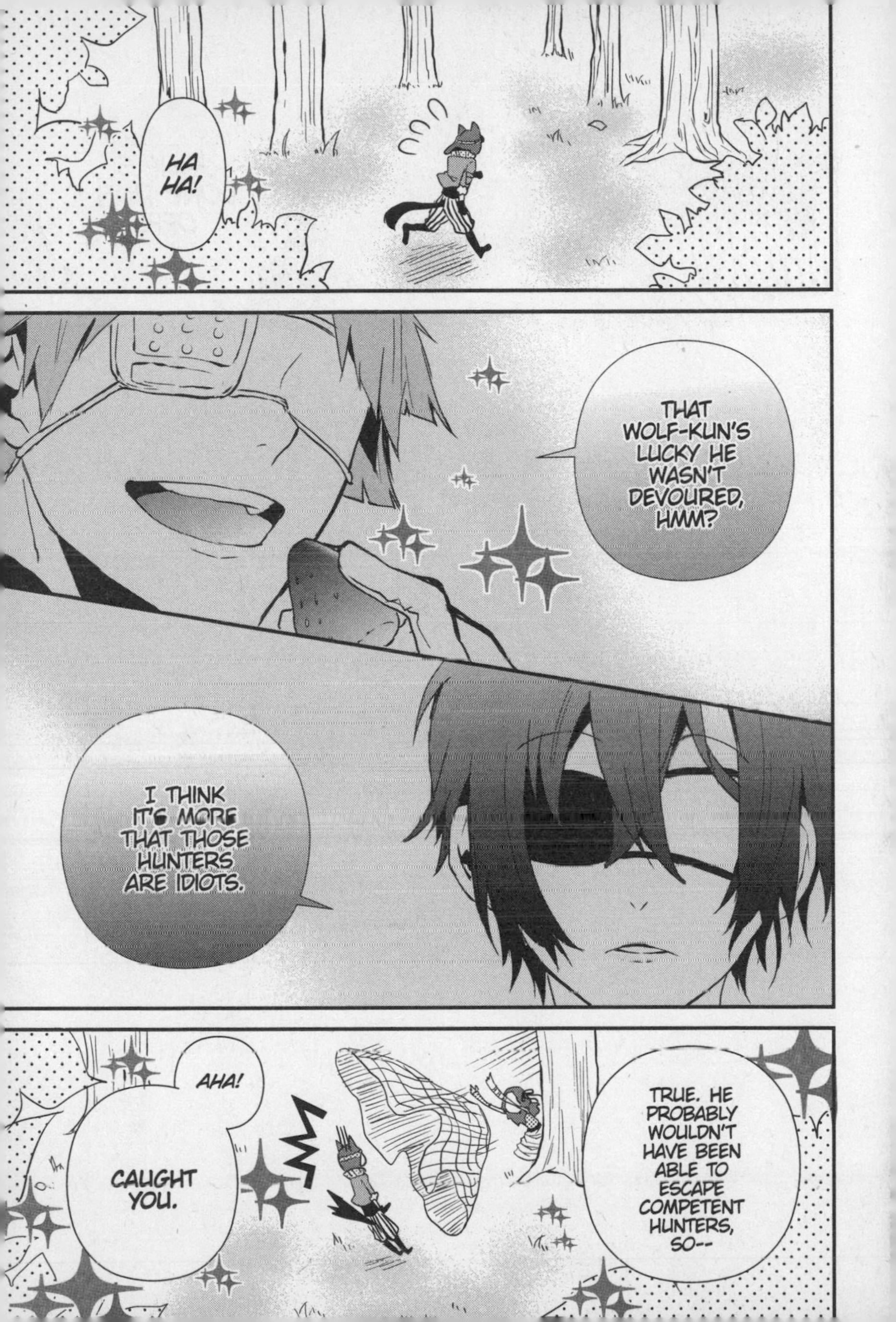
HA HA!
THAT WOLF-KUN'S LUCKY HE WASN'T DEVOURED, HMM?
I THINK IT'S MORE THAT THOSE HUNTERS ARE IDIOTS.
TRUE. HE PROBABLY WOULDN'T HAVE BEEN ABLE TO ESCAPE COMPETENT HUNTERS, SO--
AHA!
CAUGHT YOU.

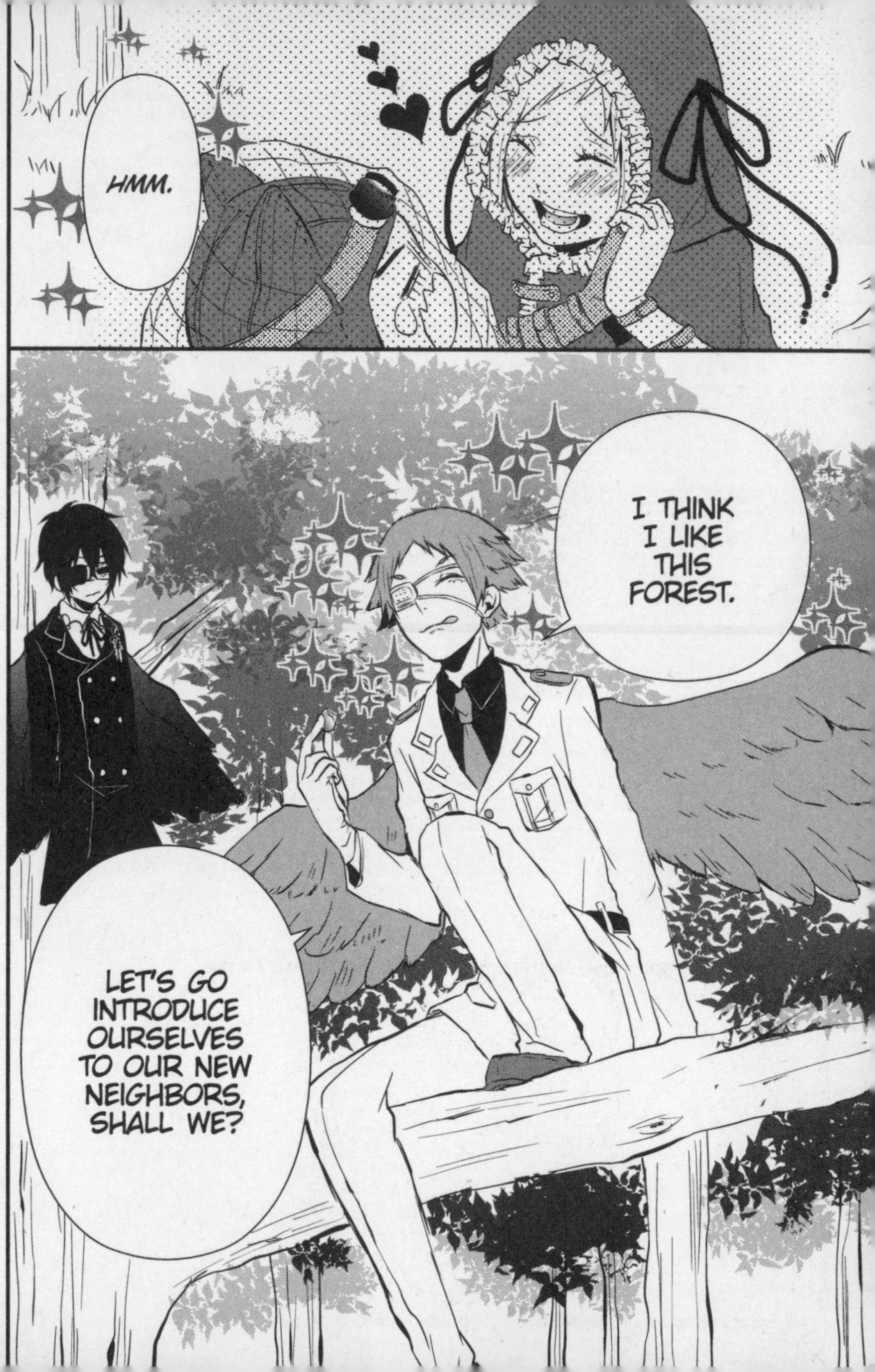
HMM.
I THINK I LIKE THIS FOREST.
LET'S GO INTRODUCE OURSELVES TO OUR NEW NEIGHBORS, SHALL WE?

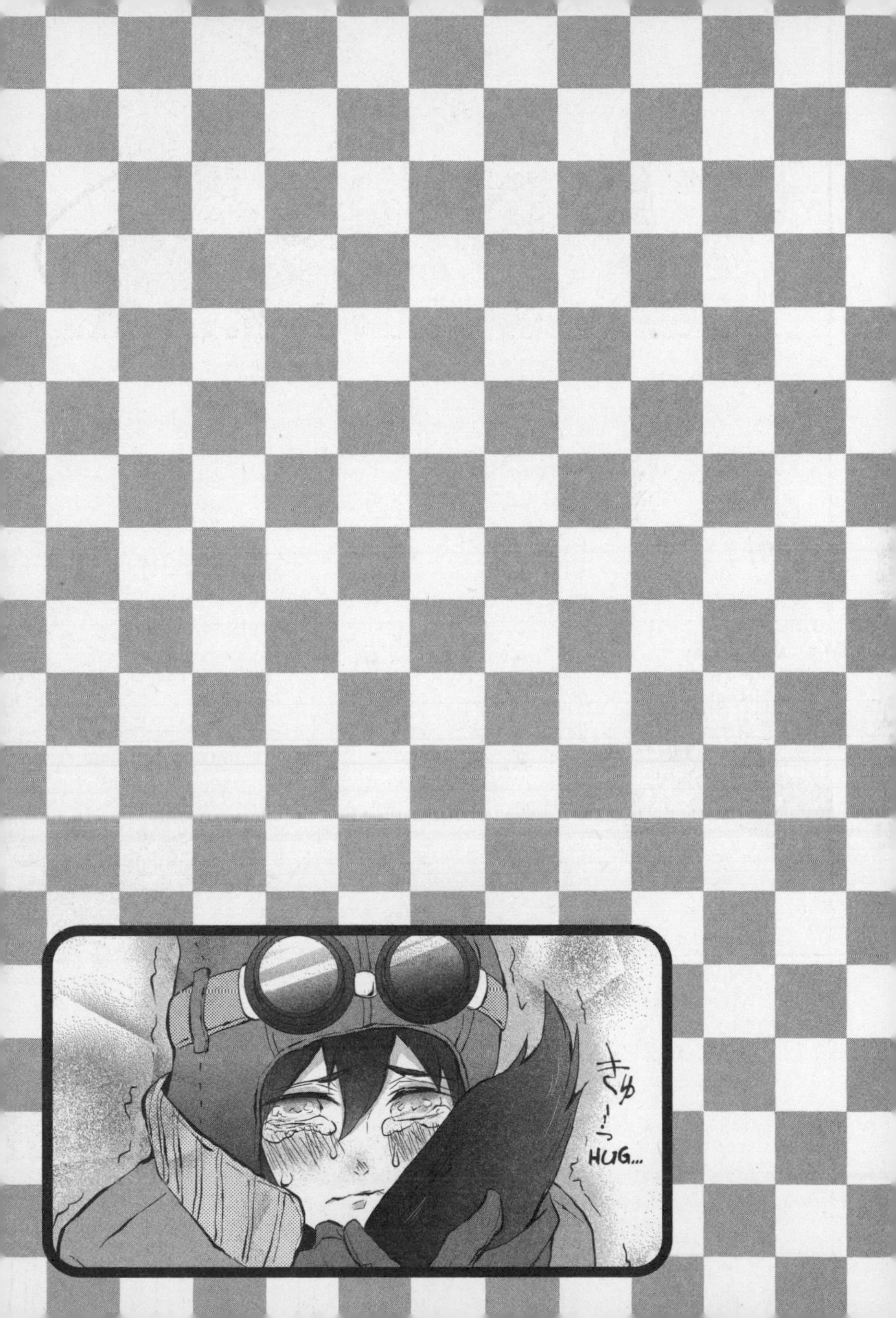
きゅ～っ
HUG...

RED RIDING HOOD AND THE BIG SAD WOLF

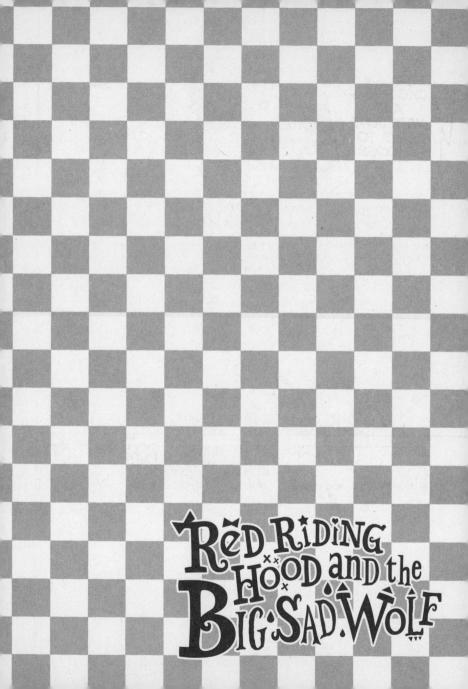

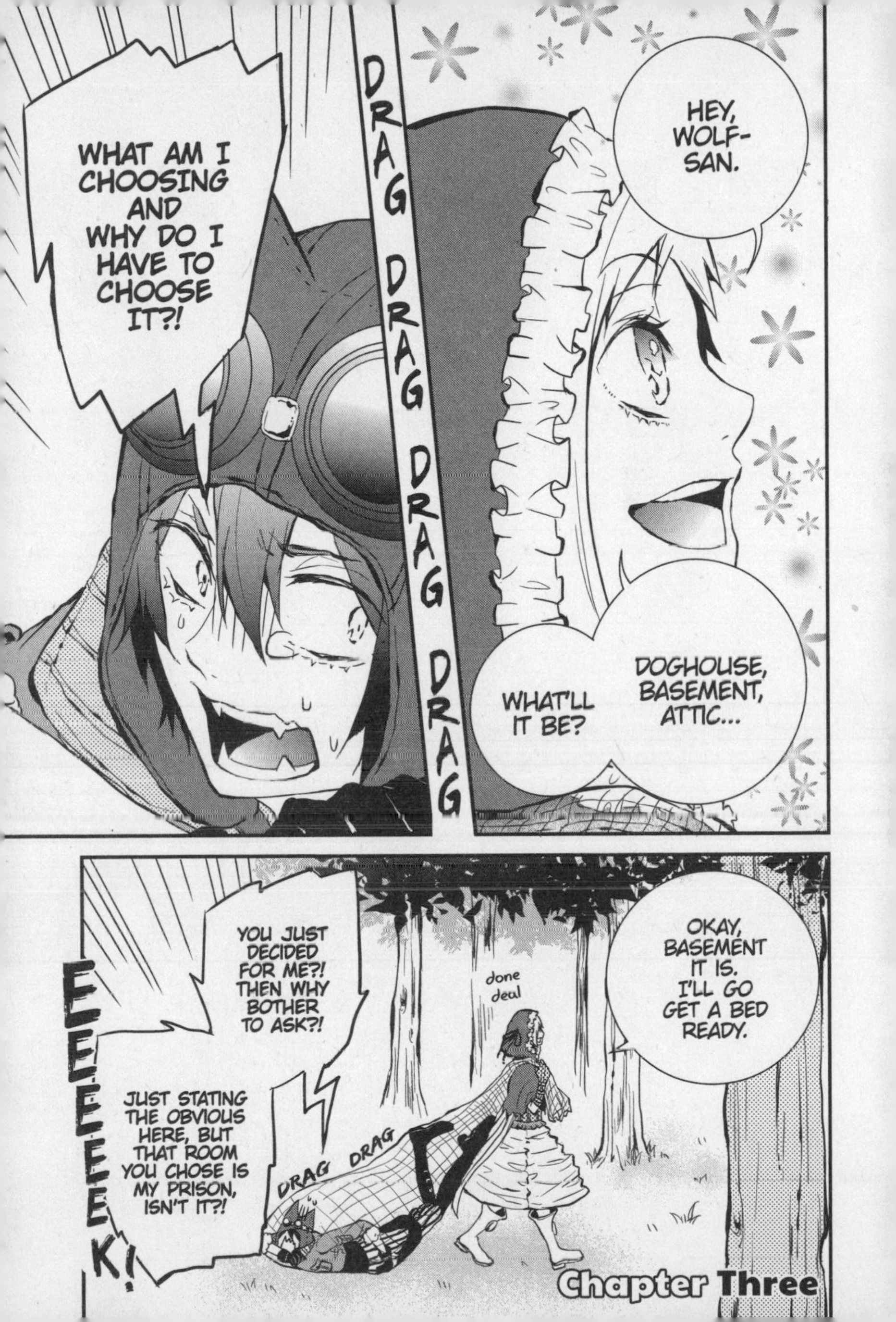
HEY, WOLF-SAN.
DOGHOUSE, BASEMENT, ATTIC...
WHAT'LL IT BE?
DRAG DRAG DRAG DRAG
WHAT AM I CHOOSING AND WHY DO I HAVE TO CHOOSE IT?!
OKAY, BASEMENT IT IS. I'LL GO GET A BED READY.
done deal
DRAG DRAG
YOU JUST DECIDED FOR ME?! THEN WHY BOTHER TO ASK?!
JUST STATING THE OBVIOUS HERE, BUT THAT ROOM YOU CHOSE IS MY PRISON, ISN'T IT?!
EEEEEEEK!
Chapter Three

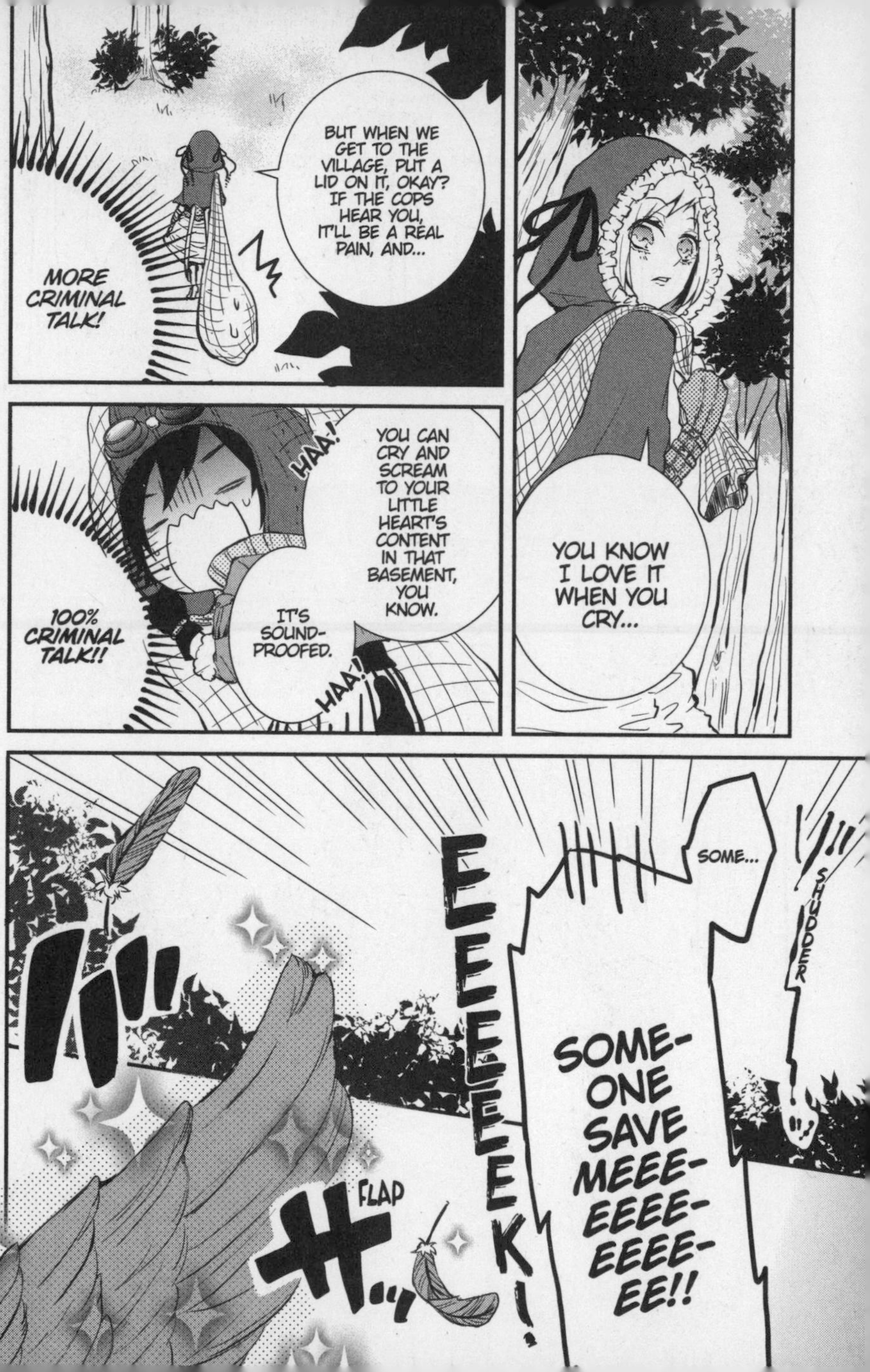
YOU KNOW I LOVE IT WHEN YOU CRY...
BUT WHEN WE GET TO THE VILLAGE, PUT A LID ON IT, OKAY? IF THE COPS HEAR YOU, IT'LL BE A REAL PAIN, AND...
MORE CRIMINAL TALK!
YOU CAN CRY AND SCREAM TO YOUR LITTLE HEART'S CONTENT IN THAT BASEMENT, YOU KNOW.
HAA!
IT'S SOUND-PROOFED.
HAA!
100% CRIMINAL TALK!!
SHUDDER
SOME...
SOME-ONE SAVE MEEEE-EEEE-EEEE-EE!!
EEEEEEEEEK!
FLAP

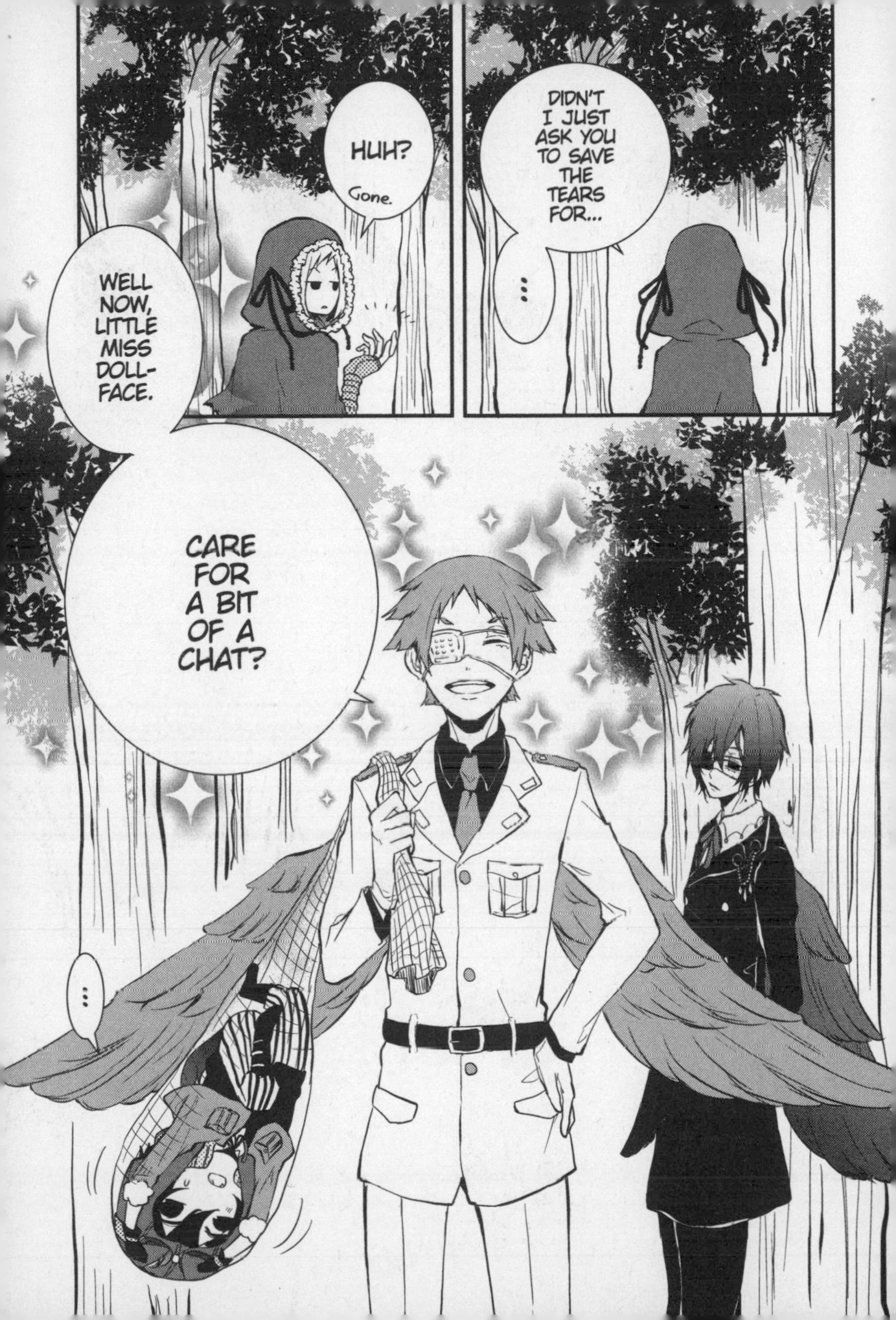
DIDN'T I JUST ASK YOU TO SAVE THE TEARS FOR...
...
HUH?
Gone.
WELL NOW, LITTLE MISS DOLL-FACE.
CARE FOR A BIT OF A CHAT?
...

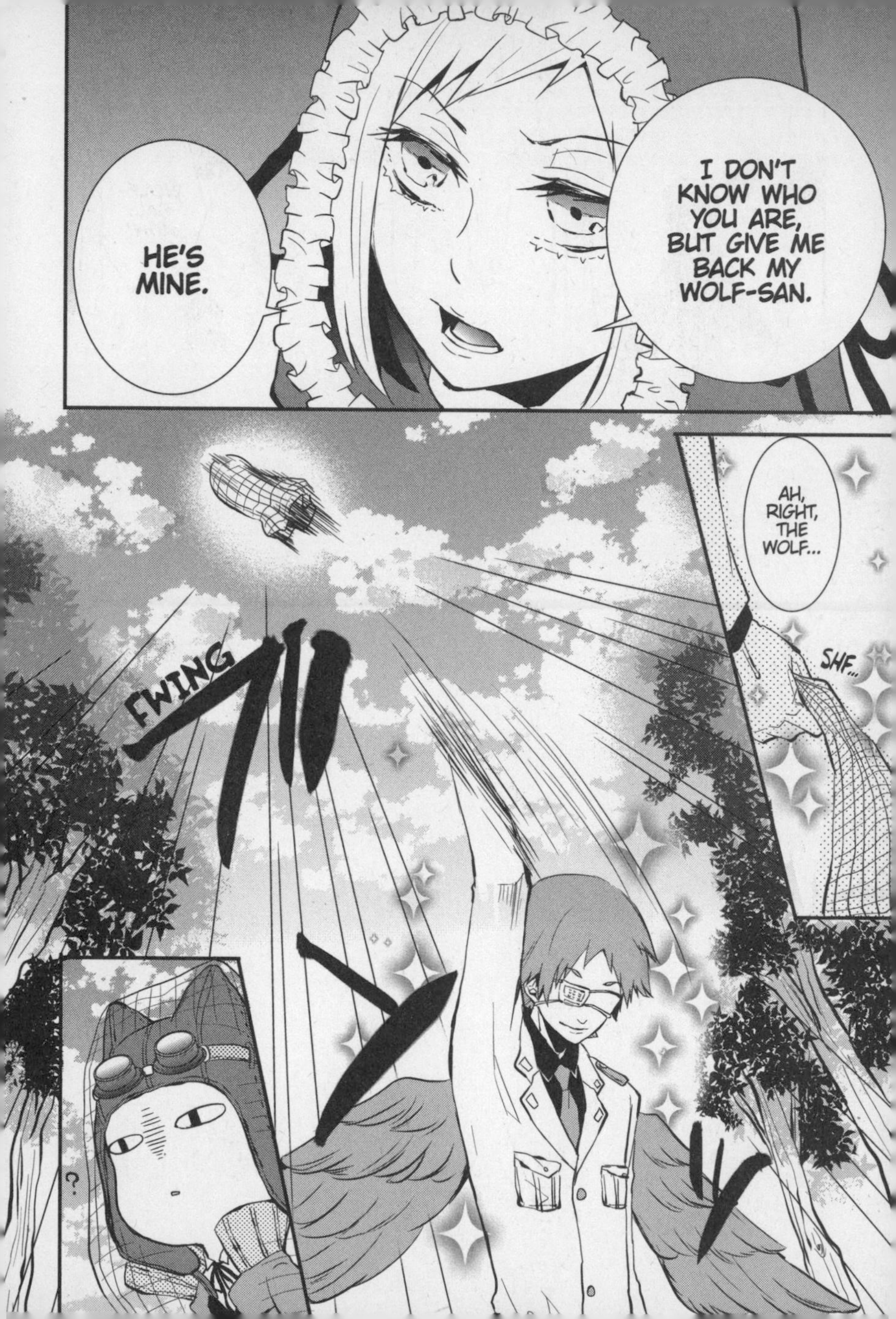
I DON'T KNOW WHO YOU ARE, BUT GIVE ME BACK MY WOLF-SAN.
HE'S MINE.
AH, RIGHT, THE WOLF...
SHF...
FWING
?

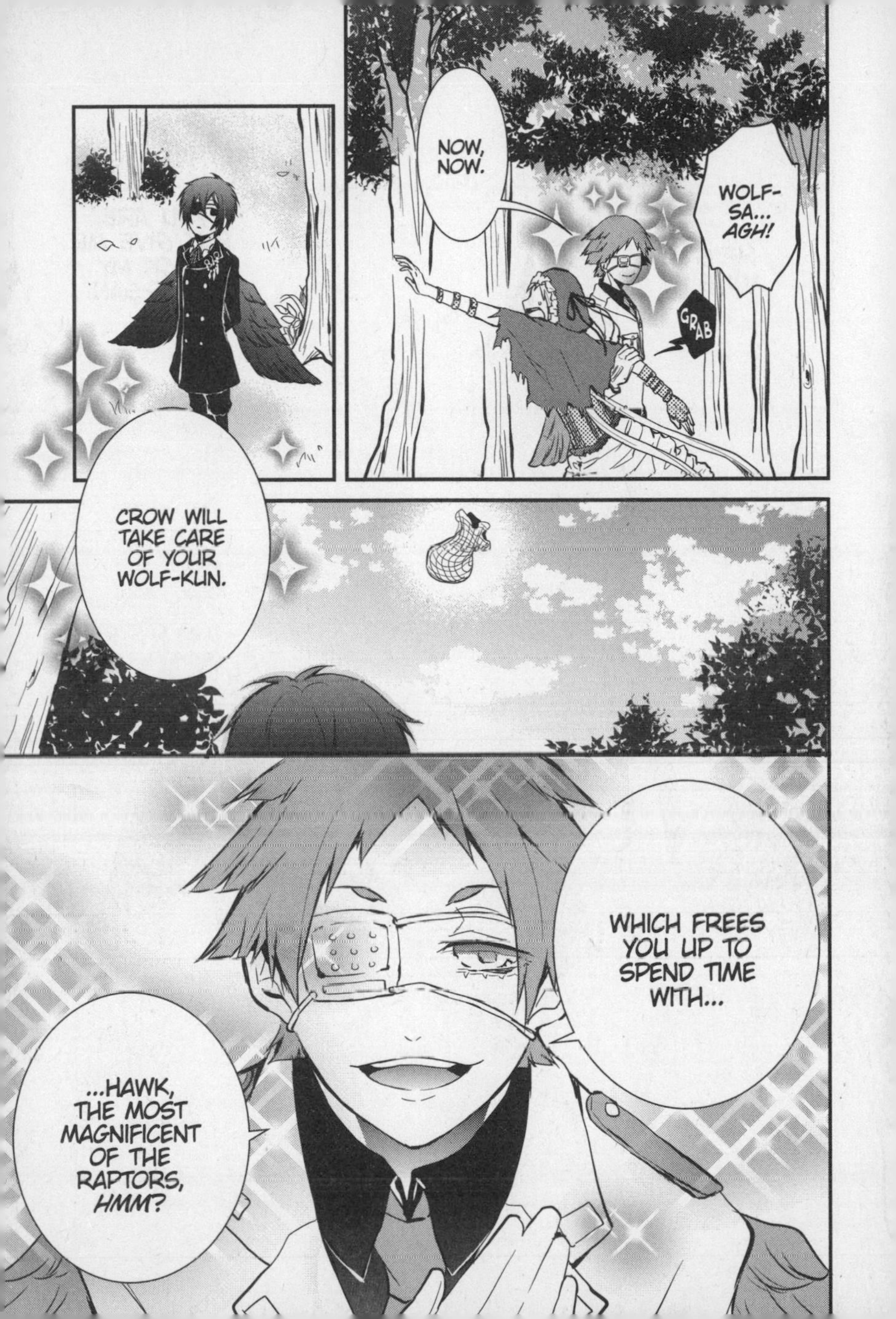
WOLF-SA... AGH!
GRAB
NOW, NOW.
CROW WILL TAKE CARE OF YOUR WOLF-KUN.
WHICH FREES YOU UP TO SPEND TIME WITH...
...HAWK, THE MOST MAGNIFICENT OF THE RAPTORS, HMM?

THE SOURCE OF KINDNESS

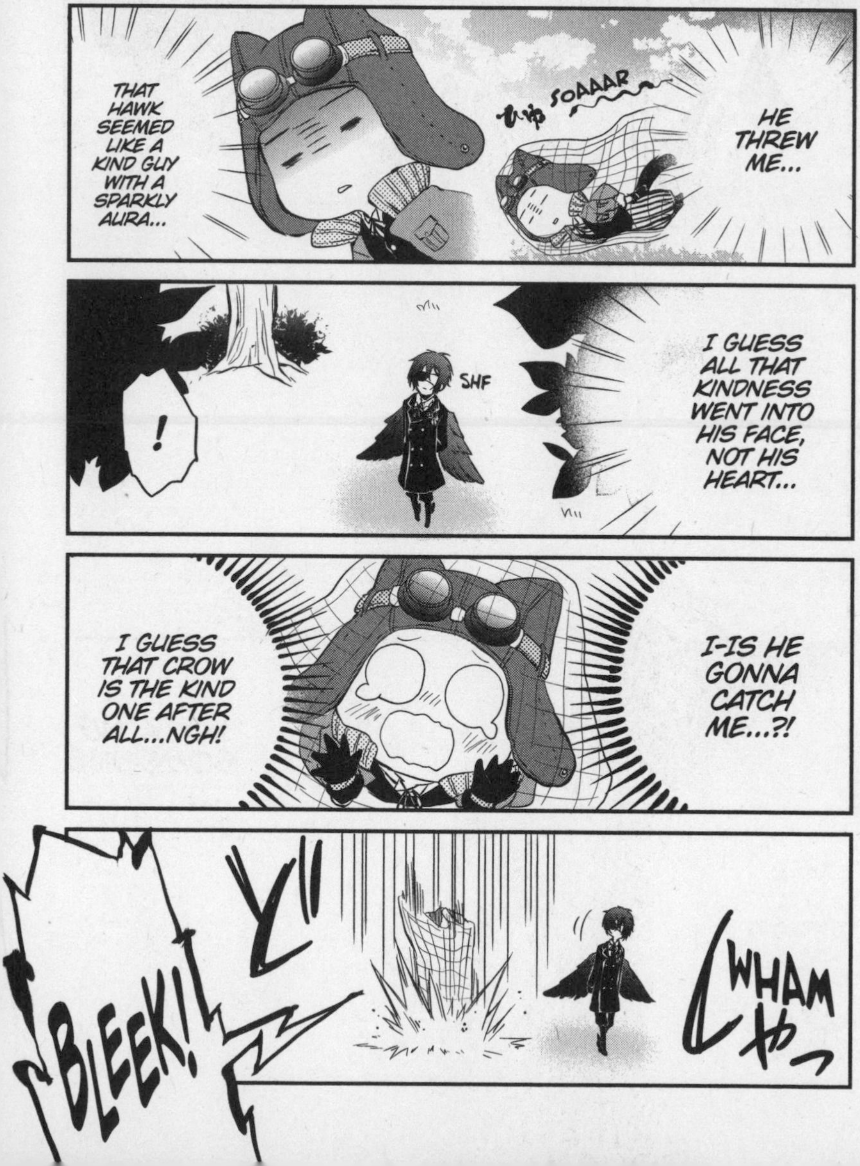
HE THREW ME...
ひゅ SOAAAR
THAT HAWK SEEMED LIKE A KIND GUY WITH A SPARKLY AURA...
I GUESS ALL THAT KINDNESS WENT INTO HIS FACE, NOT HIS HEART...
SHF
!
I-IS HE GONNA CATCH ME...?!
I GUESS THAT CROW IS THE KIND ONE AFTER ALL...NGH!
WHAM
BLEEK!

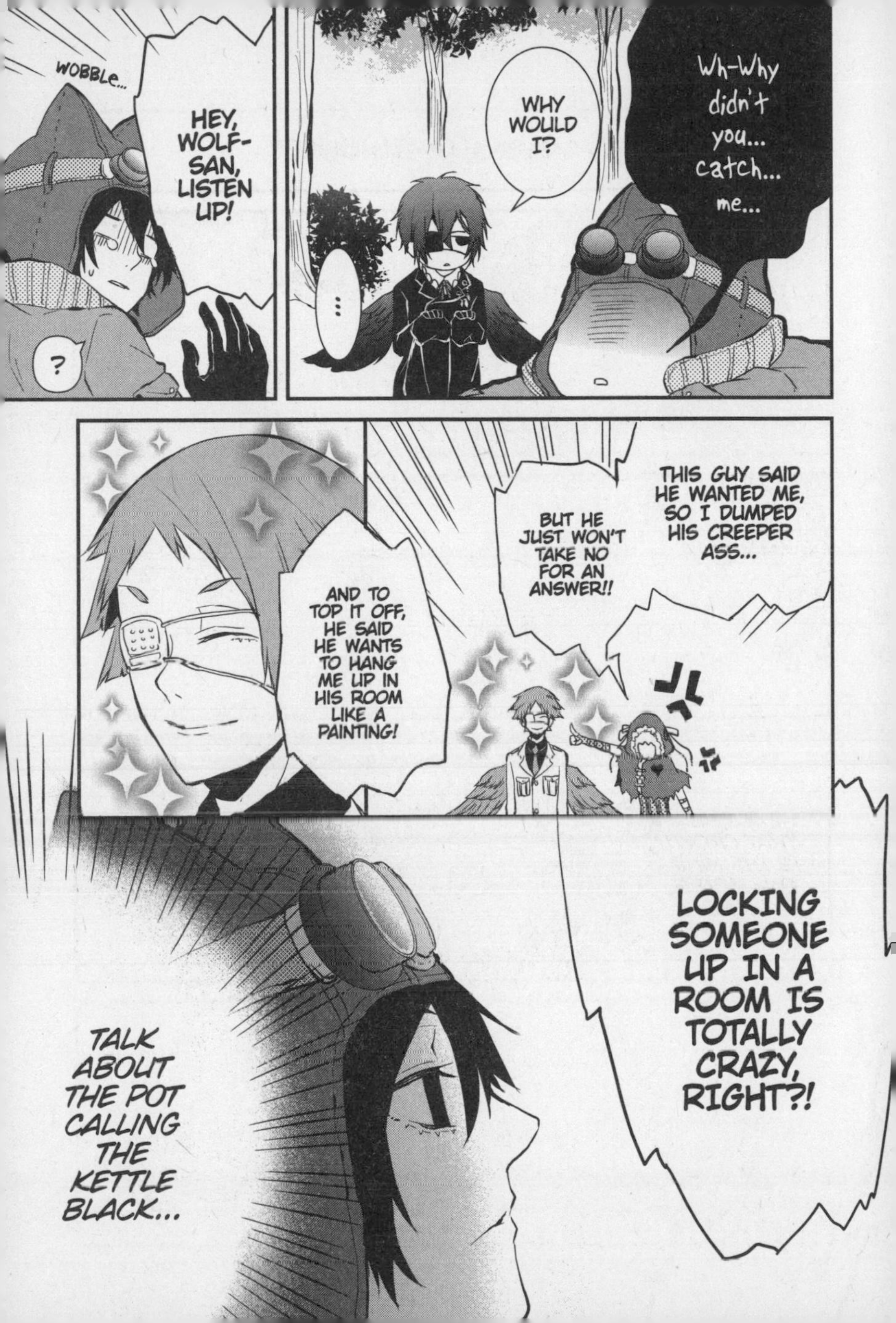
Wh-Why didn't you... catch... me...
WHY WOULD I?
...
WOBBLE...
HEY, WOLF-SAN, LISTEN UP!
?
THIS GUY SAID HE WANTED ME, SO I DUMPED HIS CREEPER ASS...
BUT HE JUST WON'T TAKE NO FOR AN ANSWER!!
AND TO TOP IT OFF, HE SAID HE WANTS TO HANG ME UP IN HIS ROOM LIKE A PAINTING!
LOCKING SOMEONE UP IN A ROOM IS TOTALLY CRAZY, RIGHT?!
TALK ABOUT THE POT CALLING THE KETTLE BLACK...

LOVE VS. POSSESSIVENESS

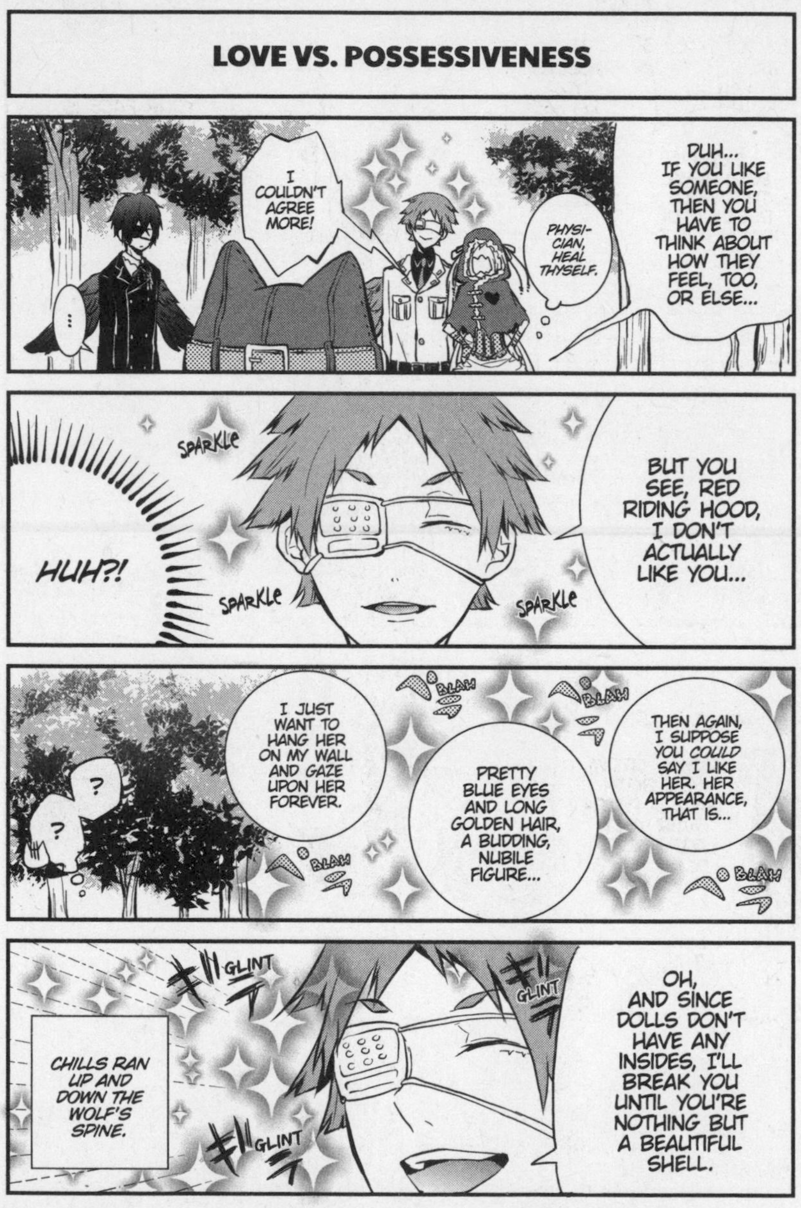
DUH... IF YOU LIKE SOMEONE, THEN YOU HAVE TO THINK ABOUT HOW THEY FEEL, TOO, OR ELSE...
PHYSICIAN, HEAL THYSELF.
I COULDN'T AGREE MORE!
...
BUT YOU SEE, RED RIDING HOOD, I DON'T ACTUALLY LIKE YOU...
SPARKLE
SPARKLE
SPARKLE
HUH?!
THEN AGAIN, I SUPPOSE YOU COULD SAY I LIKE HER. HER APPEARANCE, THAT IS...
BLAH
BLAH
PRETTY BLUE EYES AND LONG GOLDEN HAIR, A BUDDING, NUBILE FIGURE...
BLAH
I JUST WANT TO HANG HER ON MY WALL AND GAZE UPON HER FOREVER.
BLAH
?
?
OH, AND SINCE DOLLS DON'T HAVE ANY INSIDES, I'LL BREAK YOU UNTIL YOU'RE NOTHING BUT A BEAUTIFUL SHELL.
GLINT
GLINT
GLINT
CHILLS RAN UP AND DOWN THE WOLF'S SPINE.

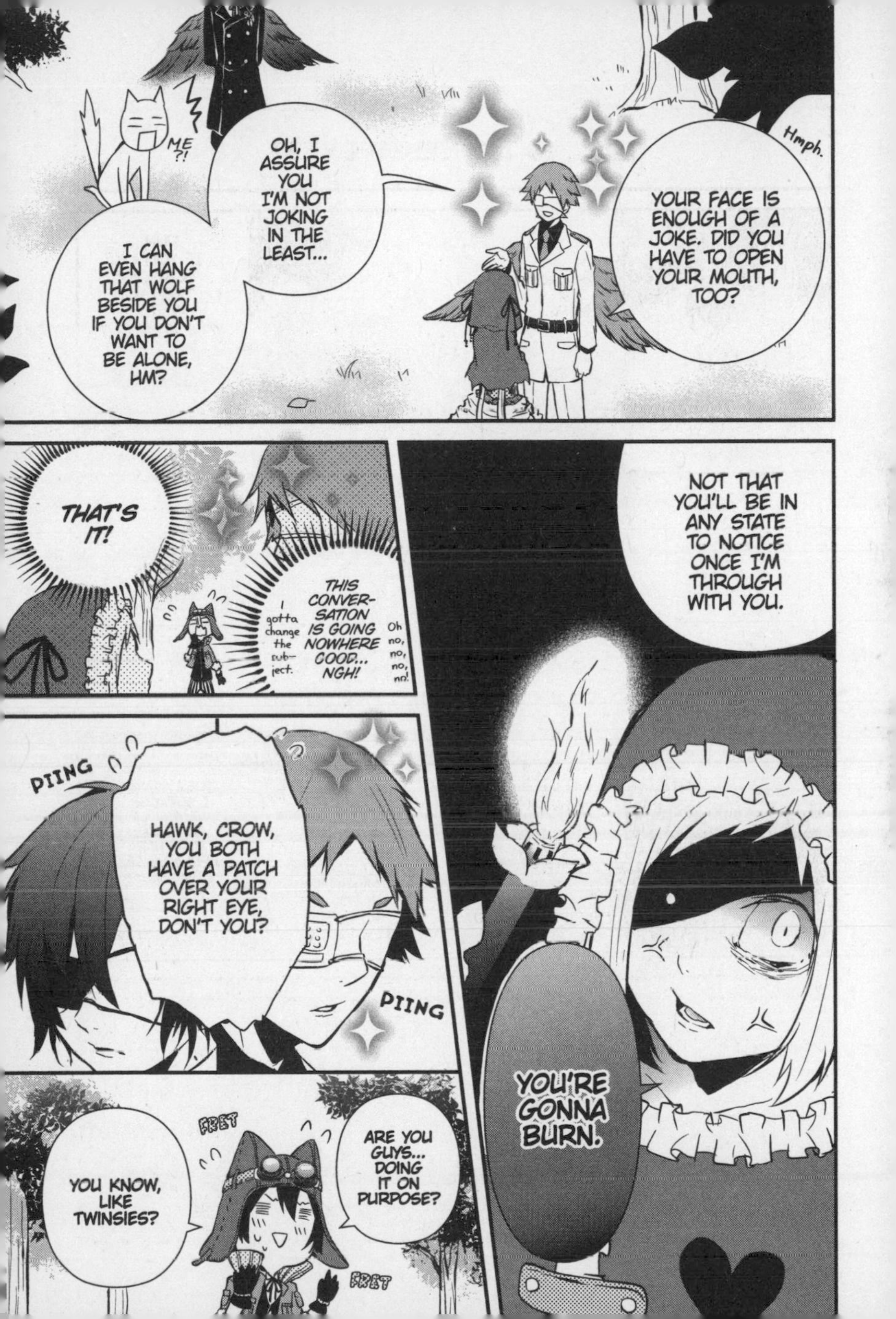
Hmph.
YOUR FACE IS ENOUGH OF A JOKE. DID YOU HAVE TO OPEN YOUR MOUTH, TOO?
OH, I ASSURE YOU I'M NOT JOKING IN THE LEAST...
I CAN EVEN HANG THAT WOLF BESIDE YOU IF YOU DON'T WANT TO BE ALONE, HM?
ME?!
NOT THAT YOU'LL BE IN ANY STATE TO NOTICE ONCE I'M THROUGH WITH YOU.
YOU'RE GONNA BURN.
Oh no, no, no, no!
THIS CONVERSATION IS GOING NOWHERE GOOD... NGH!
I gotta change the sub-ject.
THAT'S IT!
PIING
HAWK, CROW, YOU BOTH HAVE A PATCH OVER YOUR RIGHT EYE, DON'T YOU?
PIING
FRET
ARE YOU GUYS... DOING IT ON PURPOSE?
YOU KNOW, LIKE TWINSIES?
FRET

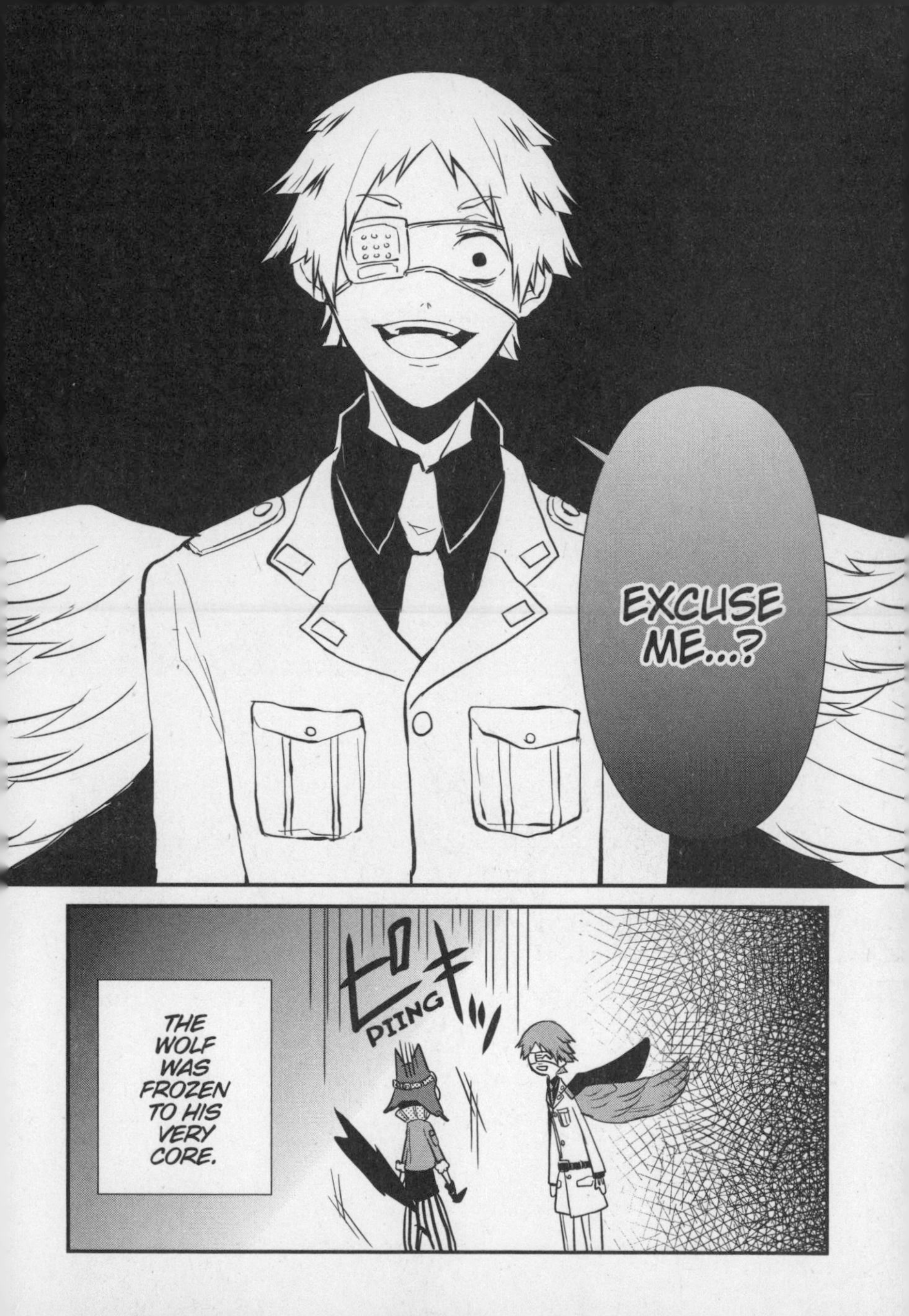
EXCUSE ME...?
PIING
THE WOLF WAS FROZEN TO HIS VERY CORE.

Chapter Four

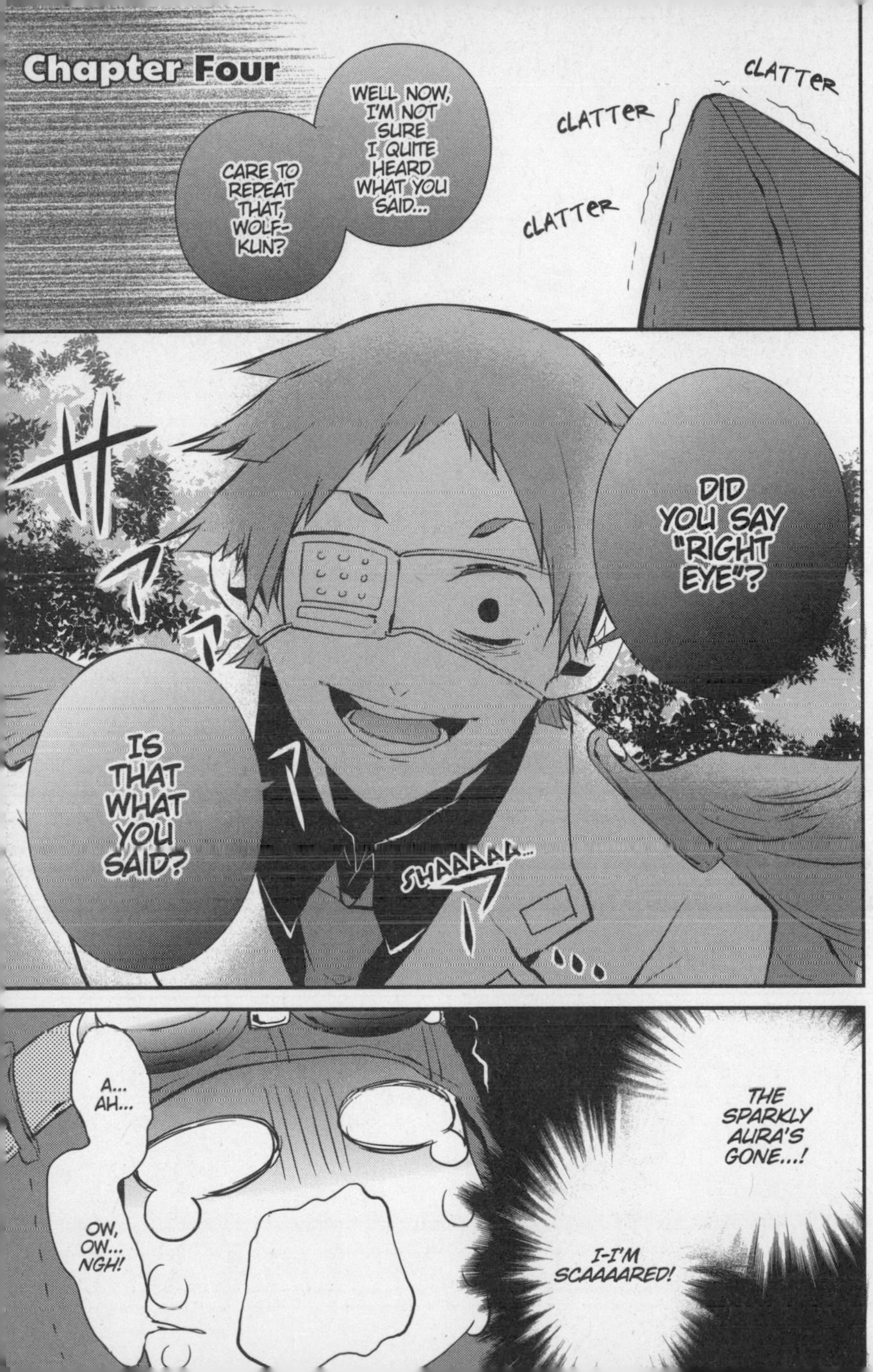
CLATTER
CLATTER
CLATTER
WELL NOW, I'M NOT SURE I QUITE HEARD WHAT YOU SAID...
CARE TO REPEAT THAT, WOLF-KUN?
DID YOU SAY "RIGHT EYE"?
IS THAT WHAT YOU SAID?
SHAAAAA...
THE SPARKLY AURA'S GONE...!
I-I'M SCAAAARED!
A... AH...
OW, OW... NGH!

TWO PEAS IN A POD

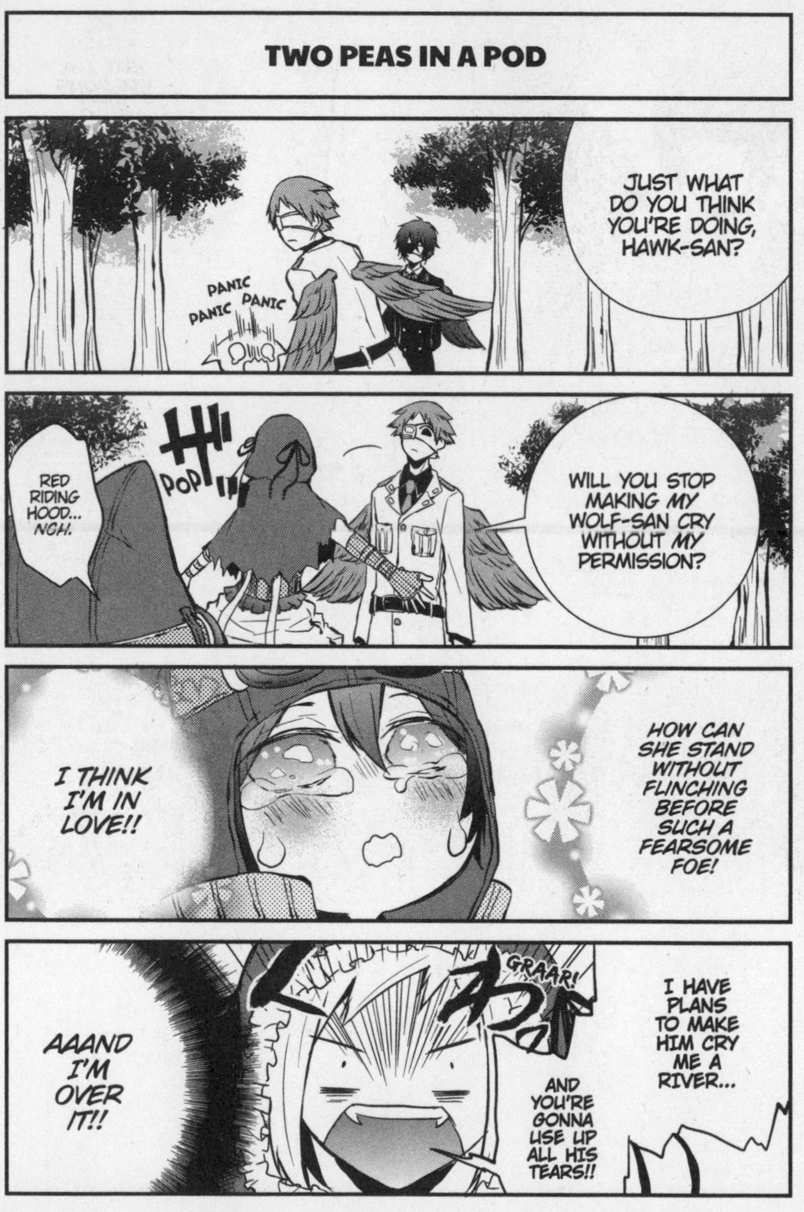

JUST WHAT DO YOU THINK YOU'RE DOING, HAWK-SAN?
PANIC PANIC PANIC
WILL YOU STOP MAKING MY WOLF-SAN CRY WITHOUT MY PERMISSION?
POP
RED RIDING HOOD... NCH.
HOW CAN SHE STAND WITHOUT FLINCHING BEFORE SUCH A FEARSOME FOE!
I THINK I'M IN LOVE!!
I HAVE PLANS TO MAKE HIM CRY ME A RIVER...
AND YOU'RE GONNA USE UP ALL HIS TEARS!!
GRAAR!
AAAND I'M OVER IT!!

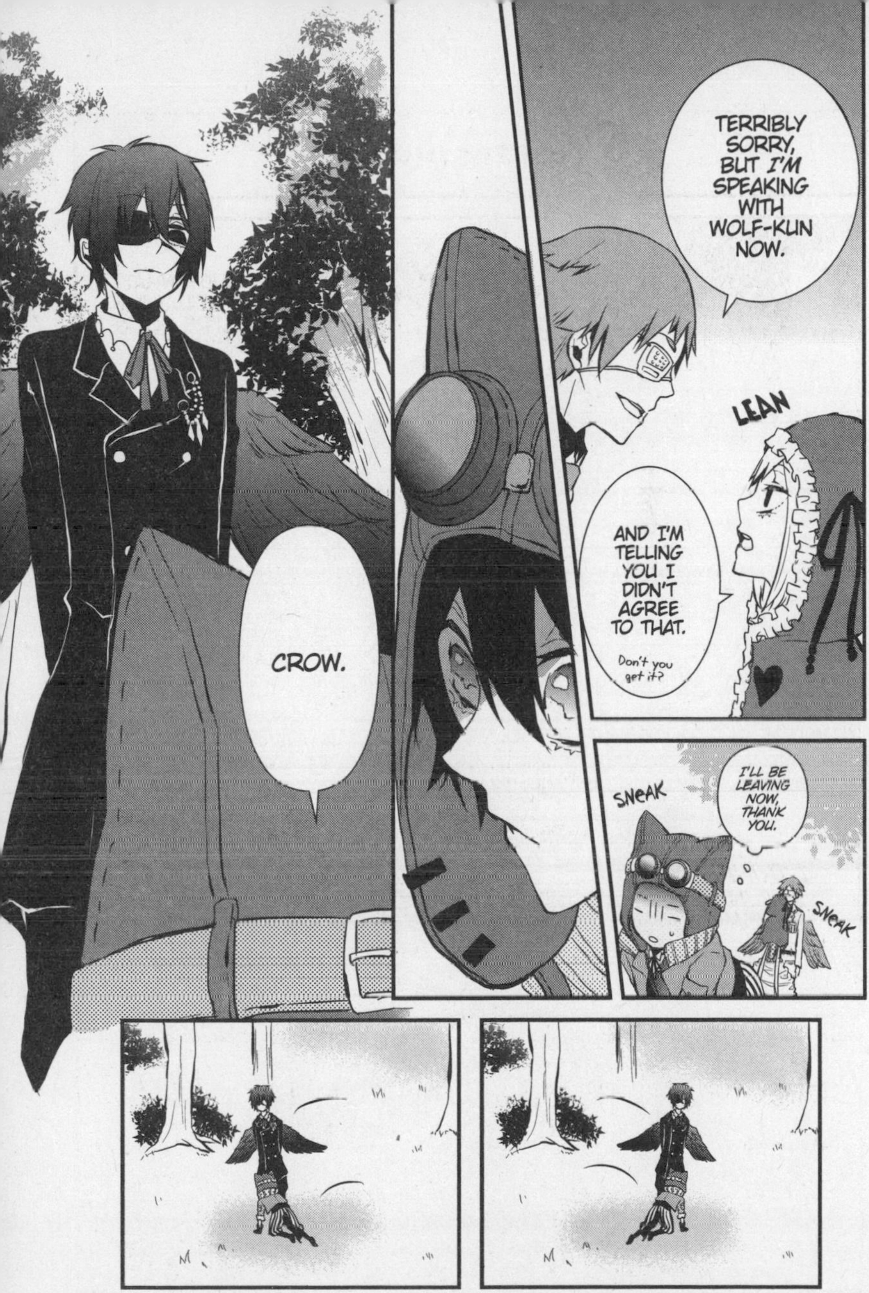
TERRIBLY SORRY, BUT I'M SPEAKING WITH WOLF-KUN NOW.
LEAN
AND I'M TELLING YOU I DIDN'T AGREE TO THAT.
Don't you get it?
SNEAK
I'LL BE LEAVING NOW, THANK YOU.
SNEAK
CROW.

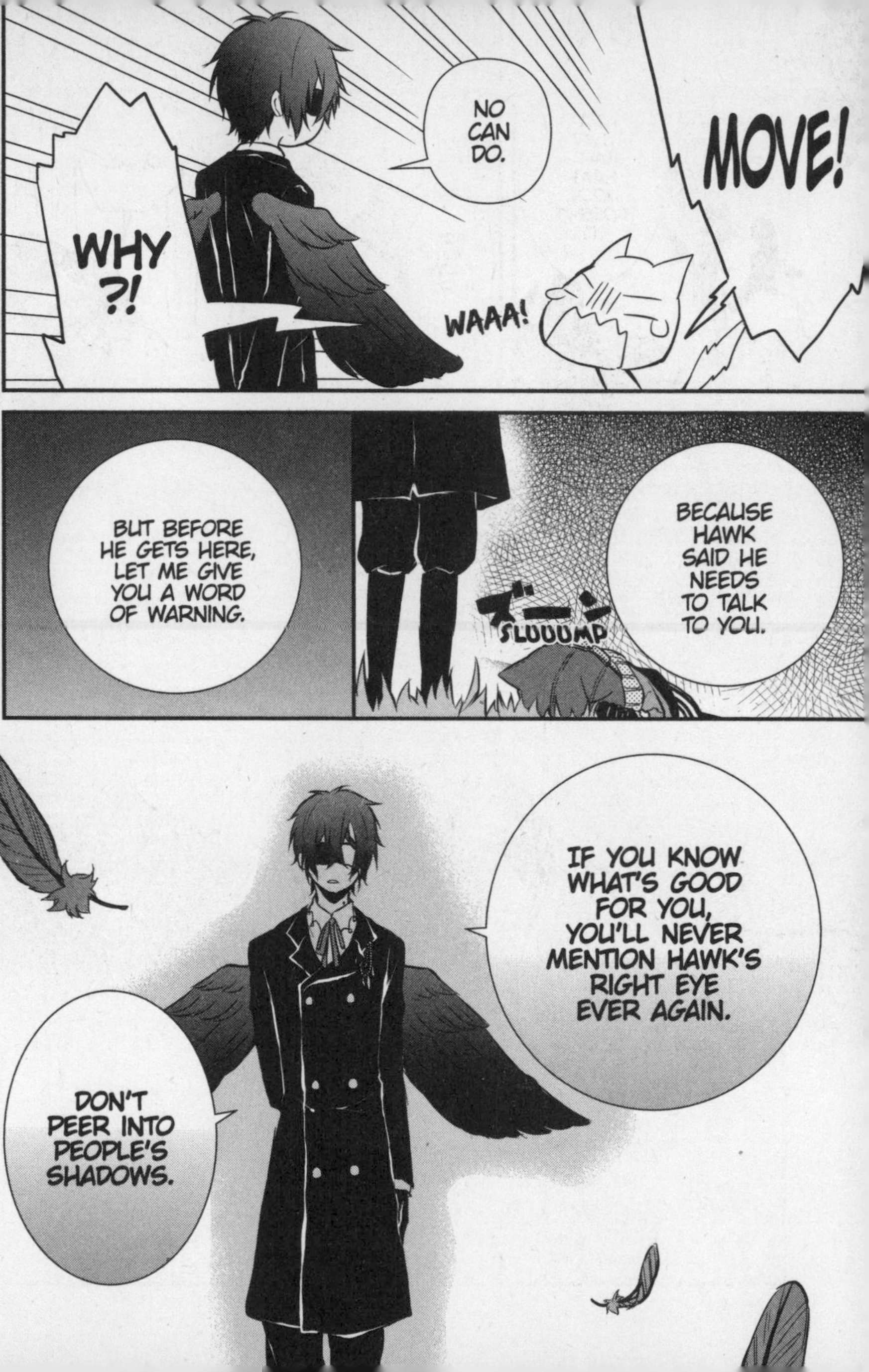
MOVE!
NO CAN DO.
WAAA!
WHY ?!
BECAUSE HAWK SAID HE NEEDS TO TALK TO YOU.
ズーン
SLUUUMP
BUT BEFORE HE GETS HERE, LET ME GIVE YOU A WORD OF WARNING.
IF YOU KNOW WHAT'S GOOD FOR YOU, YOU'LL NEVER MENTION HAWK'S RIGHT EYE EVER AGAIN.
DON'T PEER INTO PEOPLE'S SHADOWS.

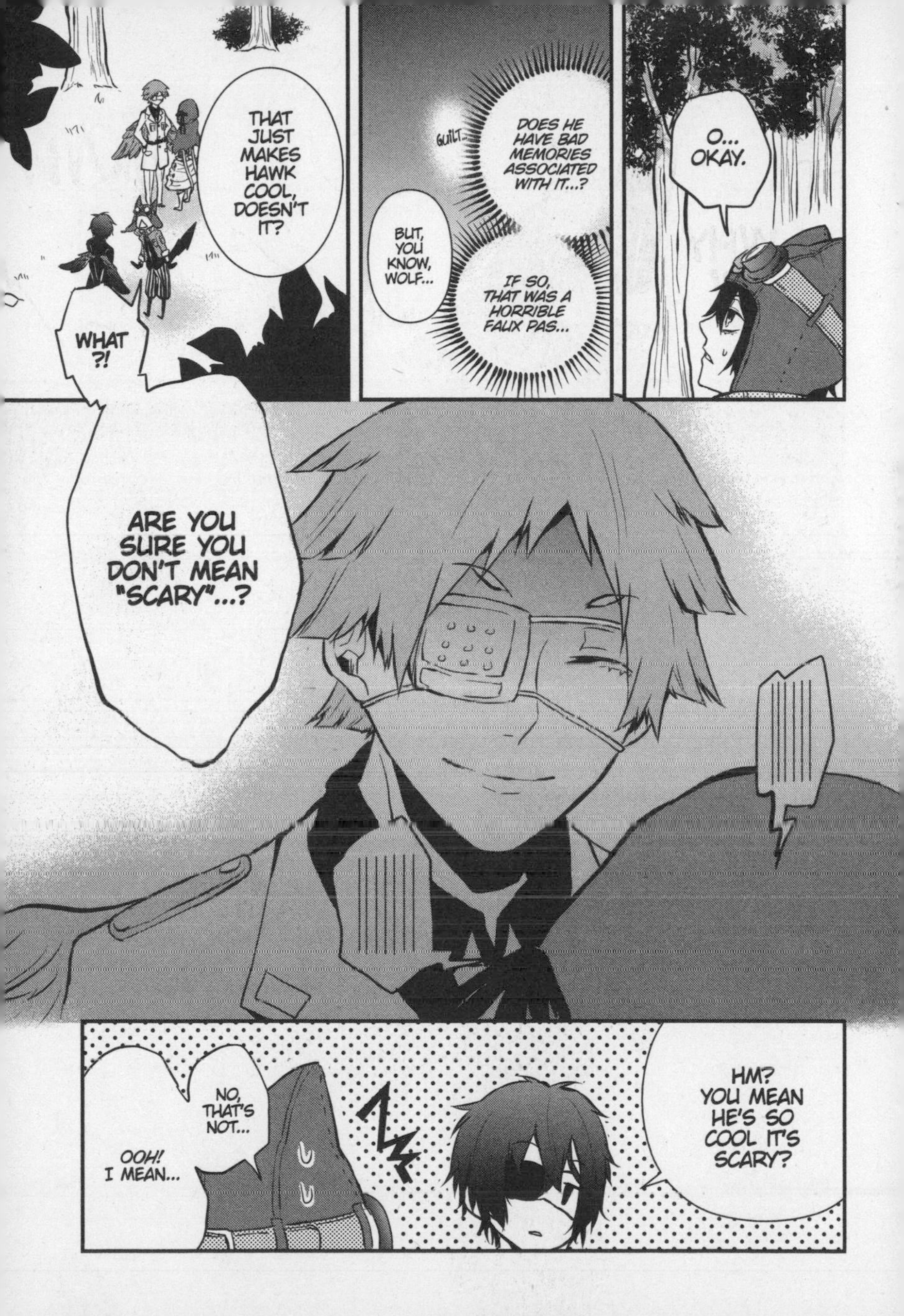
O... OKAY.
DOES HE HAVE BAD MEMORIES ASSOCIATED WITH IT...?
GUILT...
IF SO, THAT WAS A HORRIBLE FAUX PAS...
BUT, YOU KNOW, WOLF...
THAT JUST MAKES HAWK COOL, DOESN'T IT?
WHAT?!
ARE YOU SURE YOU DON'T MEAN "SCARY"...?
HM? YOU MEAN HE'S SO COOL IT'S SCARY?
NO, THAT'S NOT...
OOH! I MEAN...

CONFESSION

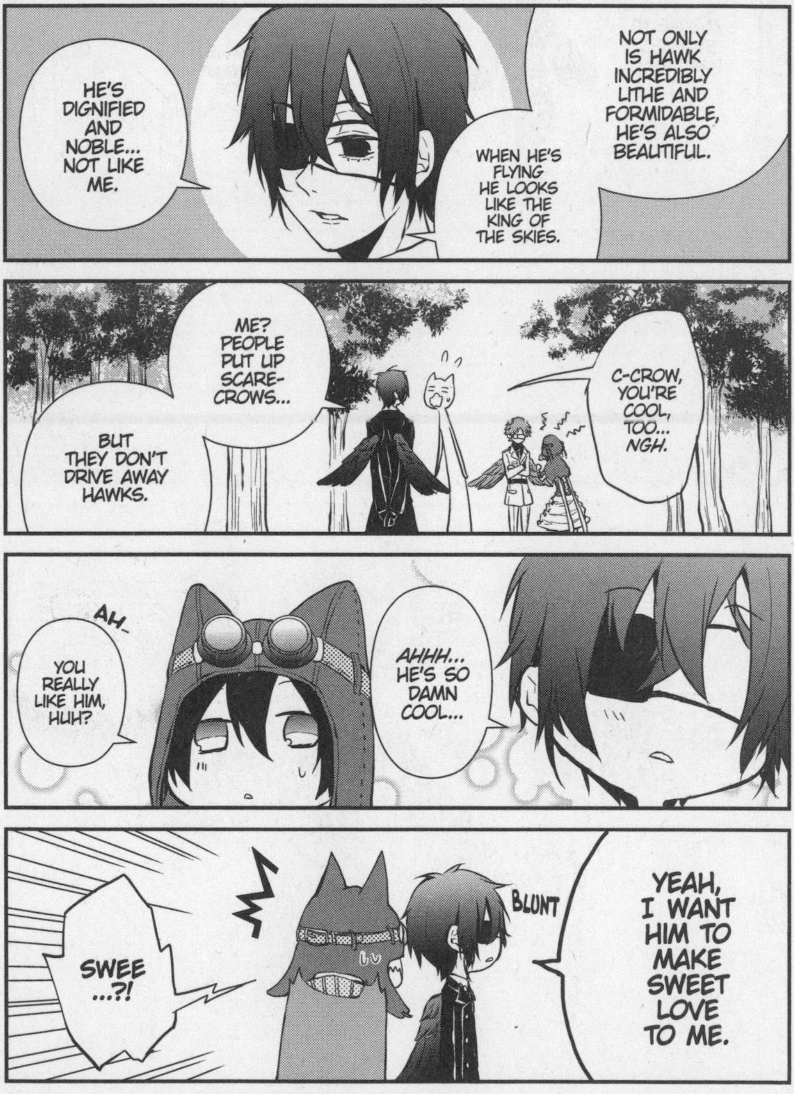
NOT ONLY IS HAWK INCREDIBLY LITHE AND FORMIDABLE, HE'S ALSO BEAUTIFUL.
WHEN HE'S FLYING HE LOOKS LIKE THE KING OF THE SKIES.
HE'S DIGNIFIED AND NOBLE... NOT LIKE ME.
C-CROW, YOU'RE COOL, TOO... NGH.
ME? PEOPLE PUT UP SCARE-CROWS...
BUT THEY DON'T DRIVE AWAY HAWKS.
AHHH... HE'S SO DAMN COOL...
AH..
YOU REALLY LIKE HIM, HUH?
YEAH, I WANT HIM TO MAKE SWEET LOVE TO ME.
BLUNT
SWEE ...?!

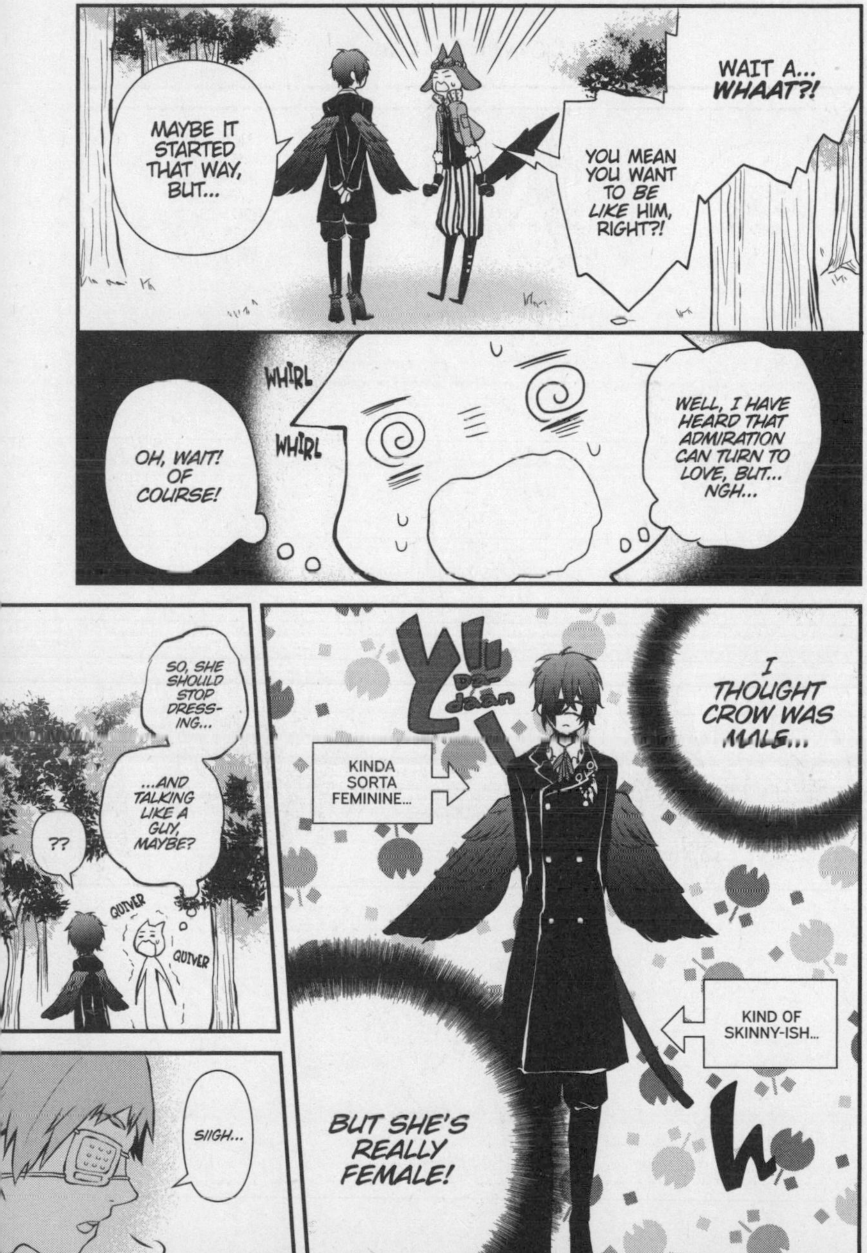
WAIT A... WHAAT?!
YOU MEAN YOU WANT TO BE LIKE HIM, RIGHT?!
MAYBE IT STARTED THAT WAY, BUT...
WELL, I HAVE HEARD THAT ADMIRATION CAN TURN TO LOVE, BUT... NGH...
WHIRL
WHIRL
OH, WAIT! OF COURSE!
I THOUGHT CROW WAS MALE...
DA-DAAN
KINDA SORTA FEMININE...
KIND OF SKINNY-ISH...
BUT SHE'S REALLY FEMALE!
SO, SHE SHOULD STOP DRESSING...
...AND TALKING LIKE A GUY, MAYBE?
??
QUIVER
QUIVER
SIIGH...

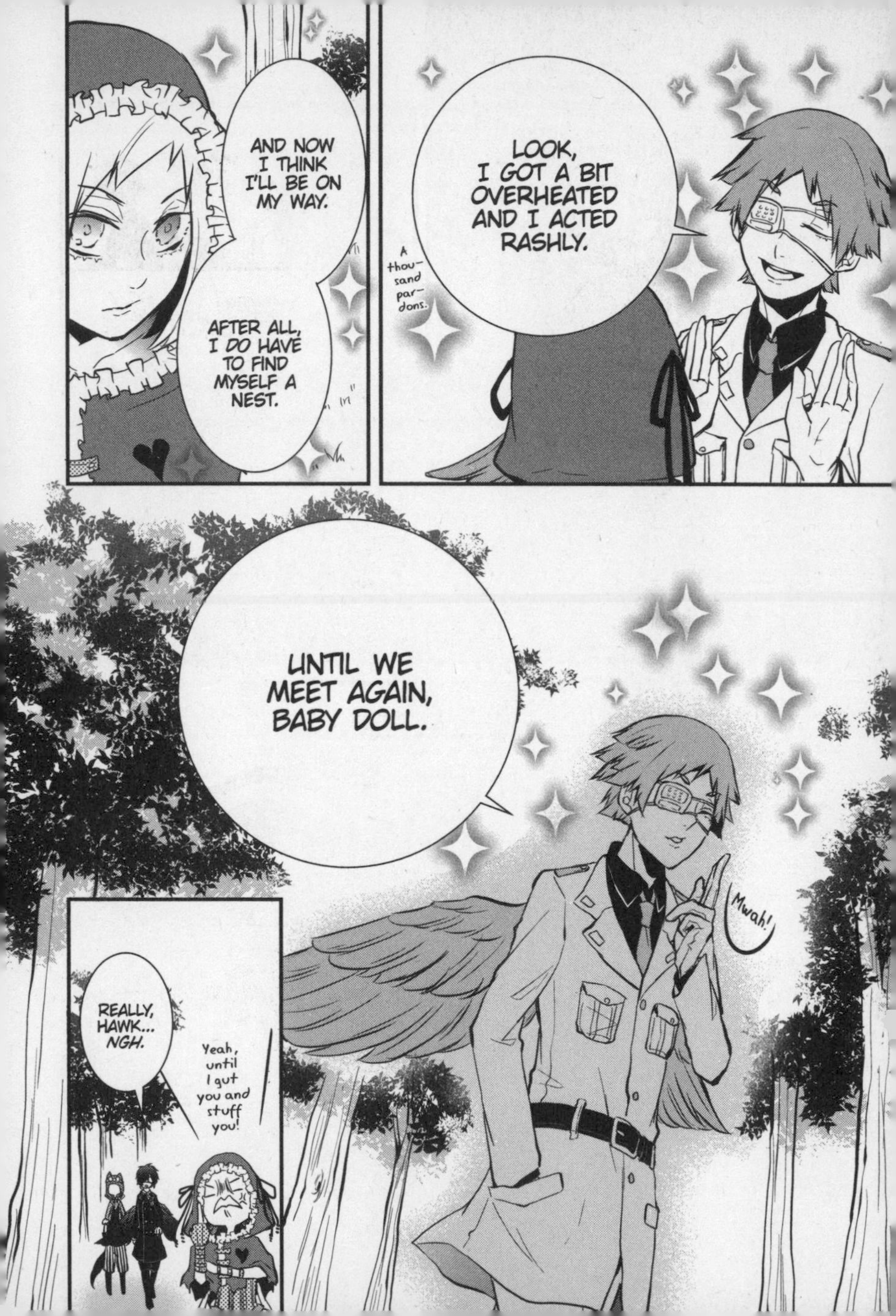
LOOK, I GOT A BIT OVERHEATED AND I ACTED RASHLY.
A thou-sand par-dons.
AND NOW I THINK I'LL BE ON MY WAY.
AFTER ALL, I DO HAVE TO FIND MYSELF A NEST.
UNTIL WE MEET AGAIN, BABY DOLL.
Mwah!
REALLY, HAWK... NGH.
Yeah, until I gut you and stuff you!

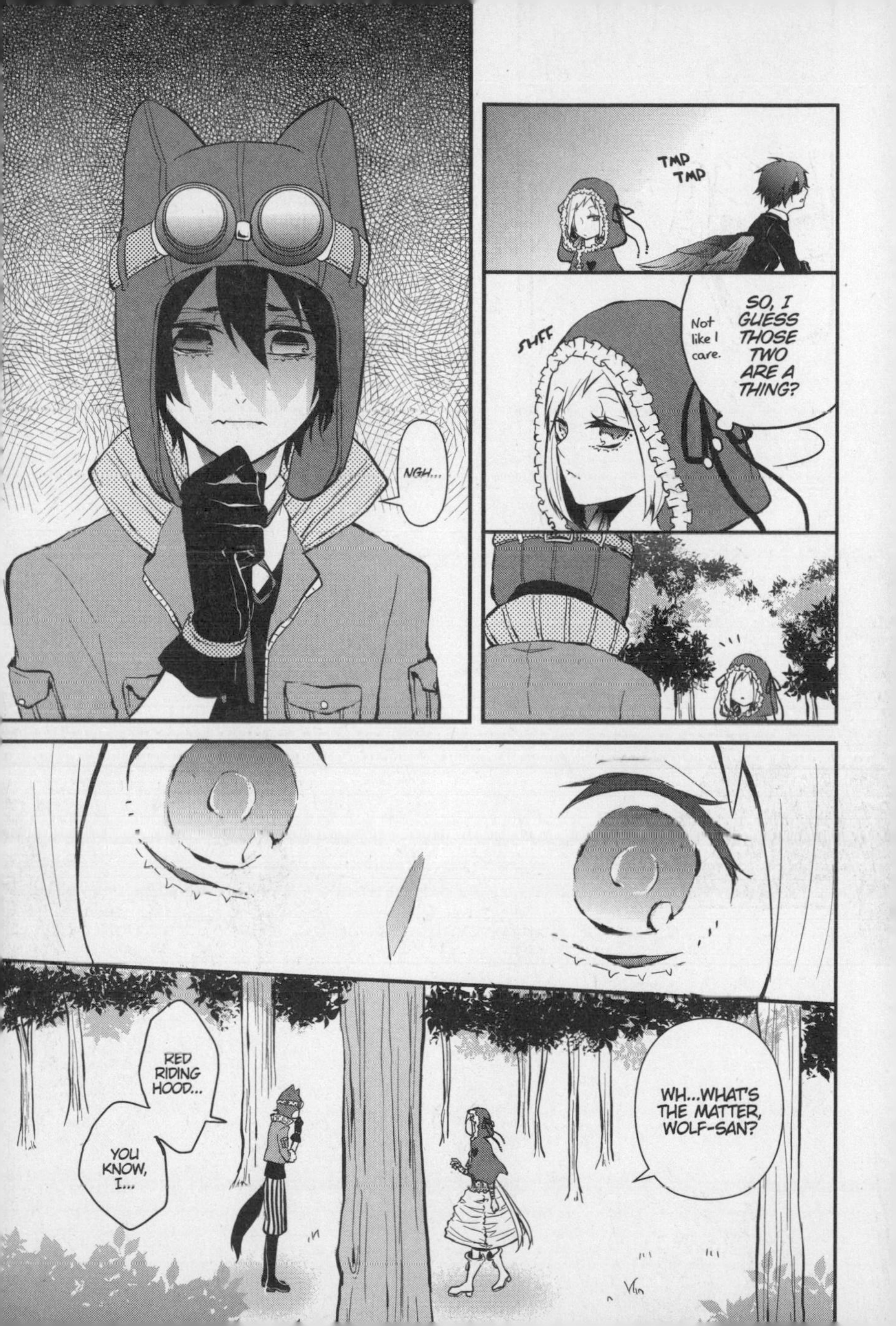
TMP TMP
SNIFF
SO, I GUESS THOSE TWO ARE A THING?
Not like I care.
NGH...
WH...WHAT'S THE MATTER, WOLF-SAN?
RED RIDING HOOD...
YOU KNOW, I...

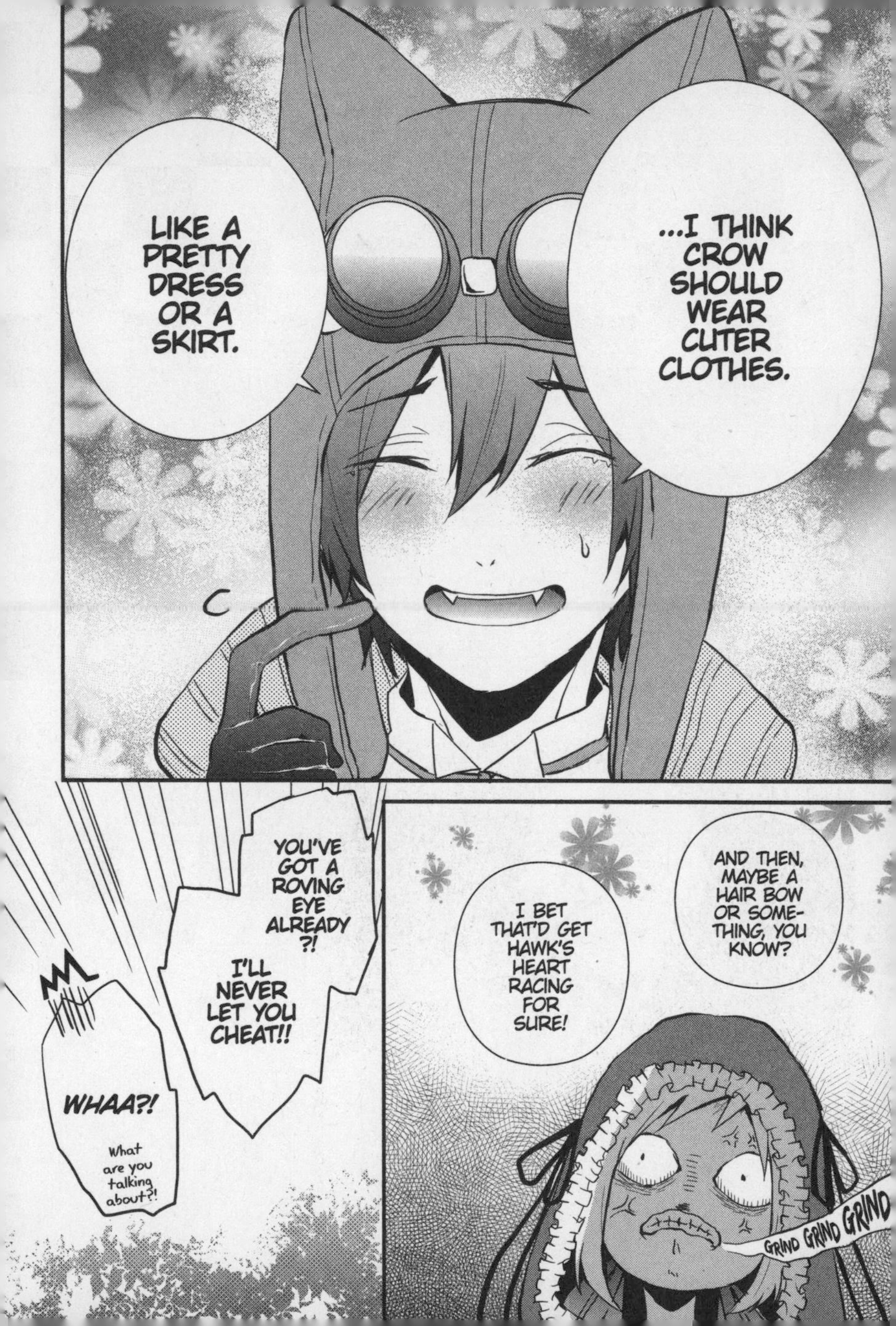
...I THINK CROW SHOULD WEAR CUTER CLOTHES.
LIKE A PRETTY DRESS OR A SKIRT.
AND THEN, MAYBE A HAIR BOW OR SOME-THING, YOU KNOW?
I BET THAT'D GET HAWK'S HEART RACING FOR SURE!
GRIND GRIND GRIND
YOU'VE GOT A ROVING EYE ALREADY?!
I'LL NEVER LET YOU CHEAT!!
WHAA?!
What are you talking about?!

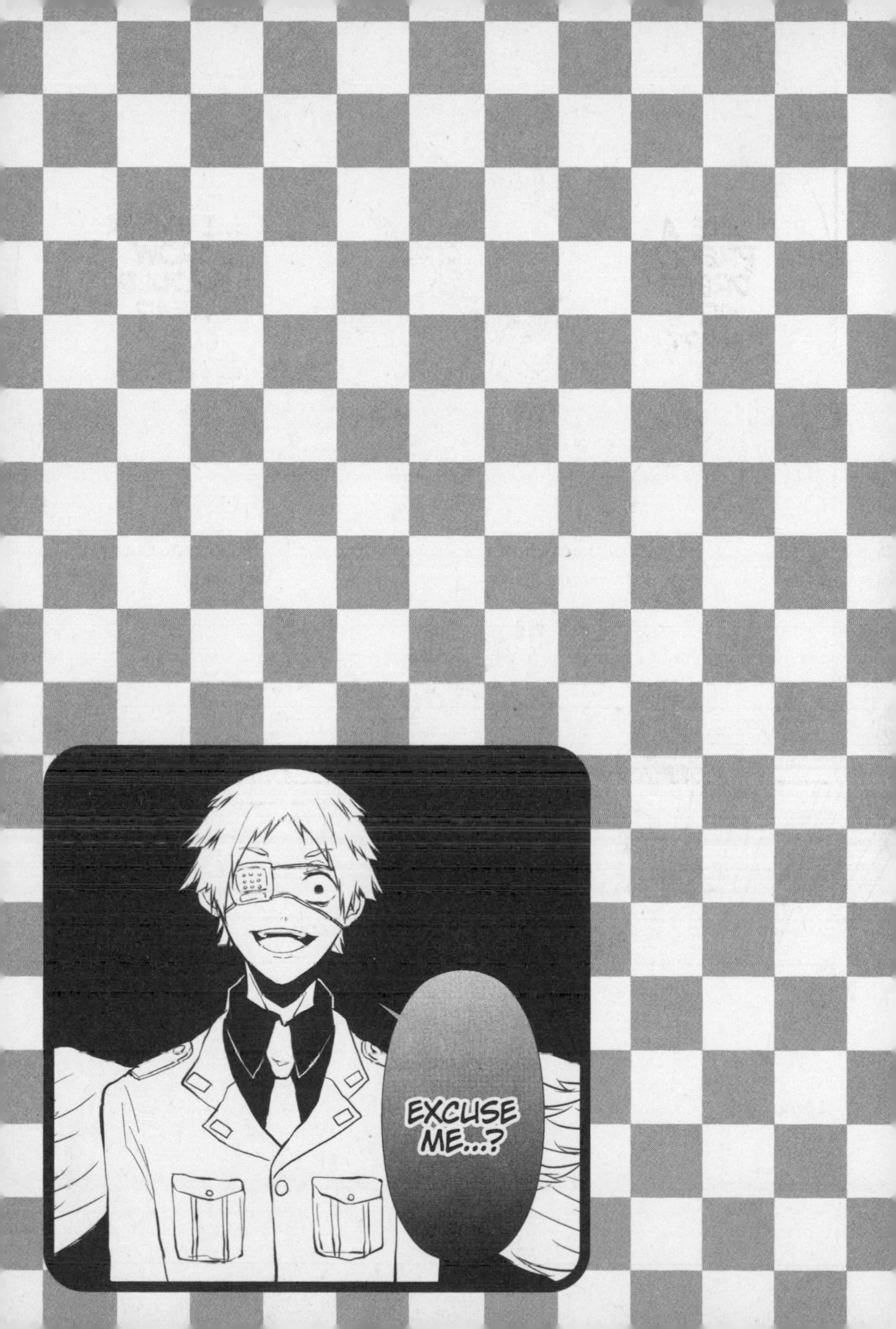
EXCUSE ME...?

Red Riding Hood and the Big Sad Wolf

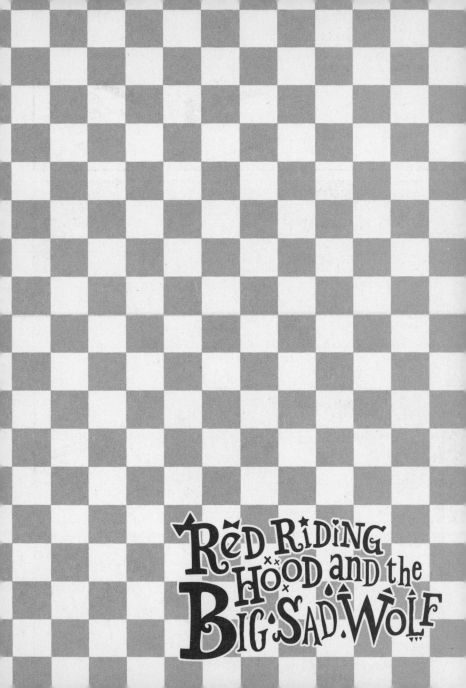

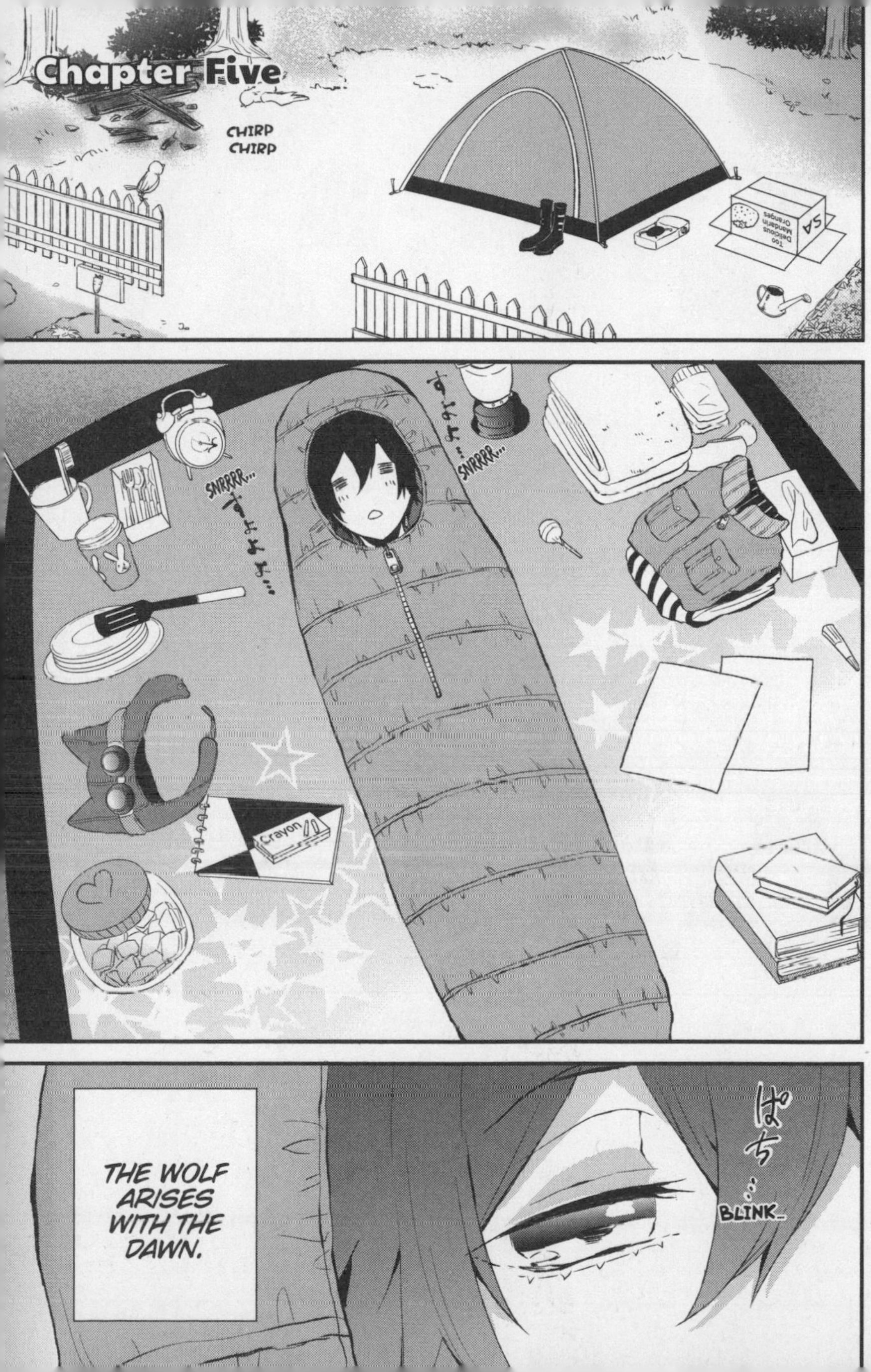
Chapter Five
CHIRP
CHIRP
SA
Too Delicious Mandarin Oranges
SNRRRR...
SNRRRR...
Crayon
THE WOLF ARISES WITH THE DAWN.
BLINK...

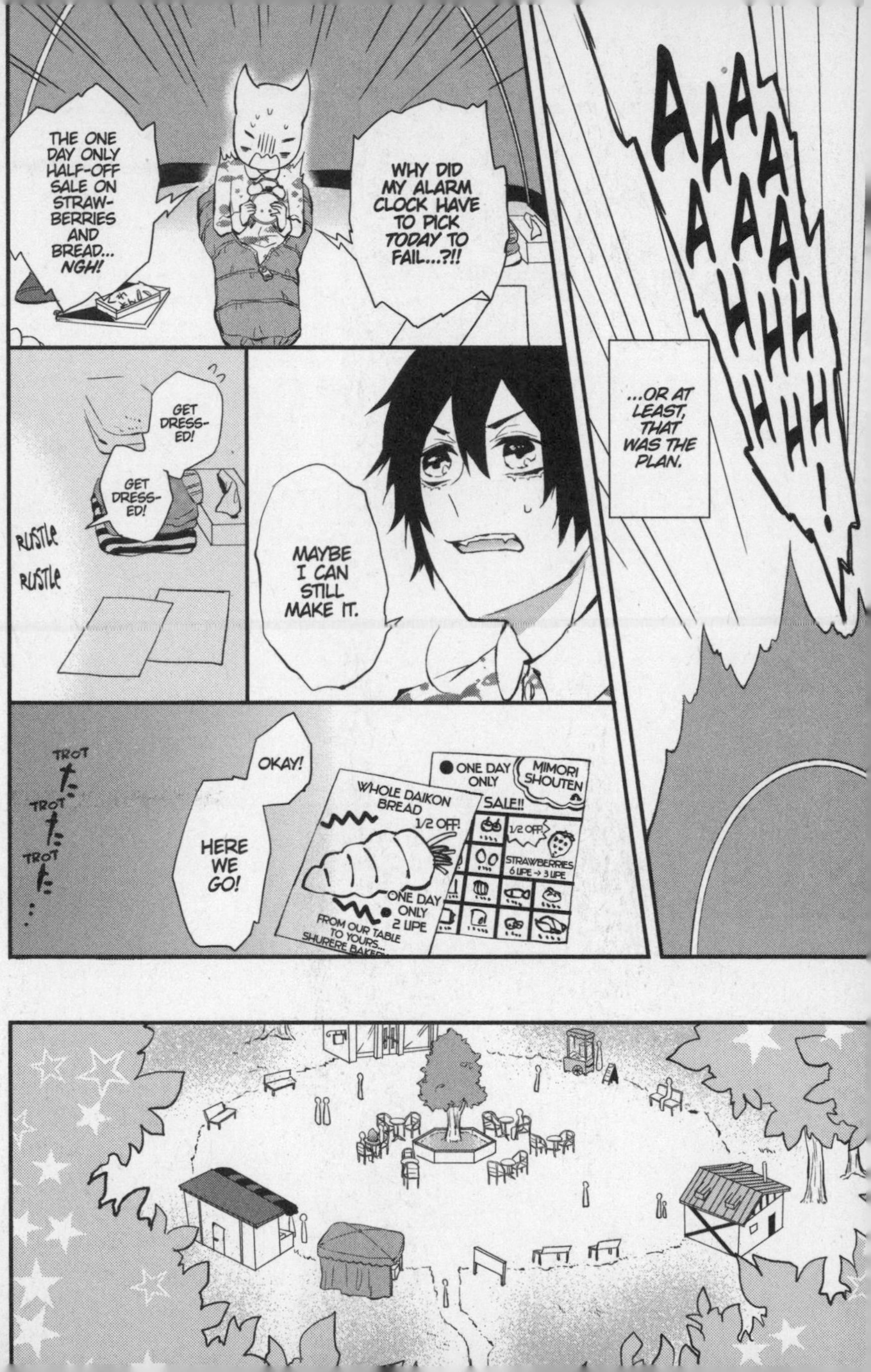
AAAAAAAAAHHHHHH!
...OR AT LEAST, THAT WAS THE PLAN.
WHY DID MY ALARM CLOCK HAVE TO PICK *TODAY* TO FAIL...?!!
THE ONE DAY ONLY HALF-OFF SALE ON STRAWBERRIES AND BREAD... *NGH!*
MAYBE I CAN STILL MAKE IT.
GET DRESSED!
GET DRESSED!
RUSTLE
RUSTLE
ONE DAY ONLY
MIMORI SHOUTEN
SALE!!
1/2 OFF
STRAWBERRIES 6 LIPE → 3 LIPE
WHOLE DAIKON BREAD
1/2 OFF!
ONE DAY ONLY 2 LIPE
FROM OUR TABLE TO YOURS... SHURERE BAKER
OKAY!
HERE WE GO!
TROT
TROT
TROT

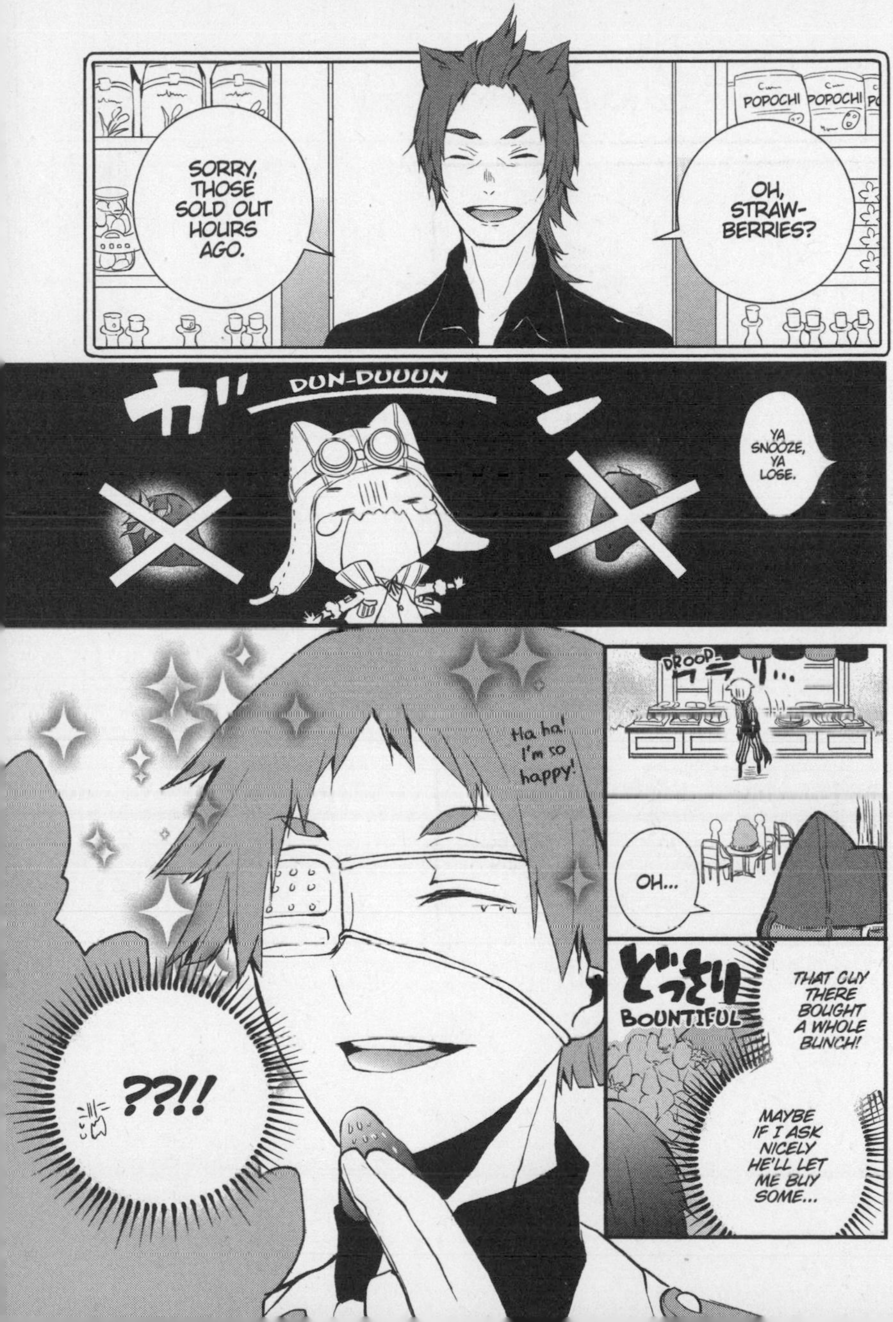
POPOCHI
POPOCHI
OH, STRAWBERRIES?
SORRY, THOSE SOLD OUT HOURS AGO.
ガーン
DUN-DUUUN
YA SNOOZE, YA LOSE.
DROOP
OH...
どっさり
BOUNTIFUL
THAT GUY THERE BOUGHT A WHOLE BUNCH!
MAYBE IF I ASK NICELY HE'LL LET ME BUY SOME...
Ha ha! I'm so happy!
??!!

TERROR VS. DESIRE

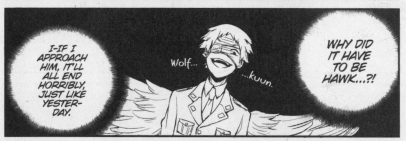

WHY DID IT HAVE TO BE HAWK...?!
Wolf...
...kuun.
I-IF I APPROACH HIM, IT'LL ALL END HORRIBLY, JUST LIKE YESTER-DAY.
NGH... BUT THEY LOOK SO YUMMY.
STRAWBER-RIES ARE ALWAYS SO EXPENSIVE, SO I JUST GO WITHOUT, BUT...
I THOUGHT I'D FINALLY GET TO EAT SOME TODAY.
OOOH... I'M SCARED BUT I REALLY WANT THEM.
WHAT SHOULD I DO... NGH.
HEY, HAWK.
THAT WOLF IS APPROACH-ING US, AND HE'S SHAKING.
SHAKE
SHAKE
SHAKE
SHAKE
HE SHOULD REALLY DO ONE AT A TIME, SHOULDN'T HE, *HMM*?

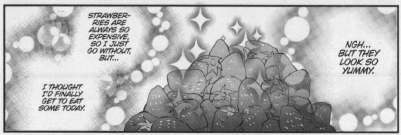

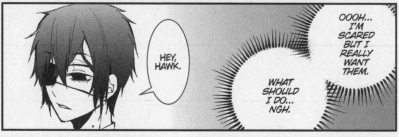

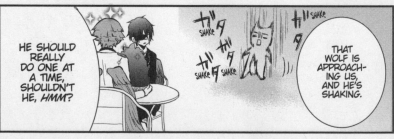

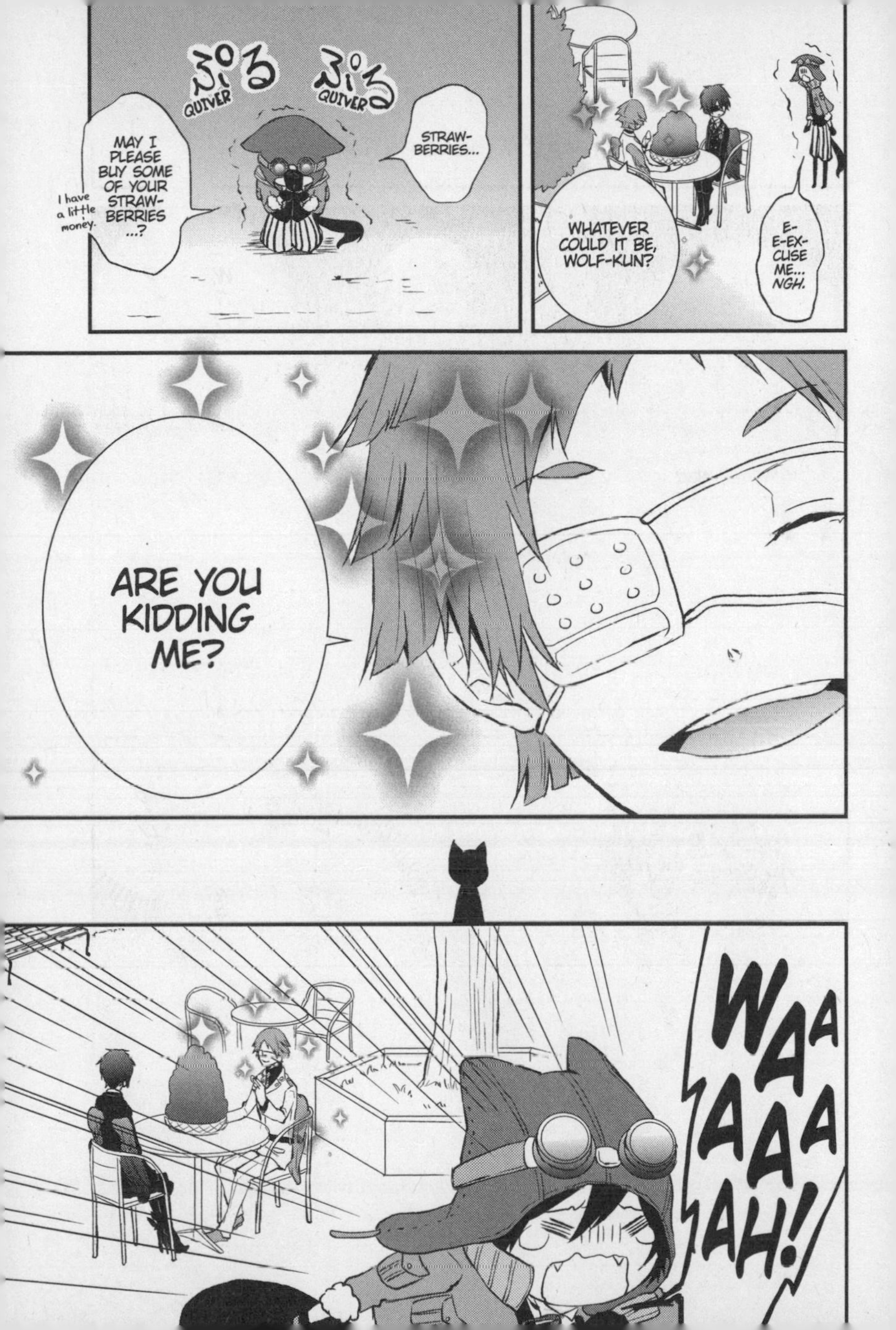
E-E-EXCUSE ME... NGH.
WHATEVER COULD IT BE, WOLF-KUN?
STRAW-BERRIES...
ぷる QUIVER
ぷる QUIVER
MAY I PLEASE BUY SOME OF YOUR STRAW-BERRIES ...?
I have a little money.
ARE YOU KIDDING ME?
WAAAAAAH!

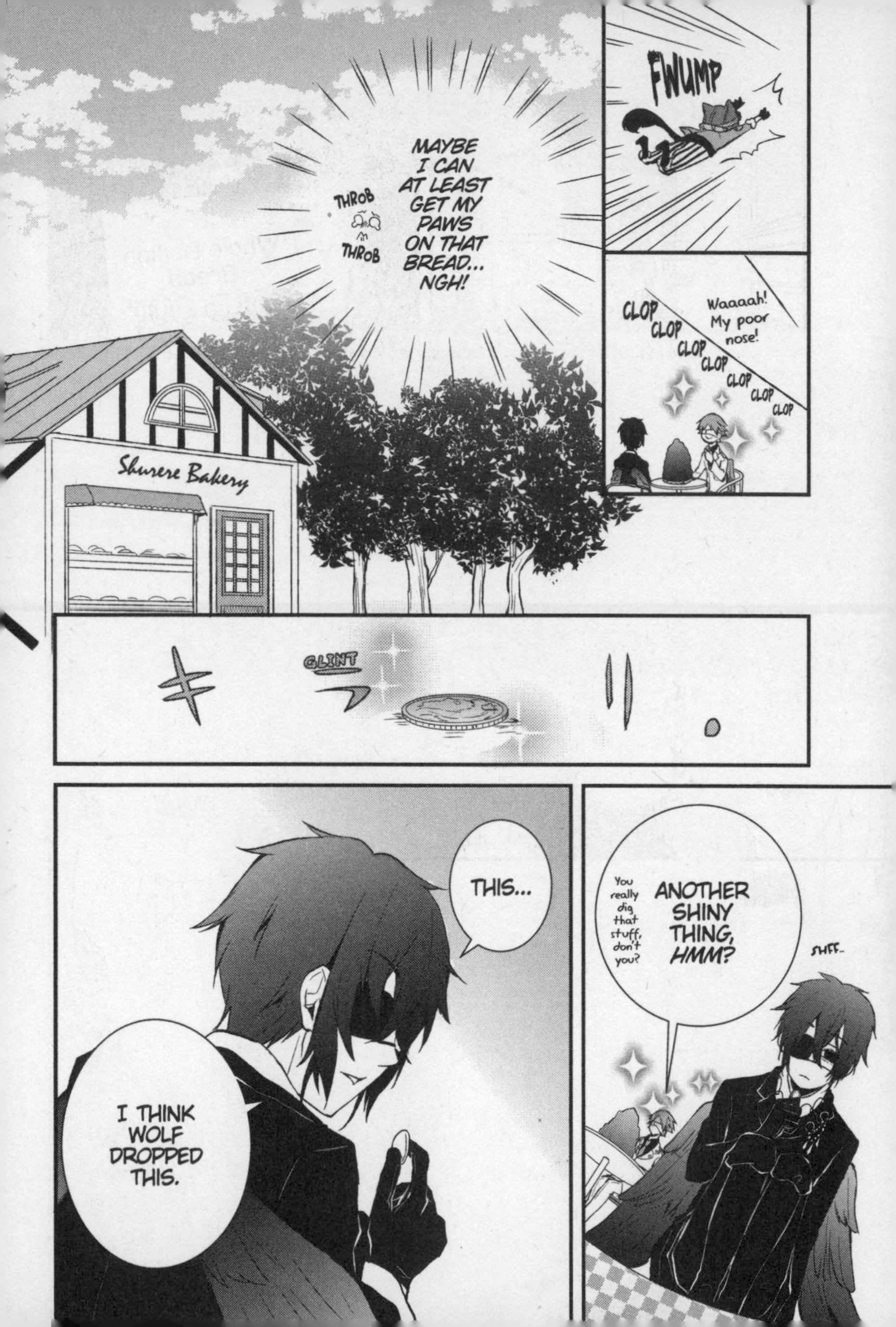
FWUMP
Waaaah! My poor nose!
CLOP CLOP CLOP CLOP CLOP CLOP CLOP
MAYBE I CAN AT LEAST GET MY PAWS ON THAT BREAD... NGH!
THROB THROB
Shurere Bakery
GLINT
ANOTHER SHINY THING, HMM?
You really dig that stuff, don't you?
SHFF..
THIS...
I THINK WOLF DROPPED THIS.

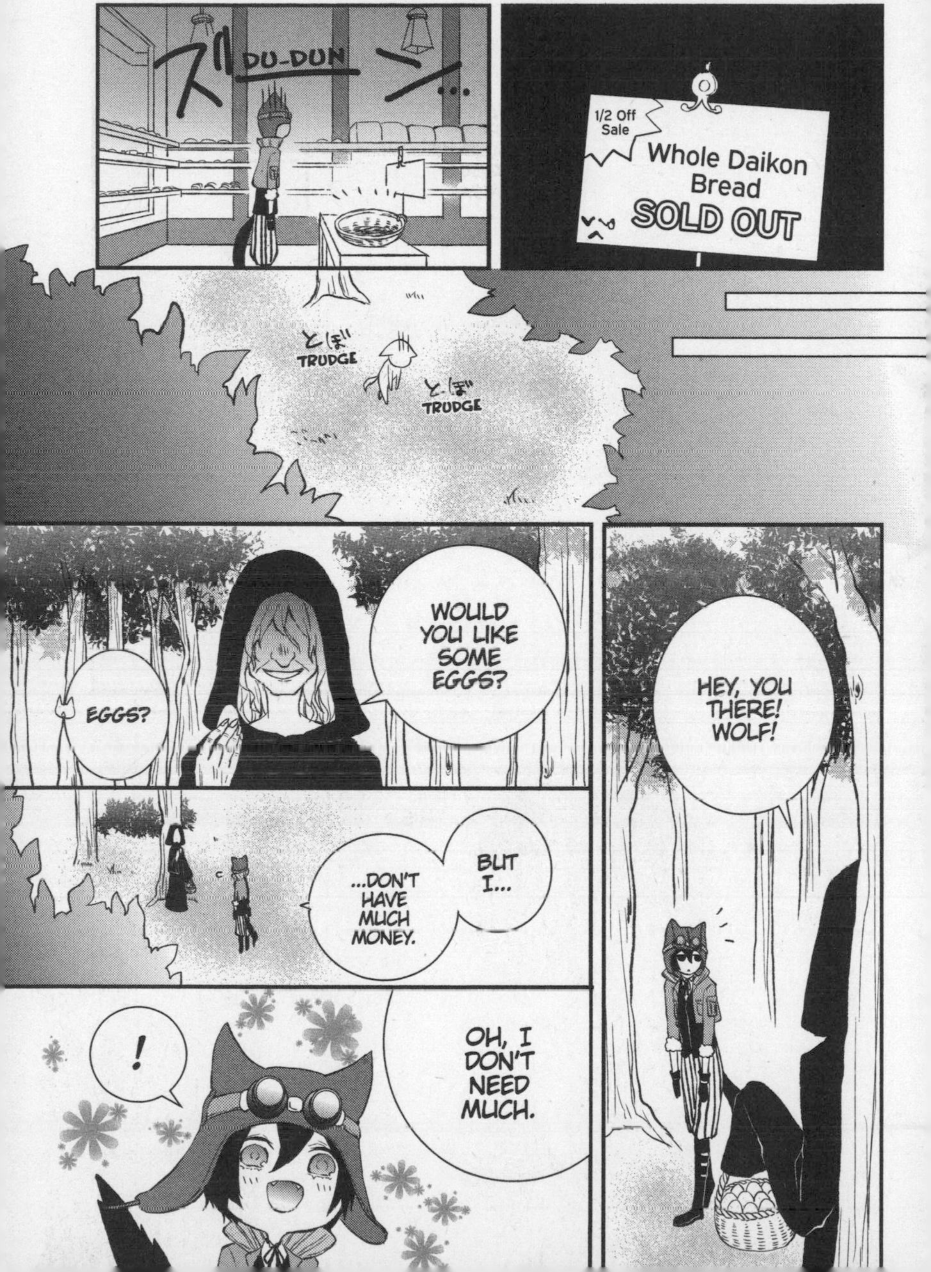
1/2 Off Sale
Whole Daikon Bread
SOLD OUT
DU-DUN
...
とぼ
TRUDGE
とぼ
TRUDGE
HEY, YOU THERE! WOLF!
WOULD YOU LIKE SOME EGGS?
EGGS?
BUT I...
...DON'T HAVE MUCH MONEY.
OH, I DON'T NEED MUCH.
!

FAMILY REUNION

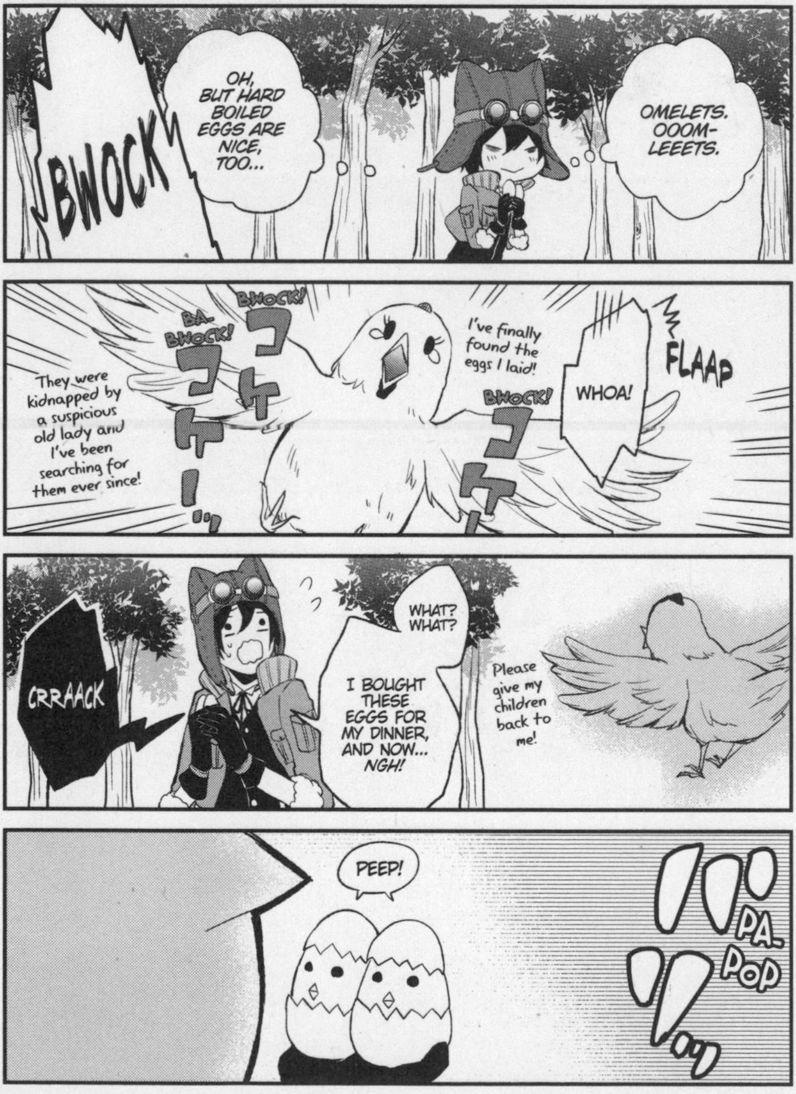

OMELETS. OOOM-LEEETS.
OH, BUT HARD BOILED EGGS ARE NICE, TOO...
BWOCK
FLAAP
WHOA!
I've finally found the eggs I laid!
BWOCK!
コケ
BWOCK!
コケ
BA-BWOCK!
コケ!..
They were kidnapped by a suspicious old lady and I've been searching for them ever since!
Please give my children back to me!
WHAT? WHAT?
I BOUGHT THESE EGGS FOR MY DINNER, AND NOW... NGH!
CRRAACK
PA-POP
PEEP!

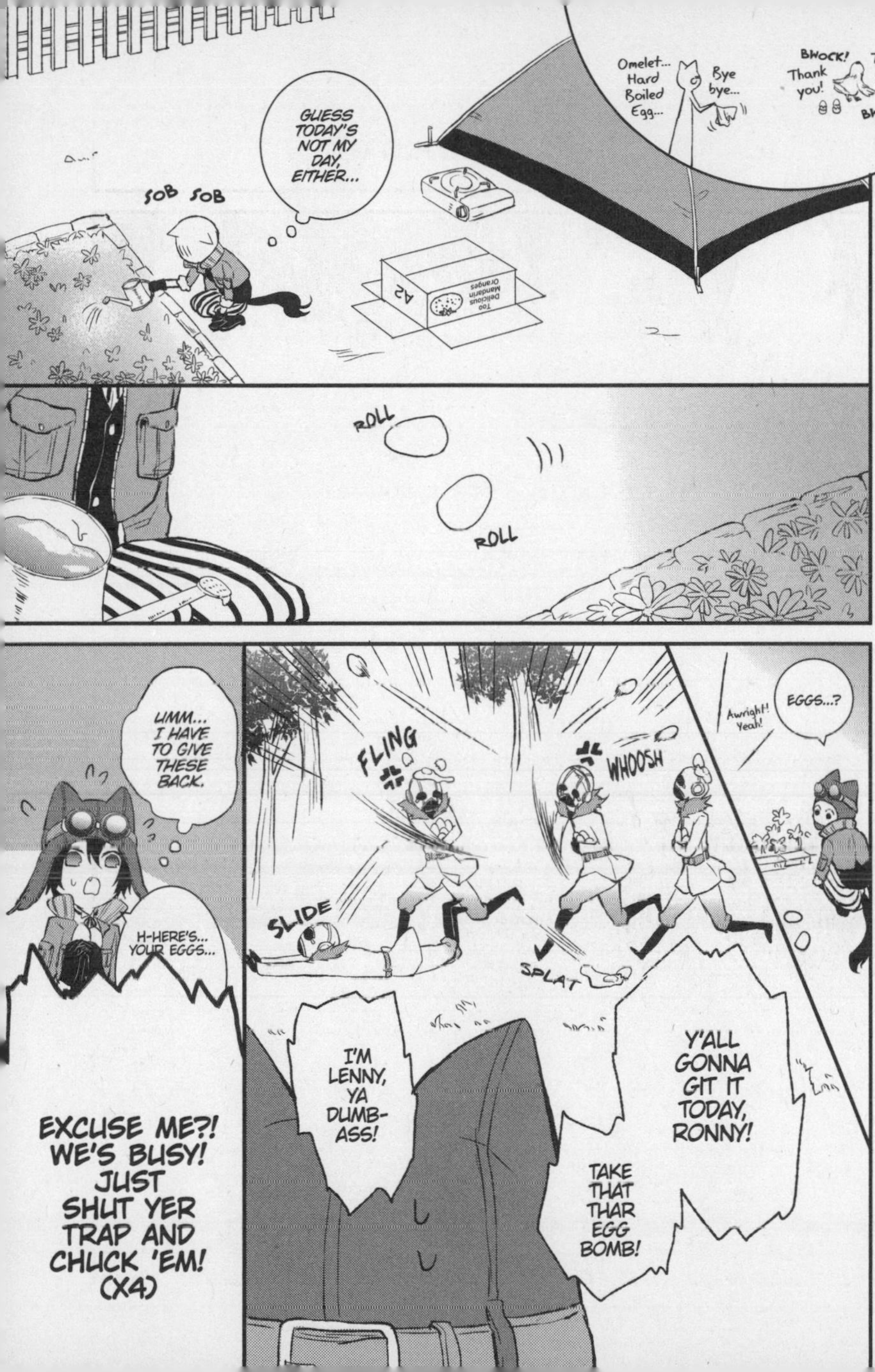
BWOCK!
Thank you!
Thank you!
BWOCK!
Omelet... Hard Boiled Egg...
Bye bye...
GUESS TODAY'S NOT MY DAY, EITHER...
SOB SOB
Too Delicious Mandarin Oranges
A2
ROLL
ROLL
EGGS...?
Awright! Yeah!
WHOOSH
FLING
SLIDE
SPLAT
Y'ALL GONNA GIT IT TODAY, RONNY!
TAKE THAT THAR EGG BOMB!
I'M LENNY, YA DUMB-ASS!
UMM... I HAVE TO GIVE THESE BACK.
H-HERE'S... YOUR EGGS...
EXCUSE ME?! WE'S BUSY! JUST SHUT YER TRAP AND CHUCK 'EM! (X4)

HMM?

SO I CAN KEEP THEM, THEN...

BWOCK

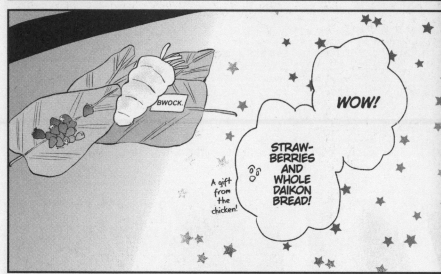

BWOCK.

A gift from the chicken!

WOW!

STRAW-BERRIES AND WHOLE DAIKON BREAD!

I LEFT THE STRAWBERRIES AND BREAD. YOU SURE YOU'RE OKAY WITH THAT?

After all, they're your favorite, Hawk.

WELL HE *DID* PAY FOR THEM, HM?

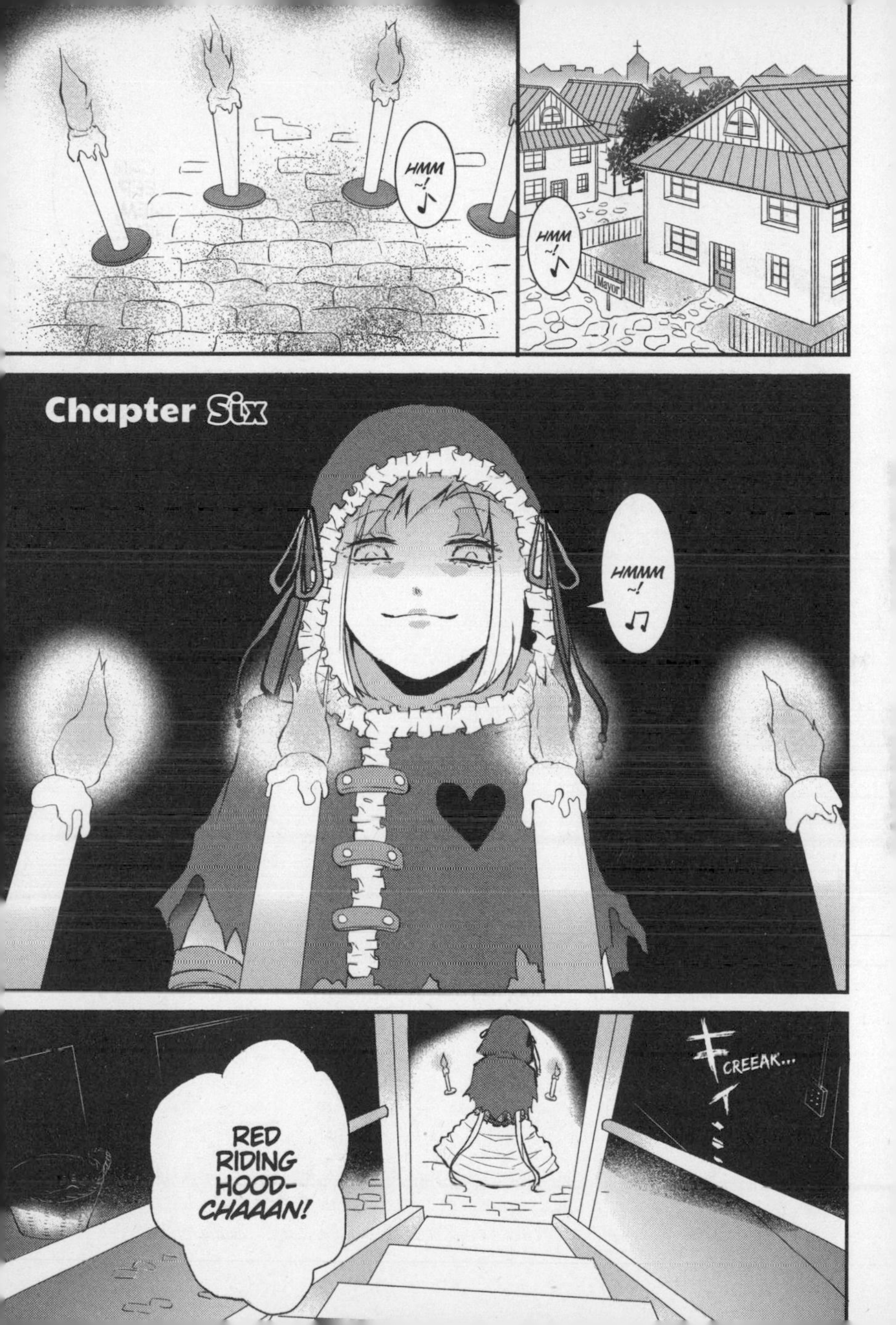

HMM ~! ♪
Mayor
HMM ~! ♪
Chapter Six
HMMM ~! ♫
CREEAK...
RED RIDING HOOD-CHAAAN!

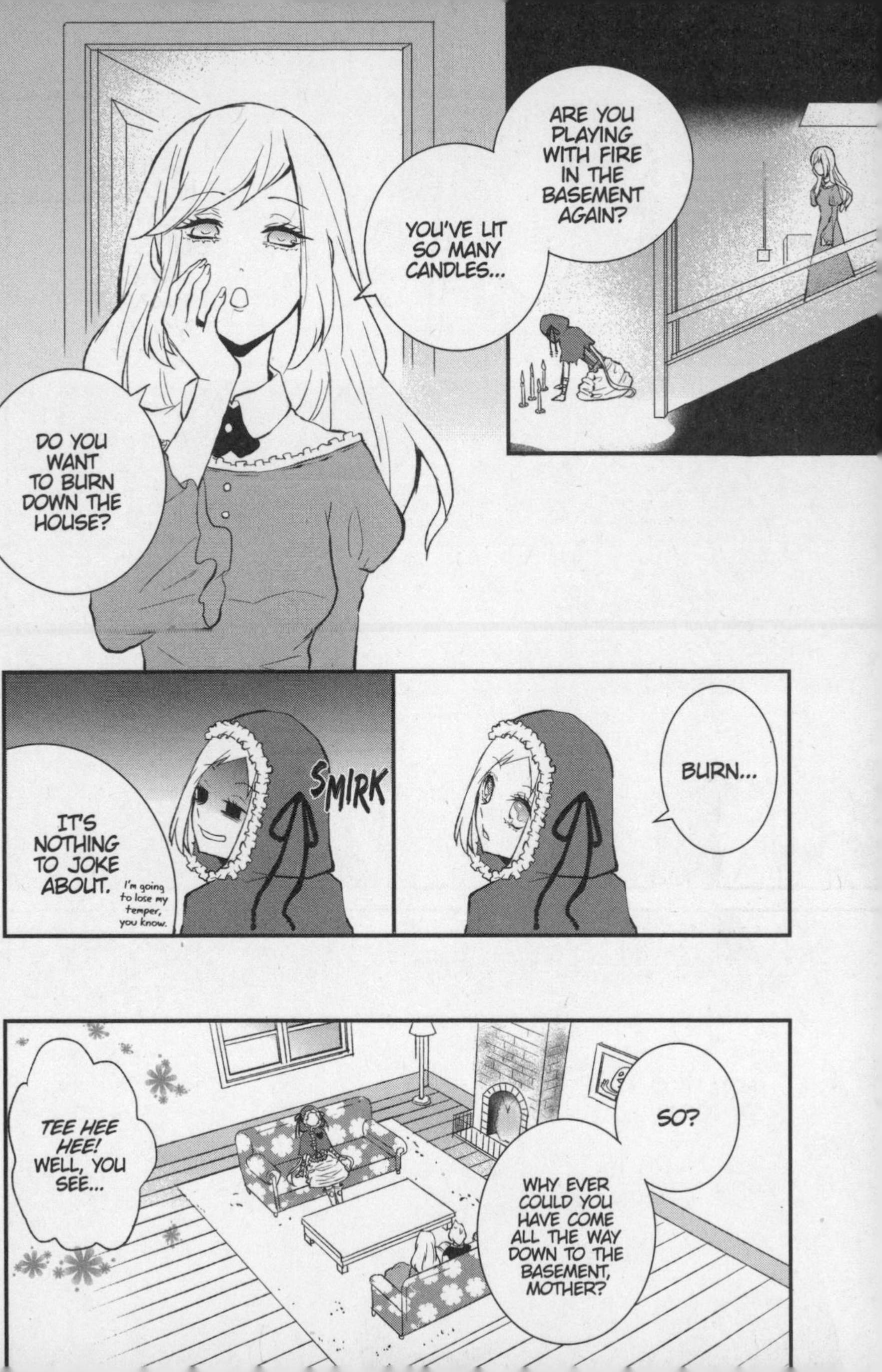
ARE YOU PLAYING WITH FIRE IN THE BASEMENT AGAIN?
YOU'VE LIT SO MANY CANDLES...
DO YOU WANT TO BURN DOWN THE HOUSE?
BURN...
SMIRK
IT'S NOTHING TO JOKE ABOUT.
I'm going to lose my temper, you know.
SO?
WHY EVER COULD YOU HAVE COME ALL THE WAY DOWN TO THE BASEMENT, MOTHER?
TEE HEE HEE! WELL, YOU SEE...

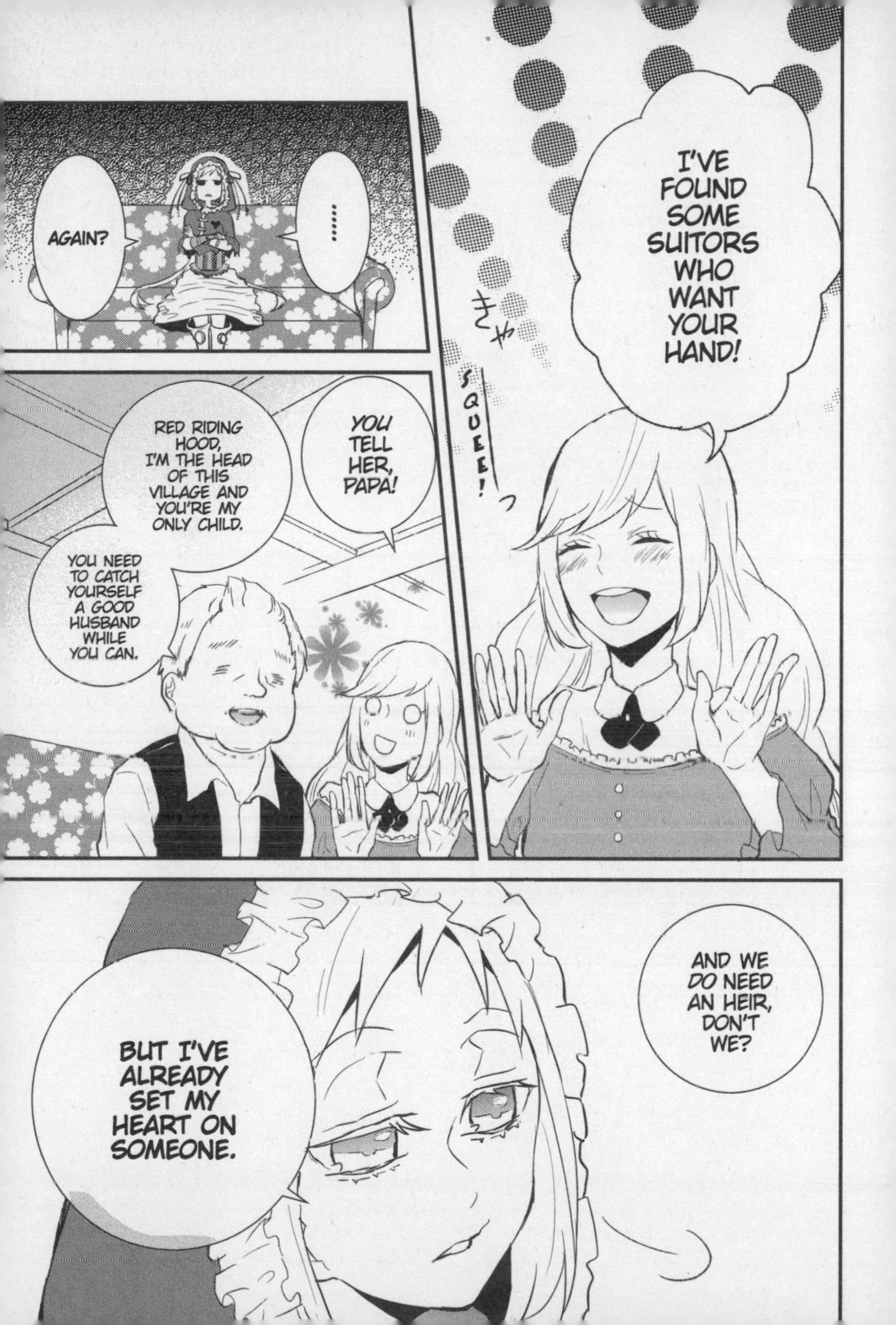
I'VE FOUND SOME SUITORS WHO WANT YOUR HAND!
きゃ
SQUEEE!
......
AGAIN?
YOU TELL HER, PAPA!
RED RIDING HOOD, I'M THE HEAD OF THIS VILLAGE AND YOU'RE MY ONLY CHILD.
YOU NEED TO CATCH YOURSELF A GOOD HUSBAND WHILE YOU CAN.
AND WE DO NEED AN HEIR, DON'T WE?
BUT I'VE ALREADY SET MY HEART ON SOMEONE.

MYSTERY MAN

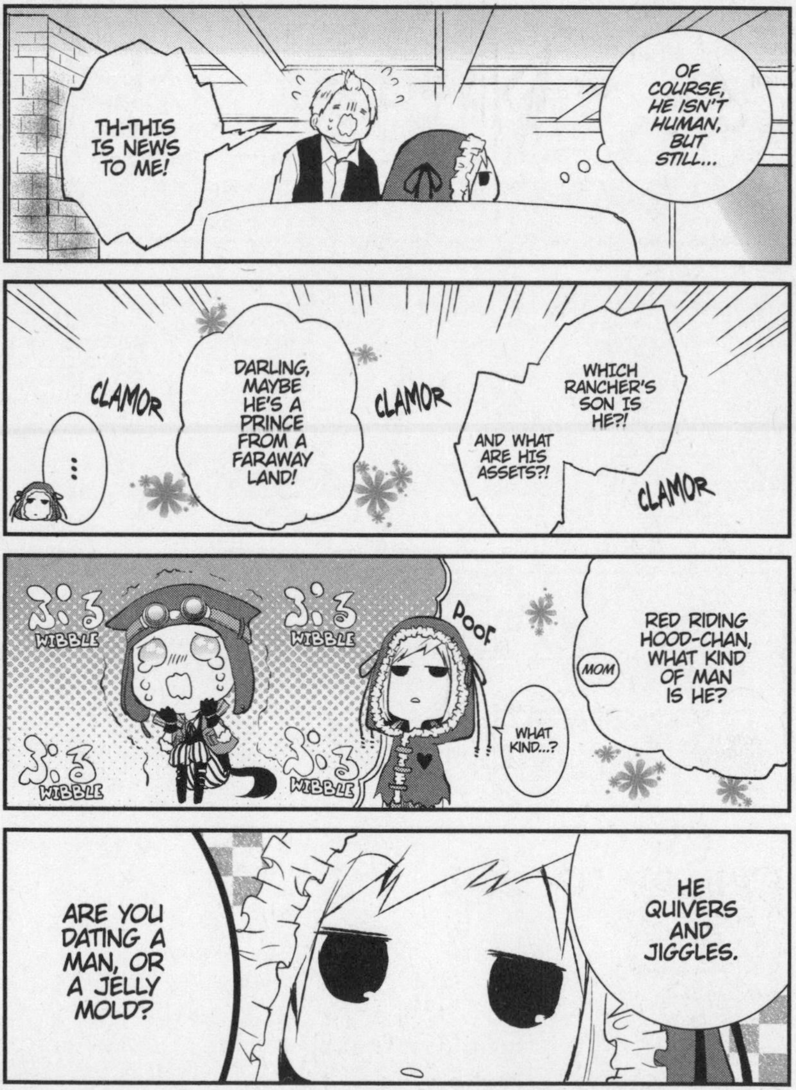

OF COURSE, HE ISN'T HUMAN, BUT STILL...
TH-THIS IS NEWS TO ME!
CLAMOR
WHICH RANCHER'S SON IS HE?!
AND WHAT ARE HIS ASSETS?!
CLAMOR
DARLING, MAYBE HE'S A PRINCE FROM A FARAWAY LAND!
CLAMOR
...
MOM
RED RIDING HOOD-CHAN, WHAT KIND OF MAN IS HE?
POOF
WHAT KIND...?
ぷる WIBBLE
ぷる WIBBLE
ぷる WIBBLE
ぷる WIBBLE
HE QUIVERS AND JIGGLES.
ARE YOU DATING A MAN, OR A JELLY MOLD?

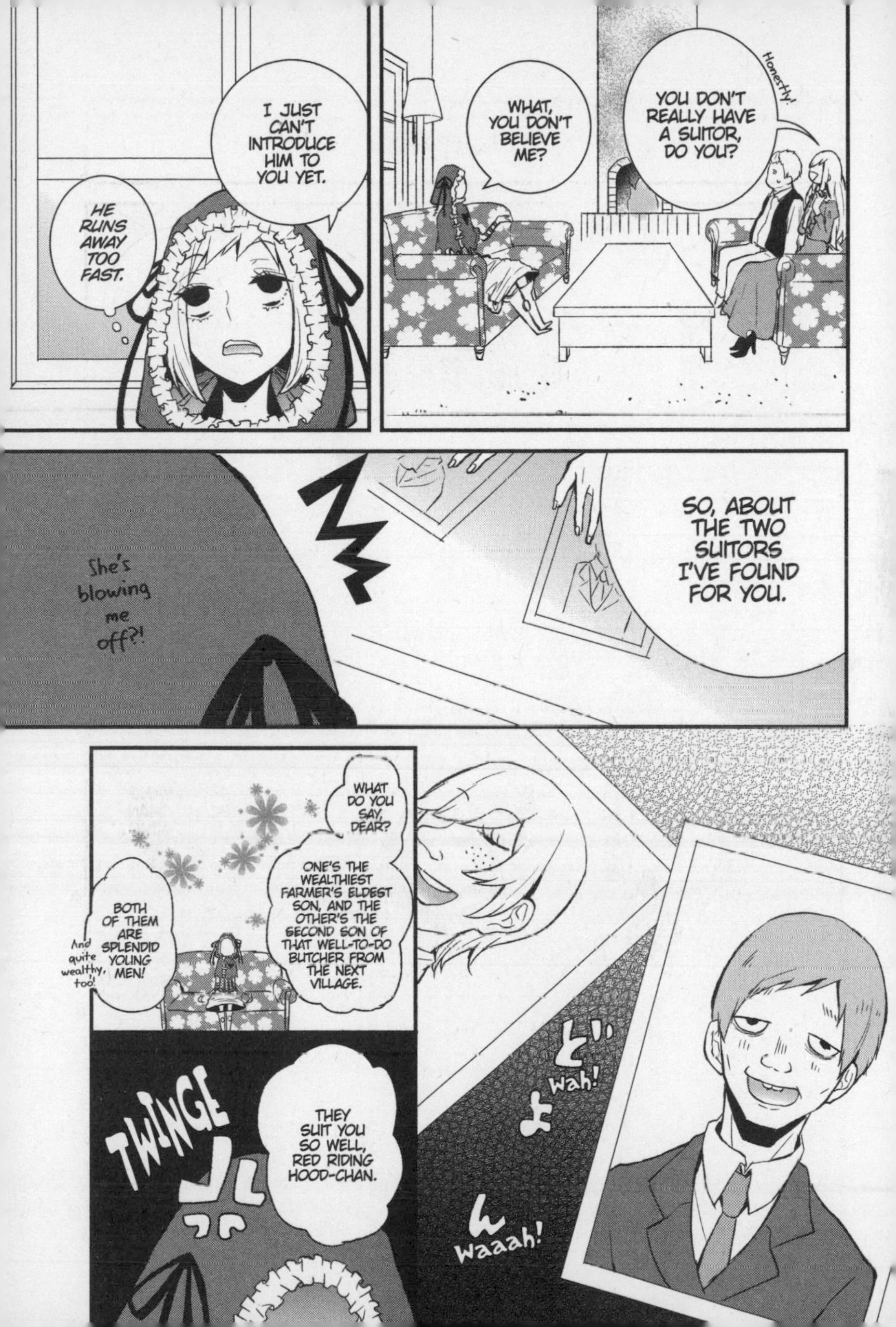
YOU DON'T REALLY HAVE A SUITOR, DO YOU?
Honestly!
WHAT, YOU DON'T BELIEVE ME?
I JUST CAN'T INTRODUCE HIM TO YOU YET.
HE RUNS AWAY TOO FAST.
SO, ABOUT THE TWO SUITORS I'VE FOUND FOR YOU.
She's blowing me off?!
wah!
waaah!
WHAT DO YOU SAY, DEAR?
ONE'S THE WEALTHIEST FARMER'S ELDEST SON, AND THE OTHER'S THE SECOND SON OF THAT WELL-TO-DO BUTCHER FROM THE NEXT VILLAGE.
BOTH OF THEM ARE SPLENDID YOUNG MEN!
And quite wealthy, too!
THEY SUIT YOU SO WELL, RED RIDING HOOD-CHAN.
TWINGE

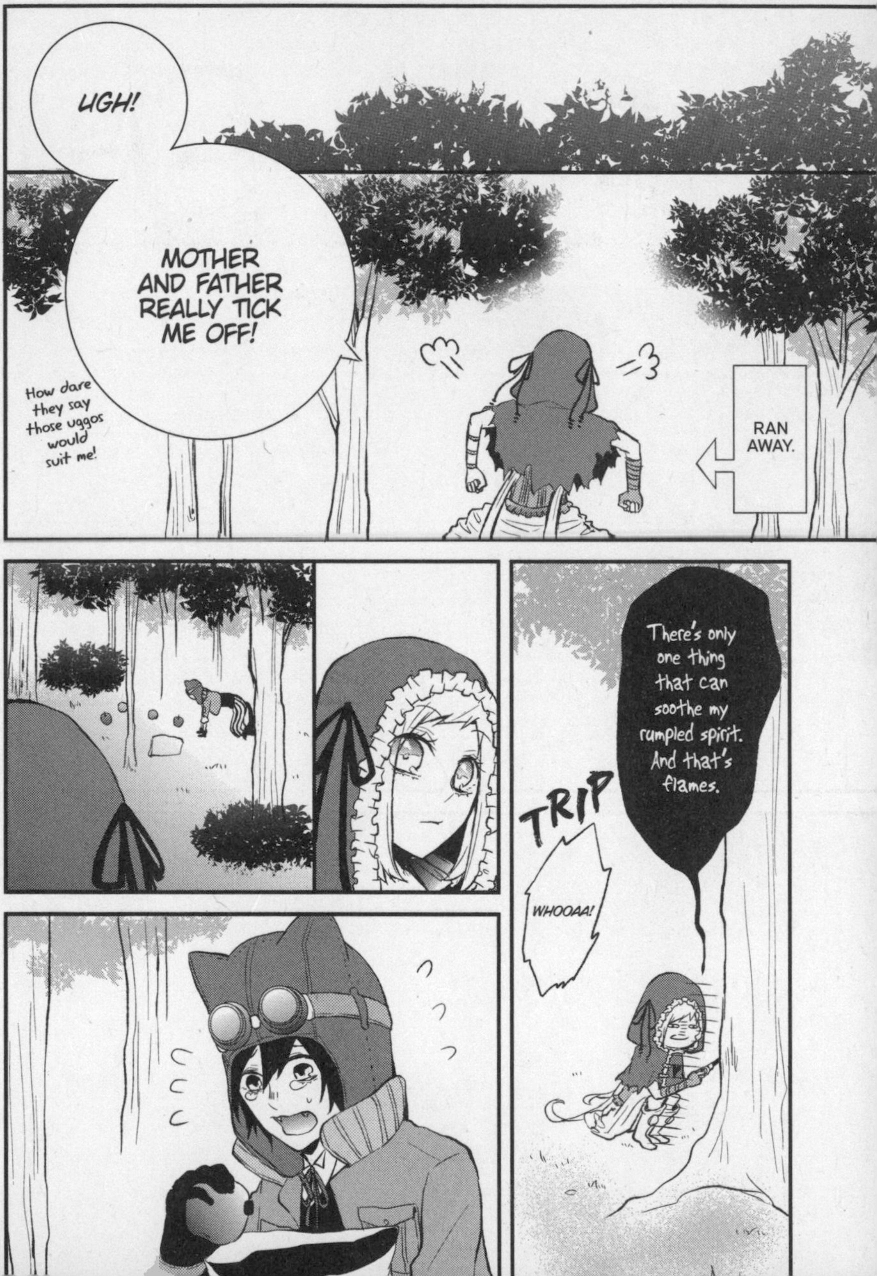
UGH!
MOTHER AND FATHER REALLY TICK ME OFF!
How dare they say those uggos would suit me!
RAN AWAY.
There's only one thing that can soothe my rumpled spirit. And that's flames.
TRIP
WHOOAA!

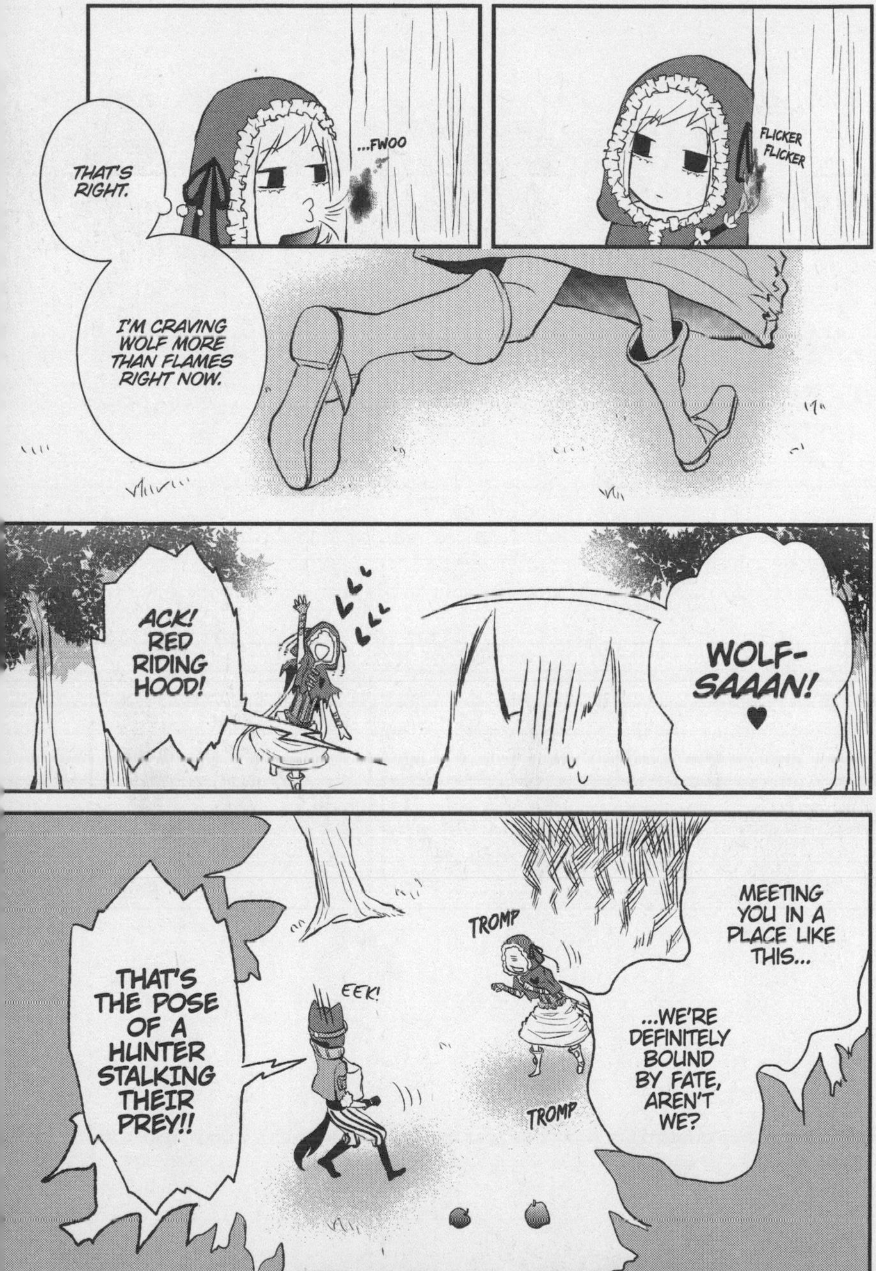
FLICKER FLICKER
...FWOO
THAT'S RIGHT.
I'M CRAVING WOLF MORE THAN FLAMES RIGHT NOW.
WOLF-SAAAN! ♥
ACK! RED RIDING HOOD!
MEETING YOU IN A PLACE LIKE THIS...
...WE'RE DEFINITELY BOUND BY FATE, AREN'T WE?
TROMP
TROMP
EEK!
THAT'S THE POSE OF A HUNTER STALKING THEIR PREY!!

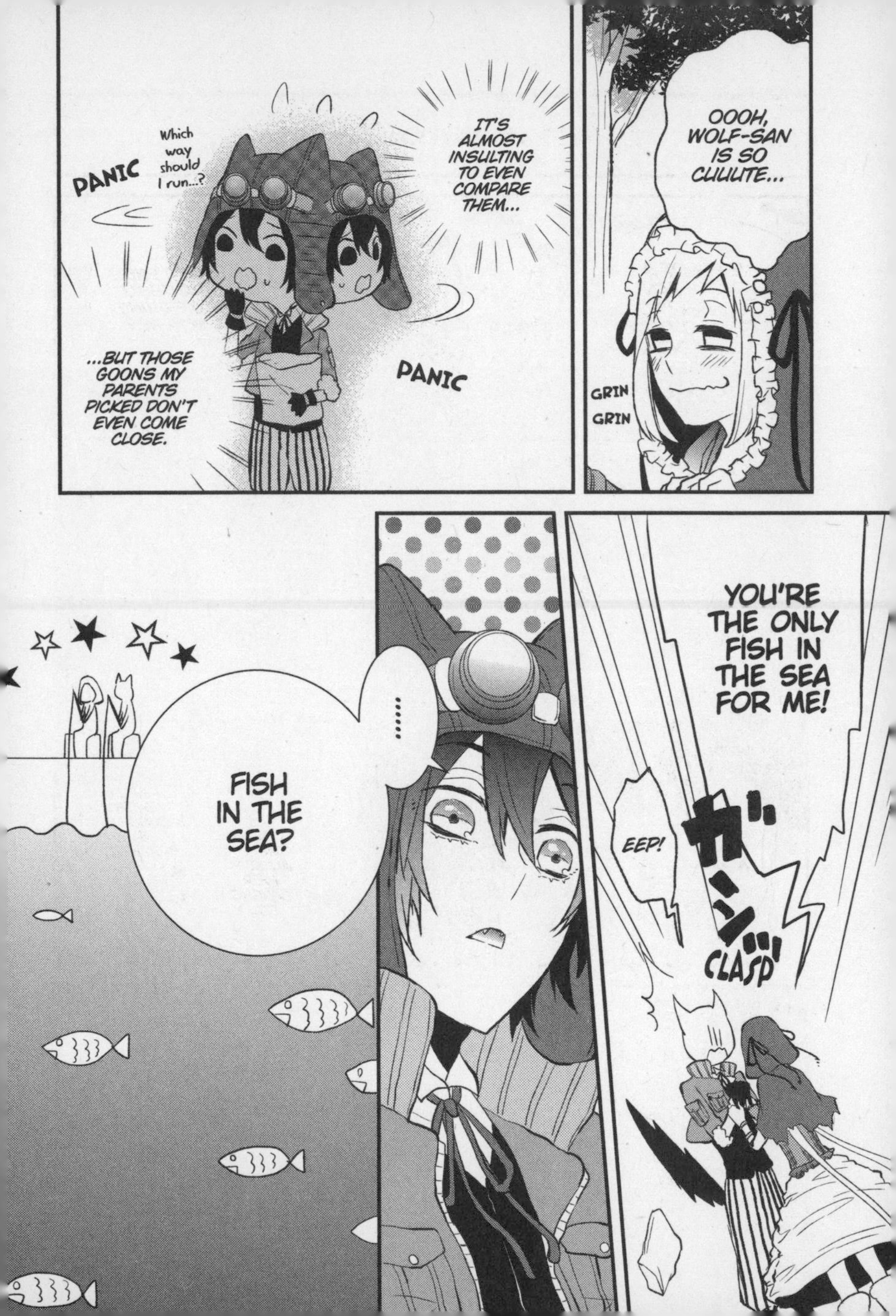
OOOH, WOLF-SAN IS SO CUUUTE...
GRIN
GRIN
IT'S ALMOST INSULTING TO EVEN COMPARE THEM...
Which way should I run...?
PANIC
...BUT THOSE GOONS MY PARENTS PICKED DON'T EVEN COME CLOSE.
PANIC
YOU'RE THE ONLY FISH IN THE SEA FOR ME!
EEP!
CLASP
......
FISH IN THE SEA?

A SIMPLE MISUNDERSTANDING

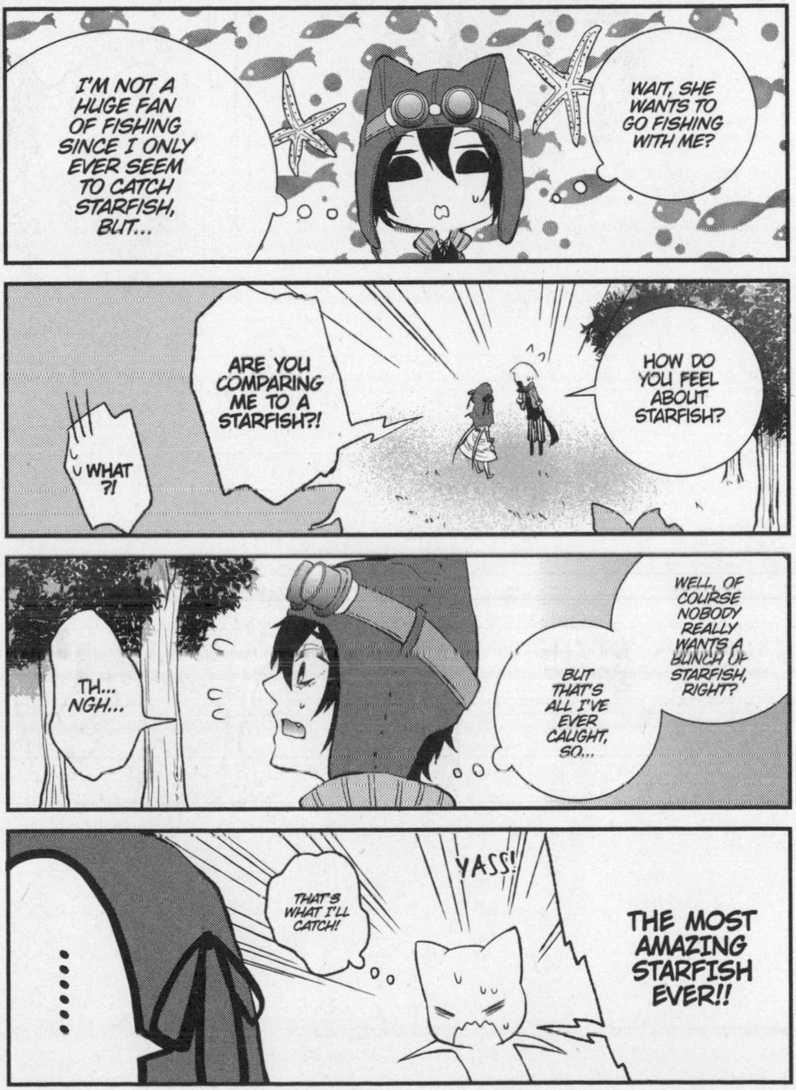
WAIT, SHE WANTS TO GO FISHING WITH ME?
I'M NOT A HUGE FAN OF FISHING SINCE I ONLY EVER SEEM TO CATCH STARFISH, BUT...
HOW DO YOU FEEL ABOUT STARFISH?
ARE YOU COMPARING ME TO A STARFISH?!
WHAT ?!
WELL, OF COURSE NOBODY REALLY WANTS A BUNCH OF STARFISH, RIGHT?
BUT THAT'S ALL I'VE EVER CAUGHT, SO...
TH... NGH...
THE MOST AMAZING STARFISH EVER!!
YASS!
THAT'S WHAT I'LL CATCH!
......

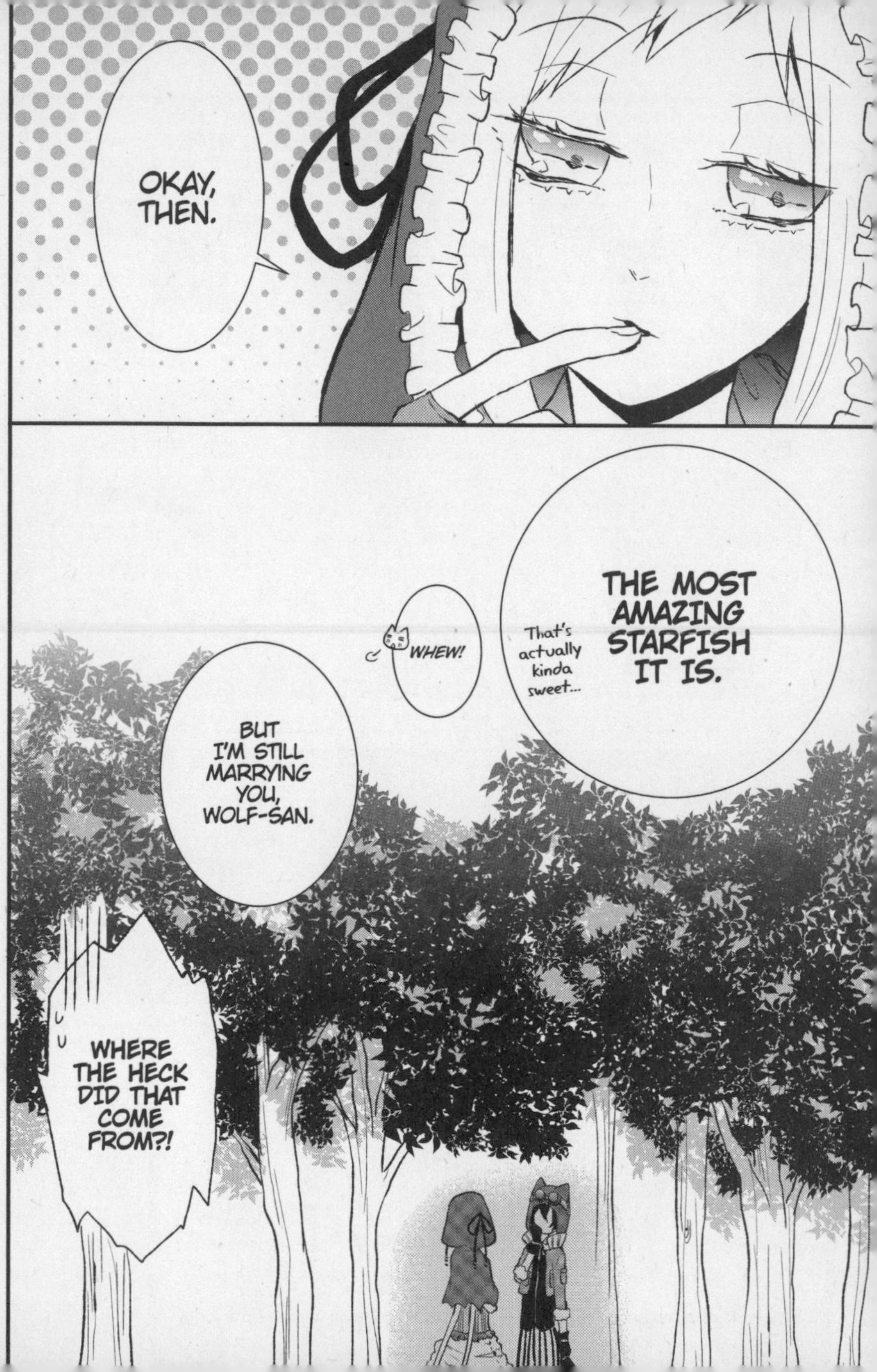
OKAY, THEN.
THE MOST AMAZING STARFISH IT IS.
That's actually kinda sweet...
WHEW!
BUT I'M STILL MARRYING YOU, WOLF-SAN.
WHERE THE HECK DID THAT COME FROM?!

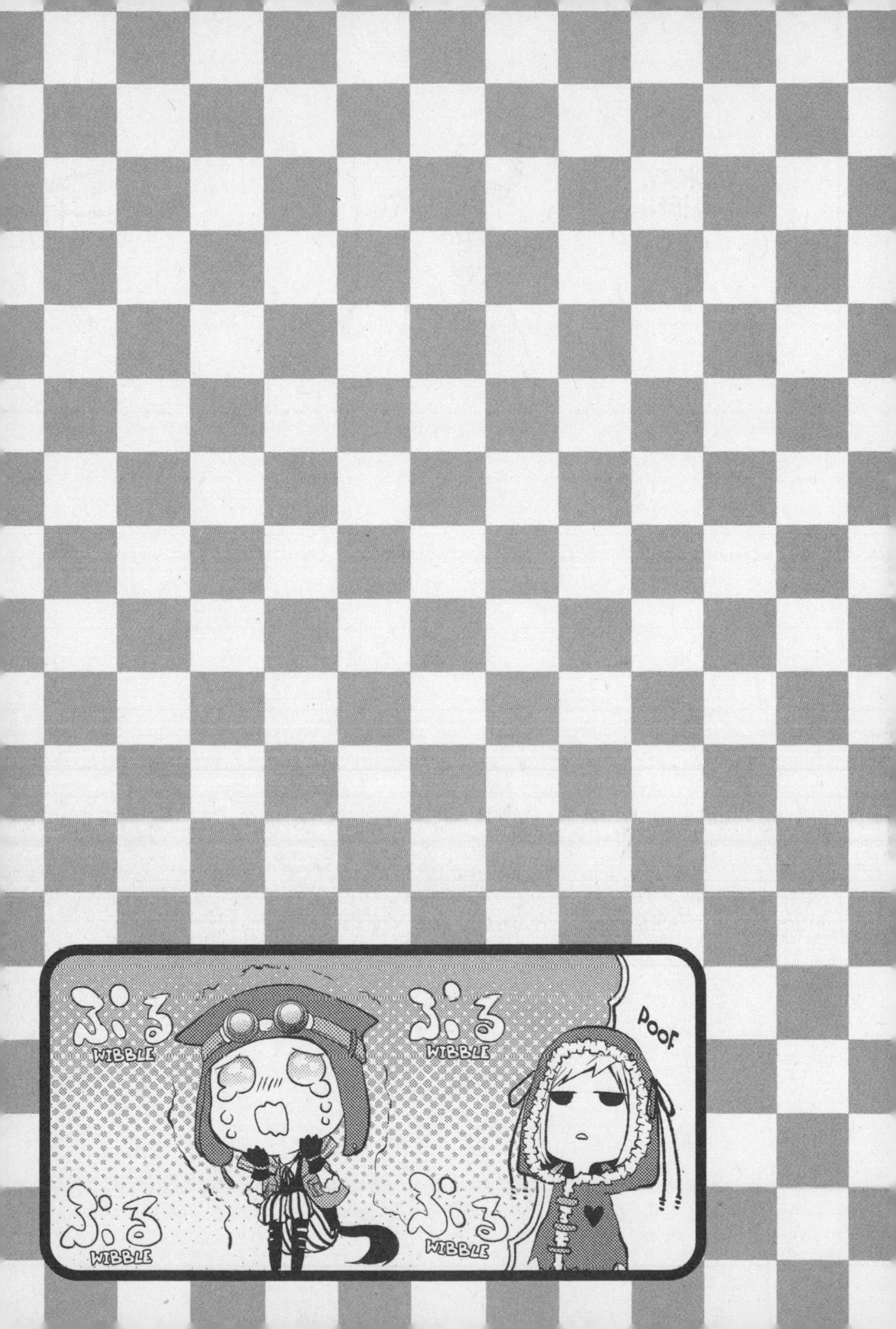
POOF
ぷる
WIBBLE
ぷる
WIBBLE
ぷる
WIBBLE
ぷる
WIBBLE

RED RIDING HOOD and the BIG SAD WOLF

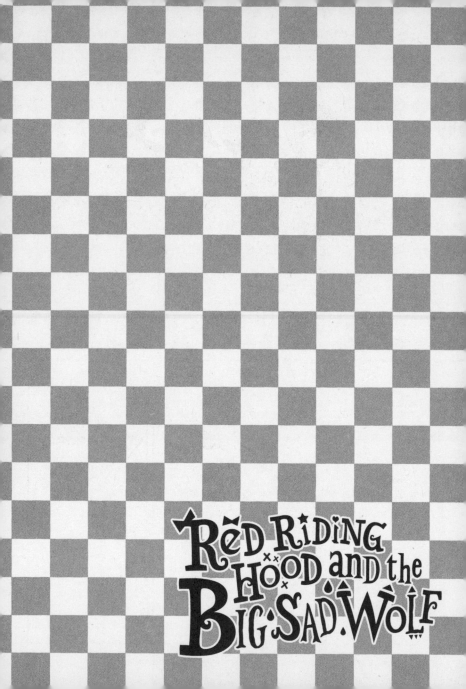

Chapter Seven

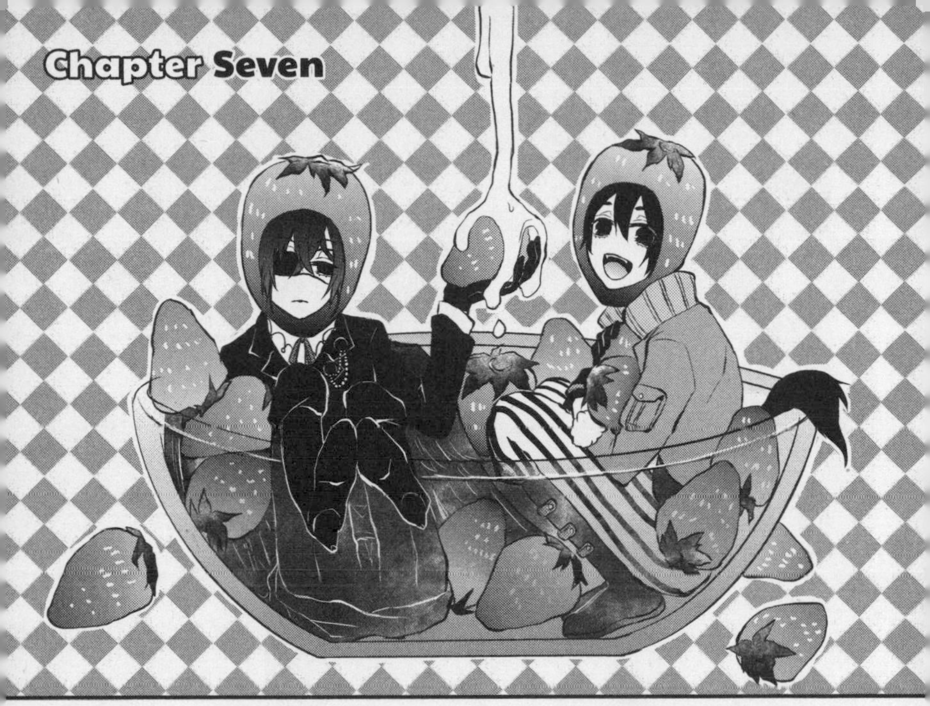

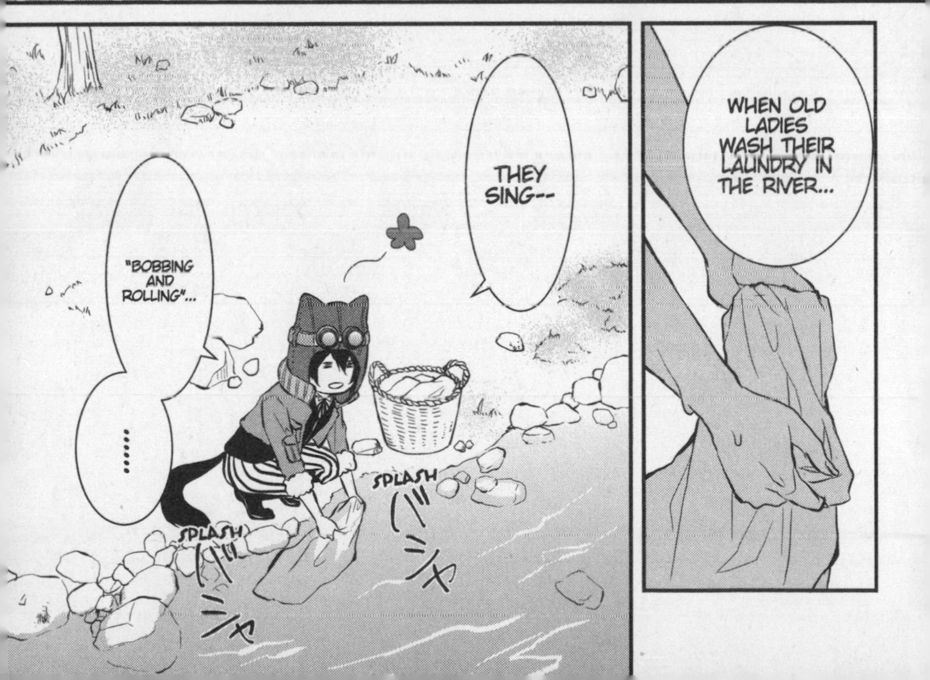
WHEN OLD LADIES WASH THEIR LAUNDRY IN THE RIVER...
THEY SING--
"BOBBING AND ROLLING"...
......
SPLASH
バシャ
SPLASH
バシャ

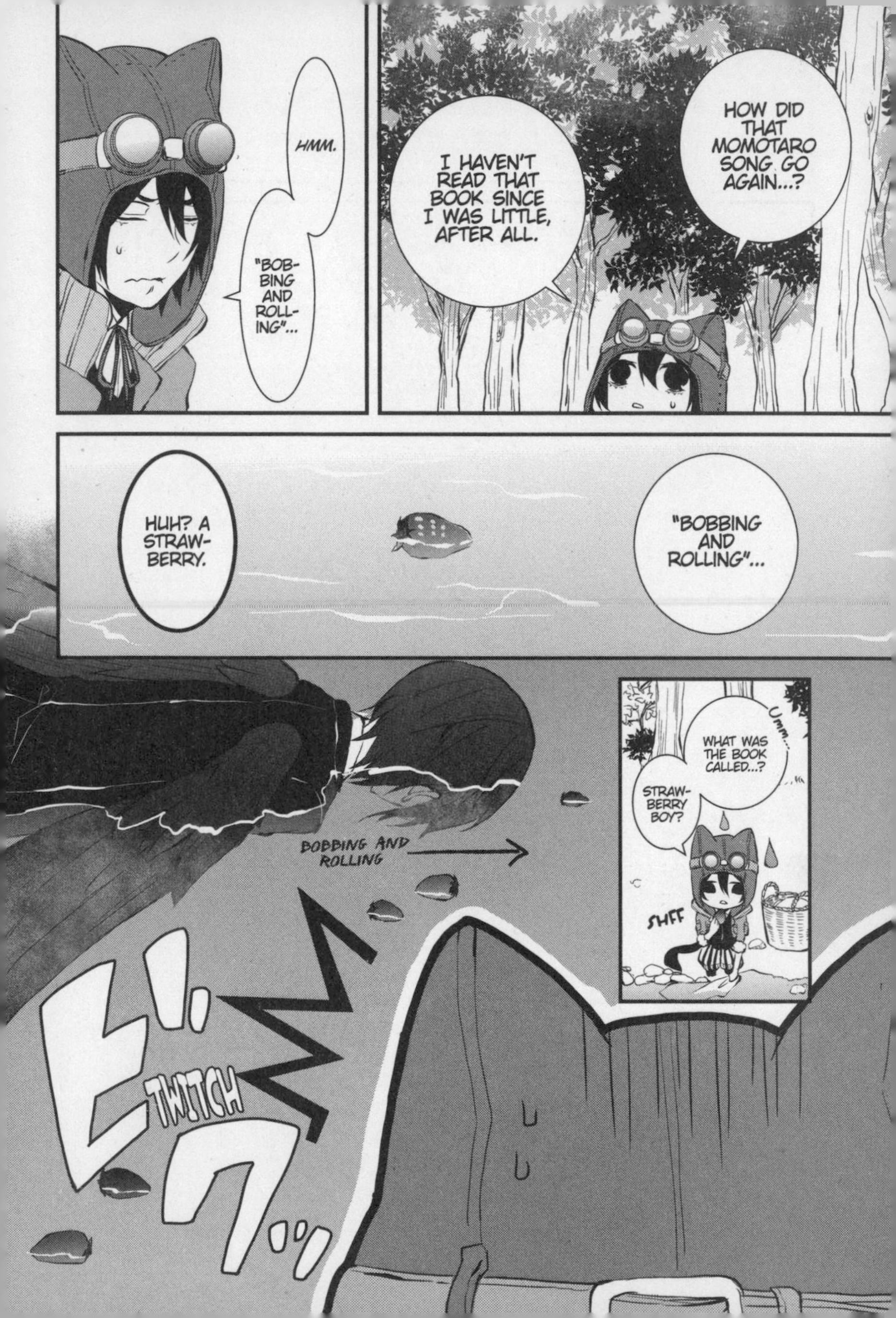
HOW DID THAT MOMOTARO SONG GO AGAIN...?
I HAVEN'T READ THAT BOOK SINCE I WAS LITTLE, AFTER ALL.
HMM.
"BOB-BING AND ROLL-ING"...
"BOBBING AND ROLLING"...
HUH? A STRAW-BERRY.
UMM...
WHAT WAS THE BOOK CALLED...?
STRAW-BERRY BOY?
SHFF
BOBBING AND ROLLING
TWITCH

CARELESS CROW

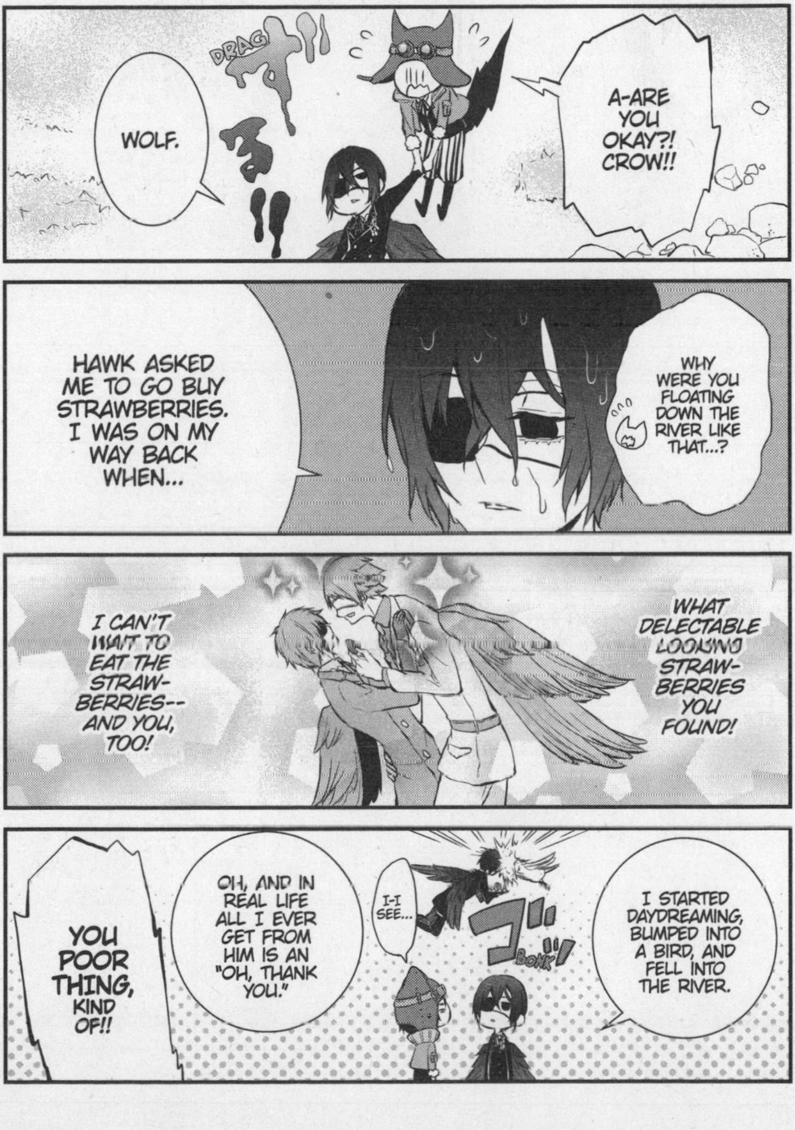
A-ARE YOU OKAY?! CROW!!
DRAG
WOLF.
WHY WERE YOU FLOATING DOWN THE RIVER LIKE THAT...?
HAWK ASKED ME TO GO BUY STRAWBERRIES. I WAS ON MY WAY BACK WHEN...
WHAT DELECTABLE LOOKING STRAWBERRIES YOU FOUND!
I CAN'T WAIT TO EAT THE STRAWBERRIES--AND YOU, TOO!
I STARTED DAYDREAMING, BUMPED INTO A BIRD, AND FELL INTO THE RIVER.
BONK
I-I SEE...
OH, AND IN REAL LIFE ALL I EVER GET FROM HIM IS AN "OH, THANK YOU."
YOU POOR THING, KIND OF!!

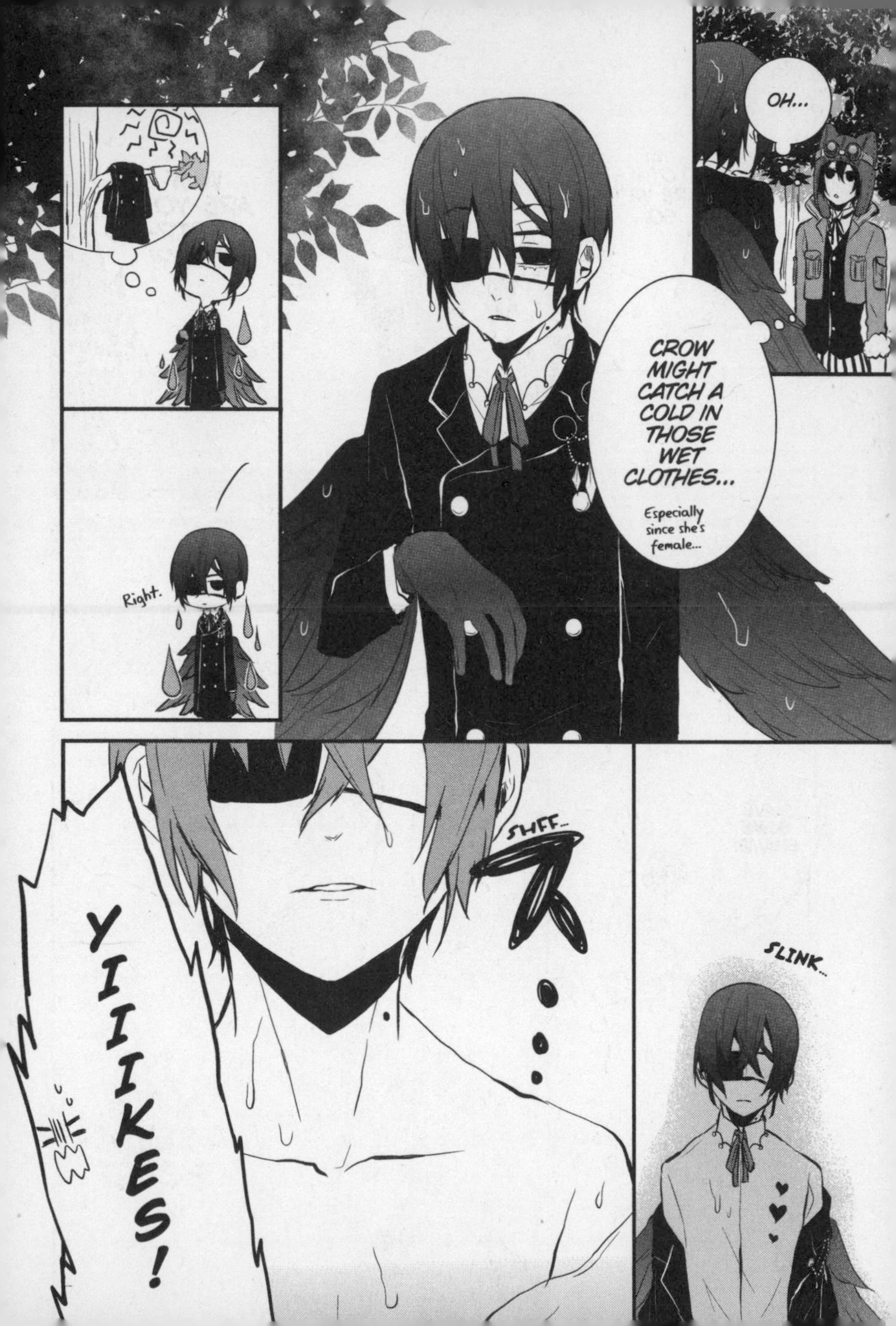
OH...
CROW MIGHT CATCH A COLD IN THOSE WET CLOTHES...
Especially since she's female...
Right.
SLINK...
SHFF...
YIIIKES!

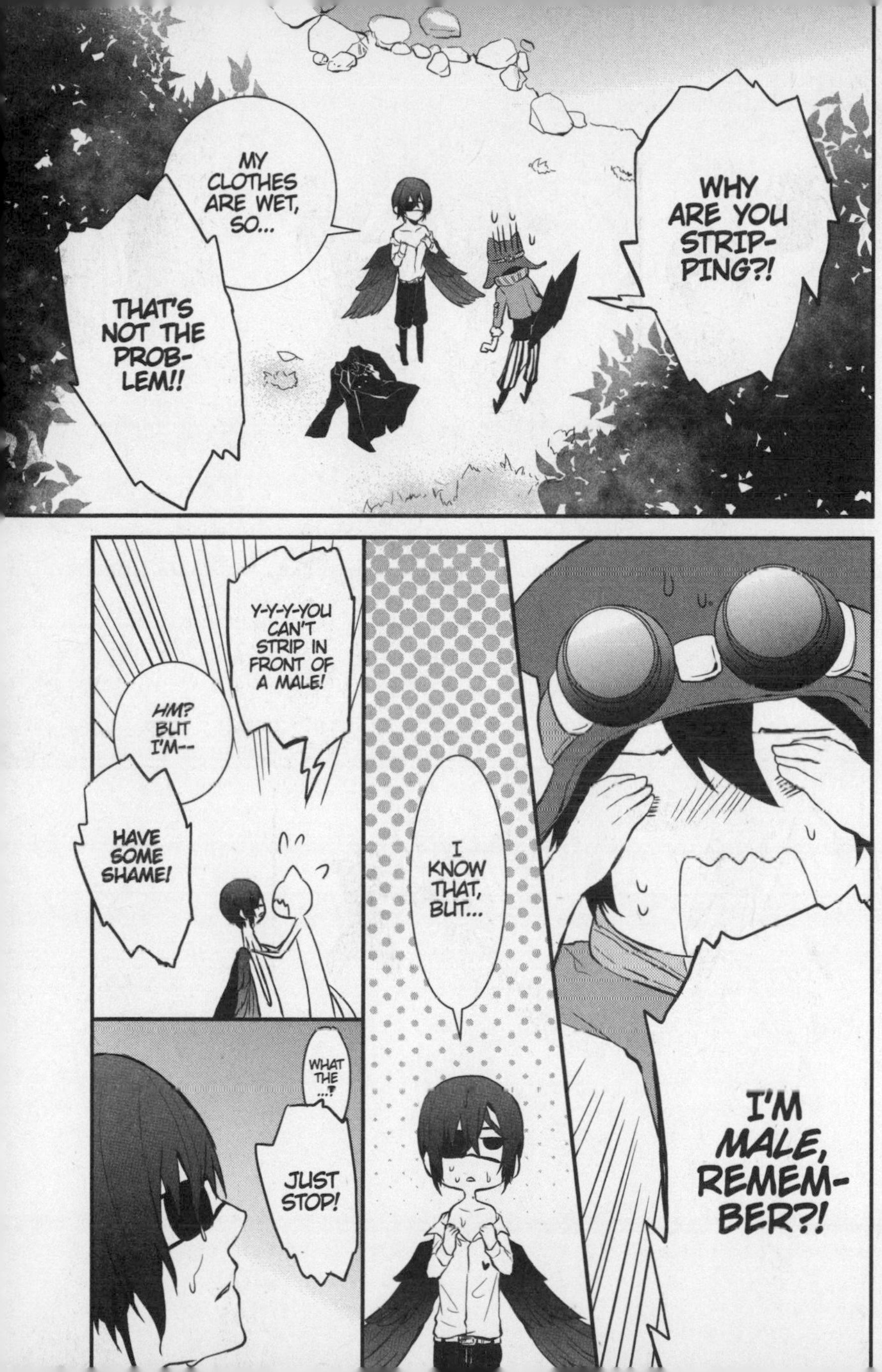
WHY ARE YOU STRIP-PING?!
MY CLOTHES ARE WET, SO...
THAT'S NOT THE PROB-LEM!!
I'M MALE, REMEM-BER?!
I KNOW THAT, BUT...
Y-Y-Y-YOU CAN'T STRIP IN FRONT OF A MALE!
HM? BUT I'M--
HAVE SOME SHAME!
WHAT THE ...?
JUST STOP!

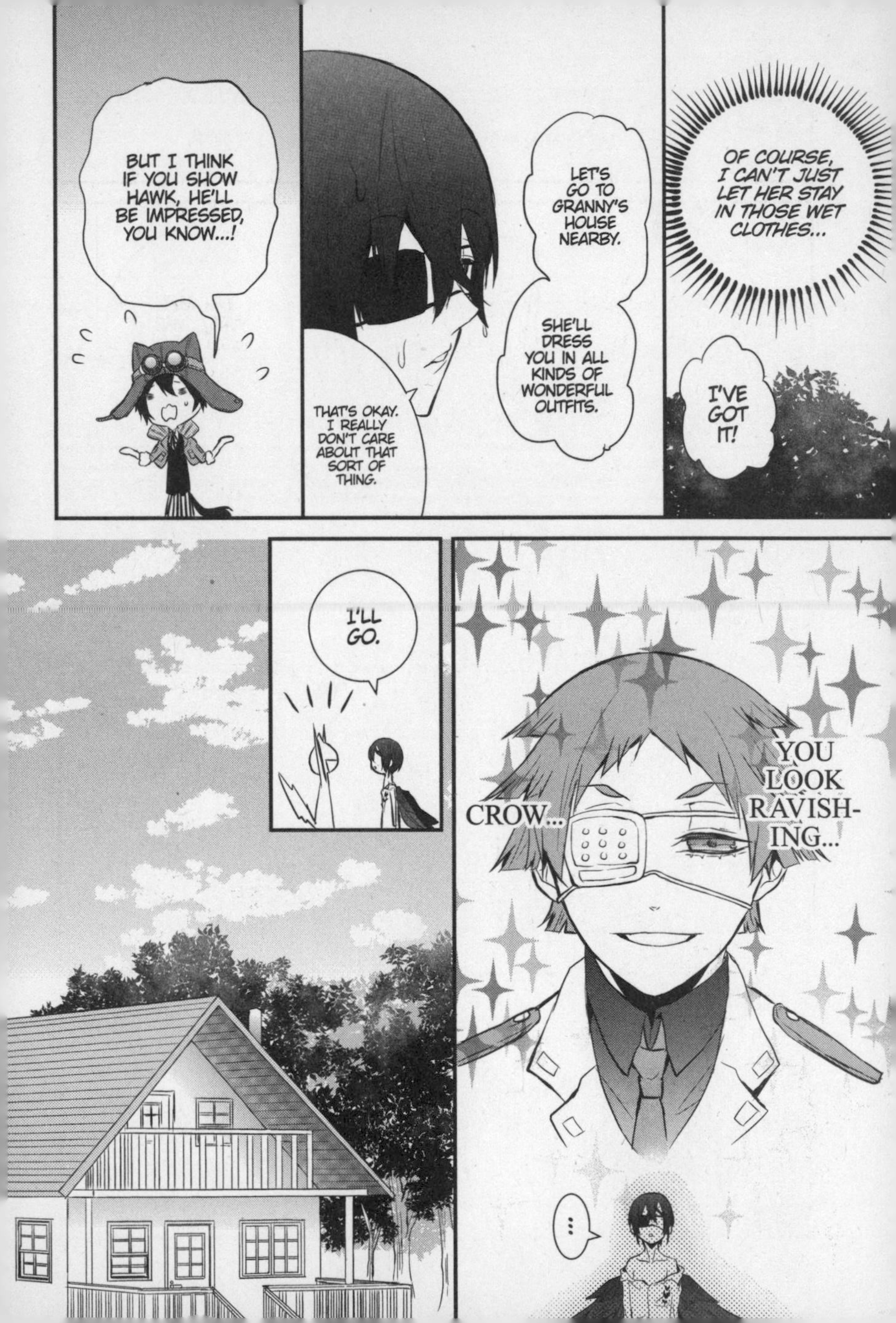
OF COURSE, I CAN'T JUST LET HER STAY IN THOSE WET CLOTHES...
I'VE GOT IT!
LET'S GO TO GRANNY'S HOUSE NEARBY.
SHE'LL DRESS YOU IN ALL KINDS OF WONDERFUL OUTFITS.
THAT'S OKAY. I REALLY DON'T CARE ABOUT THAT SORT OF THING.
BUT I THINK IF YOU SHOW HAWK, HE'LL BE IMPRESSED, YOU KNOW...!
YOU LOOK RAVISH-ING...
CROW...
...
I'LL GO.

THE GRANNY WHO GREW TOO MUCH

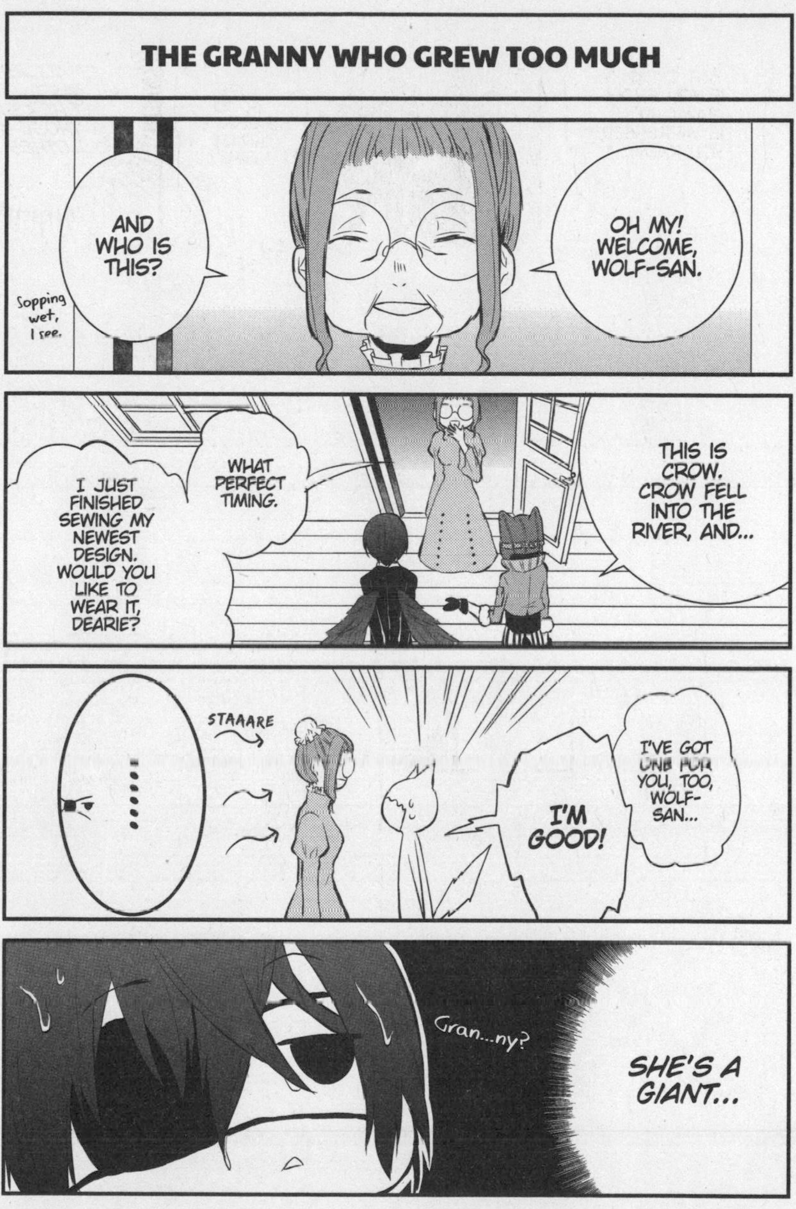
OH MY! WELCOME, WOLF-SAN.
AND WHO IS THIS?
Sopping wet, I see.
THIS IS CROW. CROW FELL INTO THE RIVER, AND...
WHAT PERFECT TIMING.
I JUST FINISHED SEWING MY NEWEST DESIGN. WOULD YOU LIKE TO WEAR IT, DEARIE?
I'VE GOT ONE FOR YOU, TOO, WOLF-SAN...
I'M GOOD!
STAAARE
......
SHE'S A GIANT...
Gran...ny?

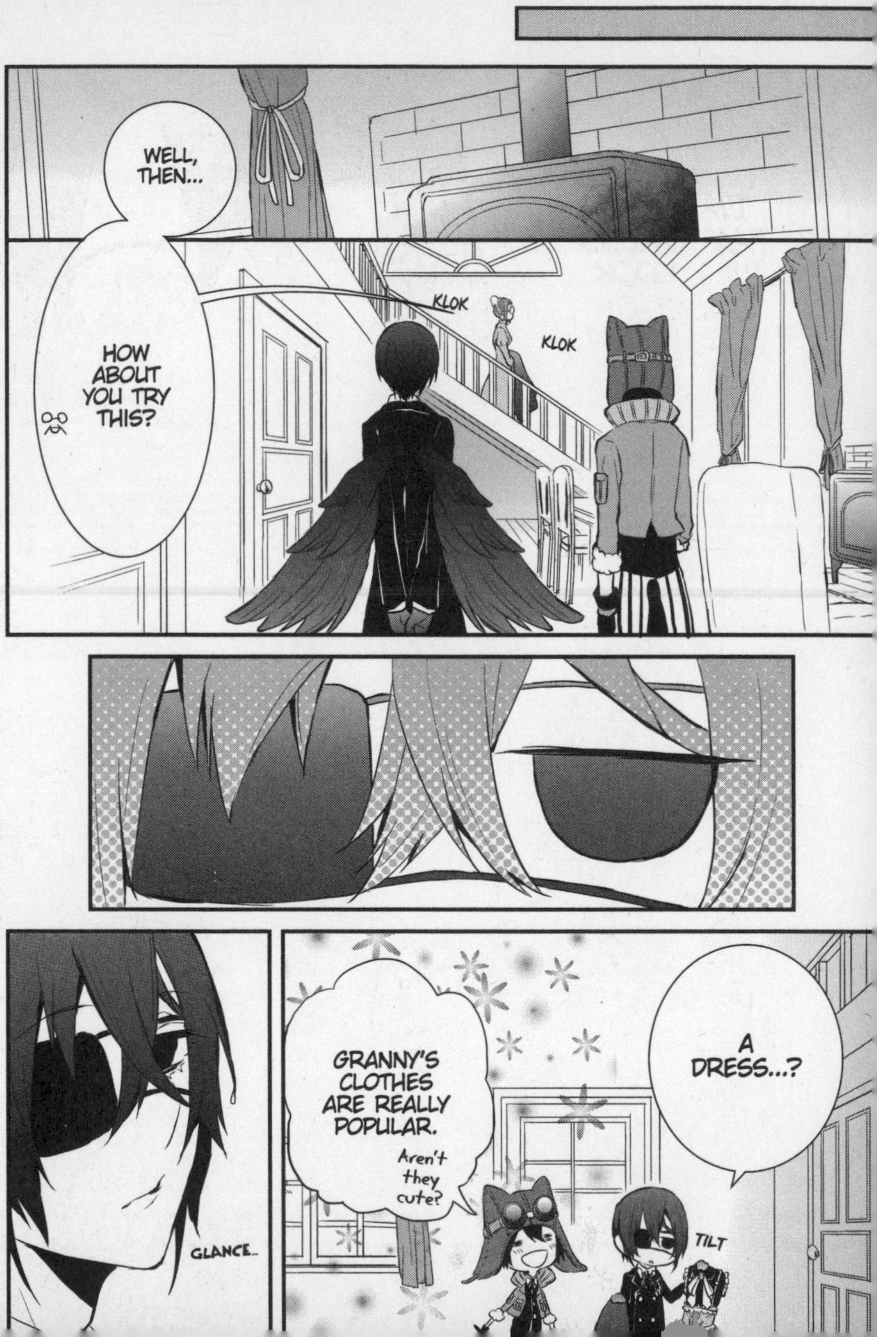
WELL, THEN...
HOW ABOUT YOU TRY THIS?
KLOK
KLOK
A DRESS...?
TILT
GRANNY'S CLOTHES ARE REALLY POPULAR.
Aren't they cute?
GLANCE..

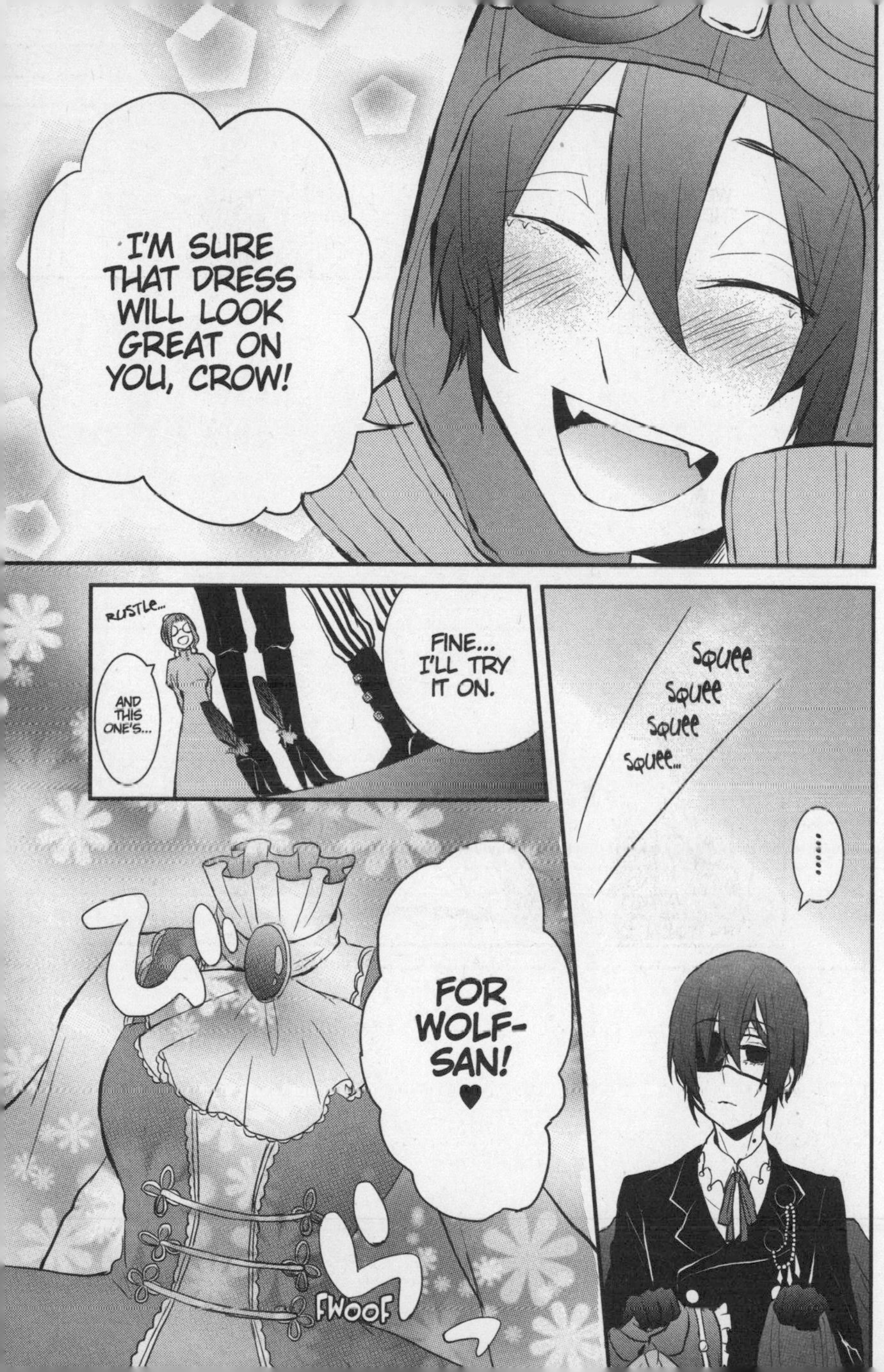
I'M SURE THAT DRESS WILL LOOK GREAT ON YOU, CROW!
SQUEE SQUEE SQUEE SQUEE...
......
FINE... I'LL TRY IT ON.
RUSTLE...
AND THIS ONE'S...
FOR WOLF-SAN! ♥
FWOOF

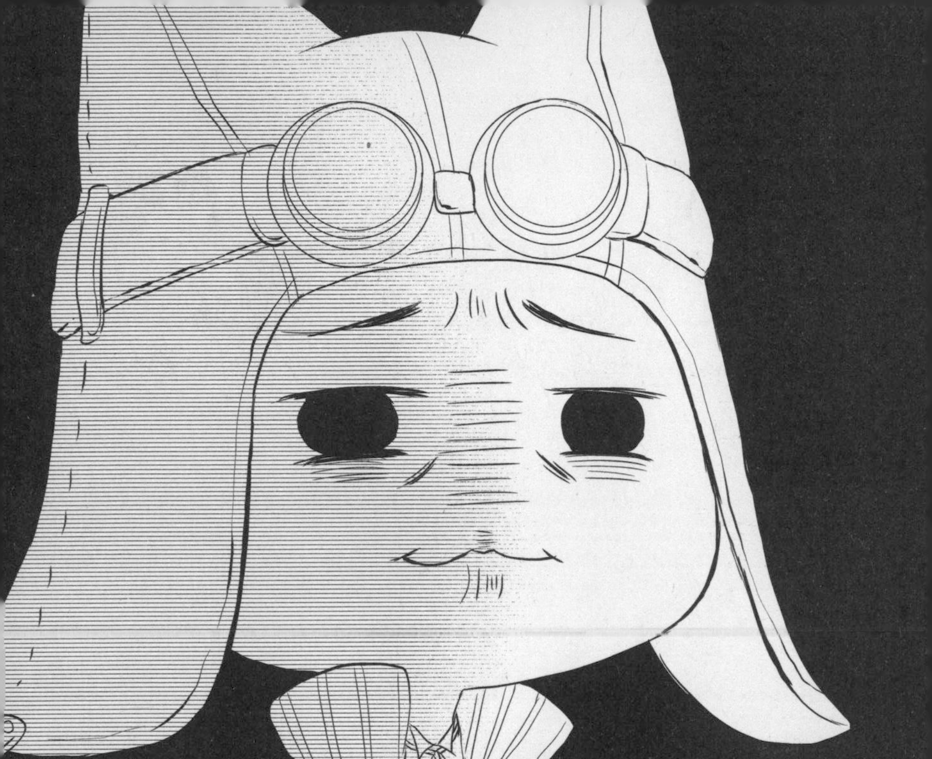

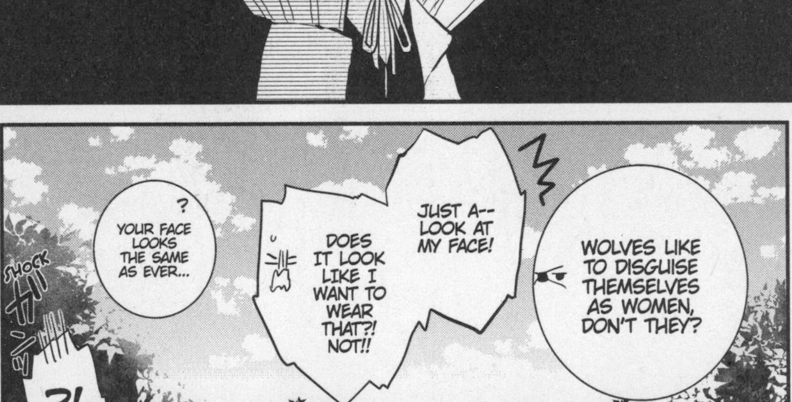
WOLVES LIKE TO DISGUISE THEMSELVES AS WOMEN, DON'T THEY?
JUST A-- LOOK AT MY FACE!
DOES IT LOOK LIKE I WANT TO WEAR THAT?! NOT!!
?
YOUR FACE LOOKS THE SAME AS EVER...
SHOCK
?!

Chapter Eight

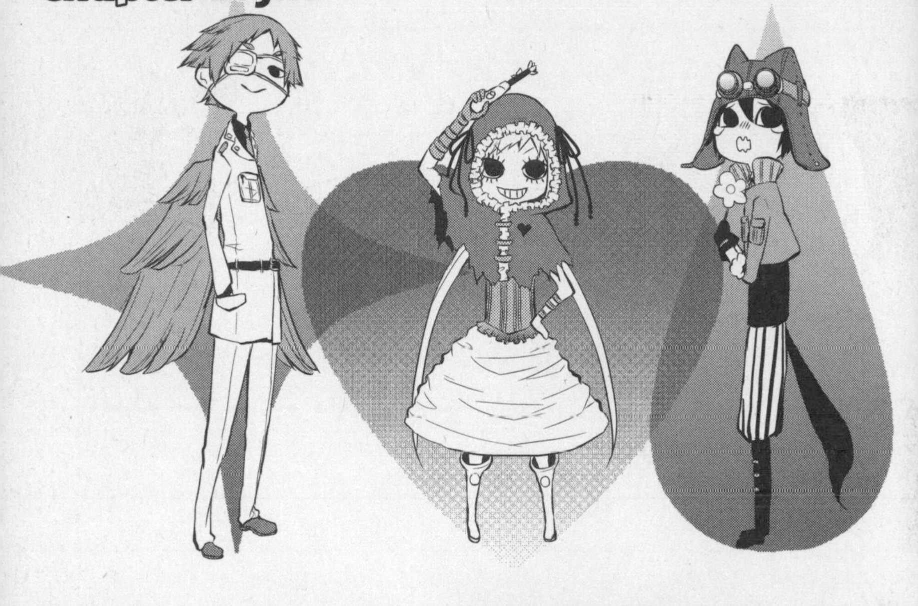

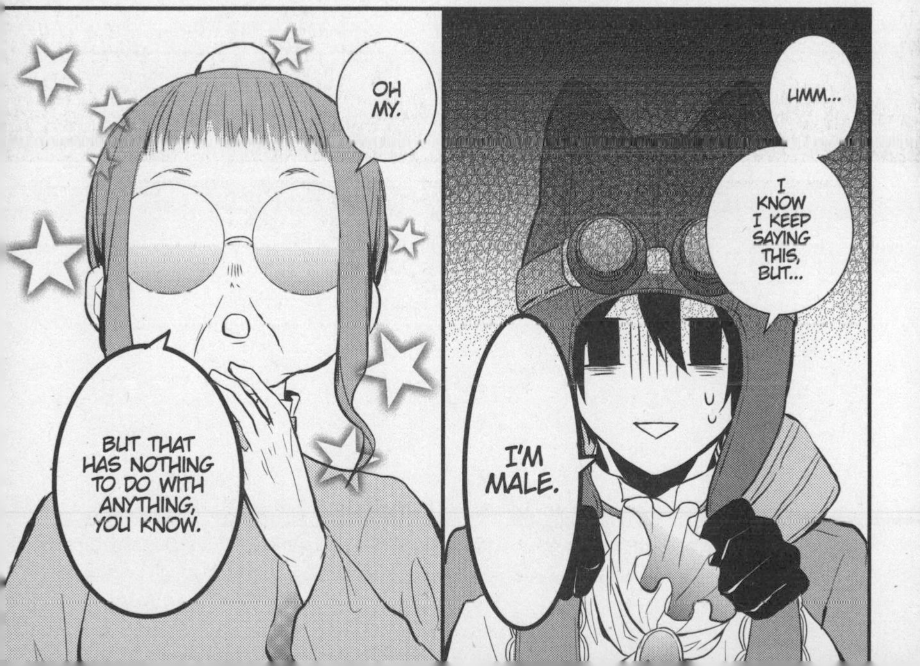
UMM...
I KNOW I KEEP SAYING THIS, BUT...
I'M MALE.
OH MY.
BUT THAT HAS NOTHING TO DO WITH ANYTHING, YOU KNOW.

THE WALL BETWEEN THE SEXES

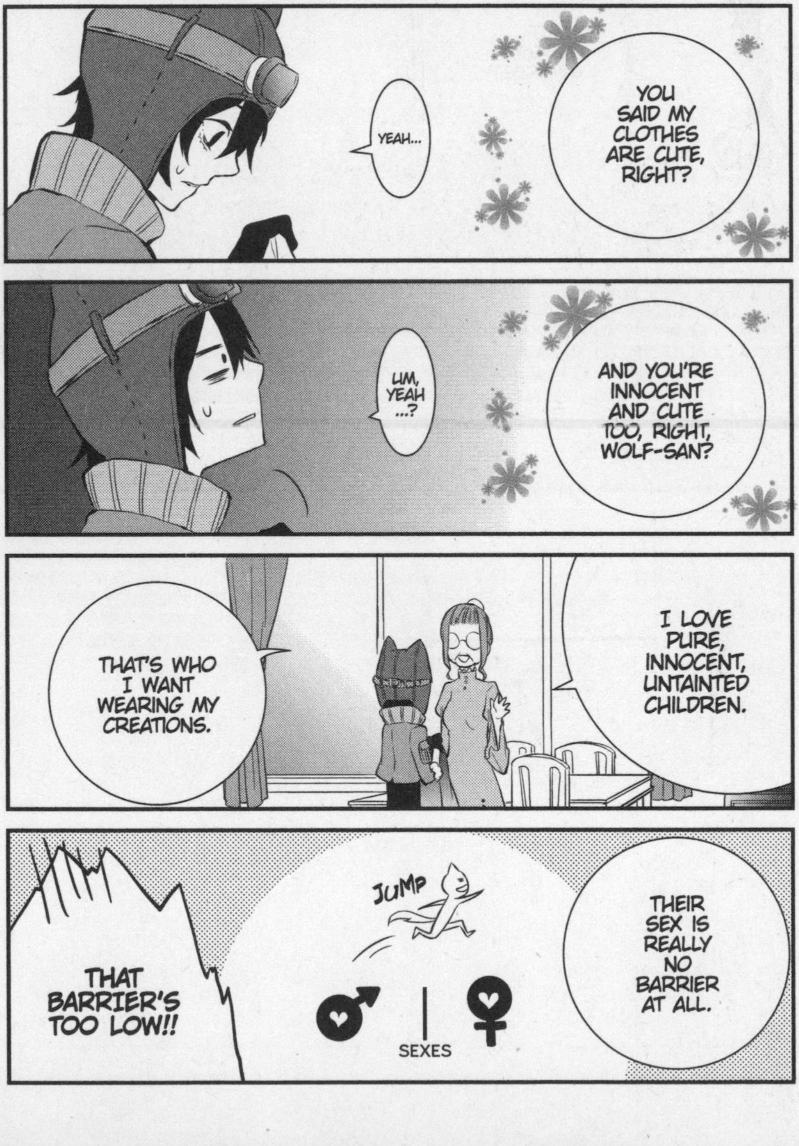
YOU SAID MY CLOTHES ARE CUTE, RIGHT?
YEAH...
AND YOU'RE INNOCENT AND CUTE TOO, RIGHT, WOLF-SAN?
UM, YEAH ...?
I LOVE PURE, INNOCENT, UNTAINTED CHILDREN.
THAT'S WHO I WANT WEARING MY CREATIONS.
THEIR SEX IS REALLY NO BARRIER AT ALL.
JUMP
SEXES
THAT BARRIER'S TOO LOW!!

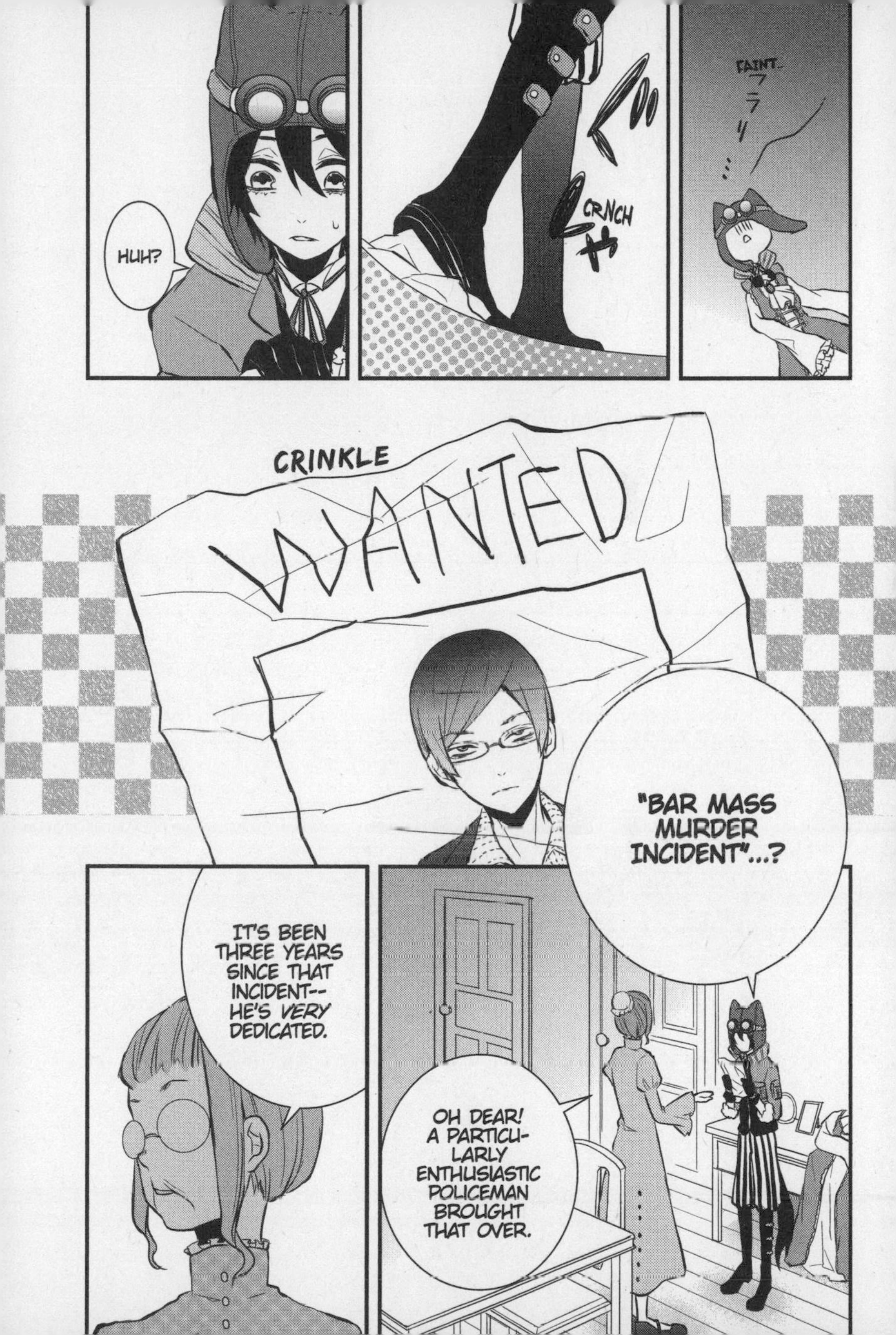
FAINT...
フラリ…
CRNCH
HUH?
CRINKLE
WANTED
"BAR MASS MURDER INCIDENT"...?
OH DEAR! A PARTICU-LARLY ENTHUSIASTIC POLICEMAN BROUGHT THAT OVER.
IT'S BEEN THREE YEARS SINCE THAT INCIDENT-- HE'S *VERY* DEDICATED.

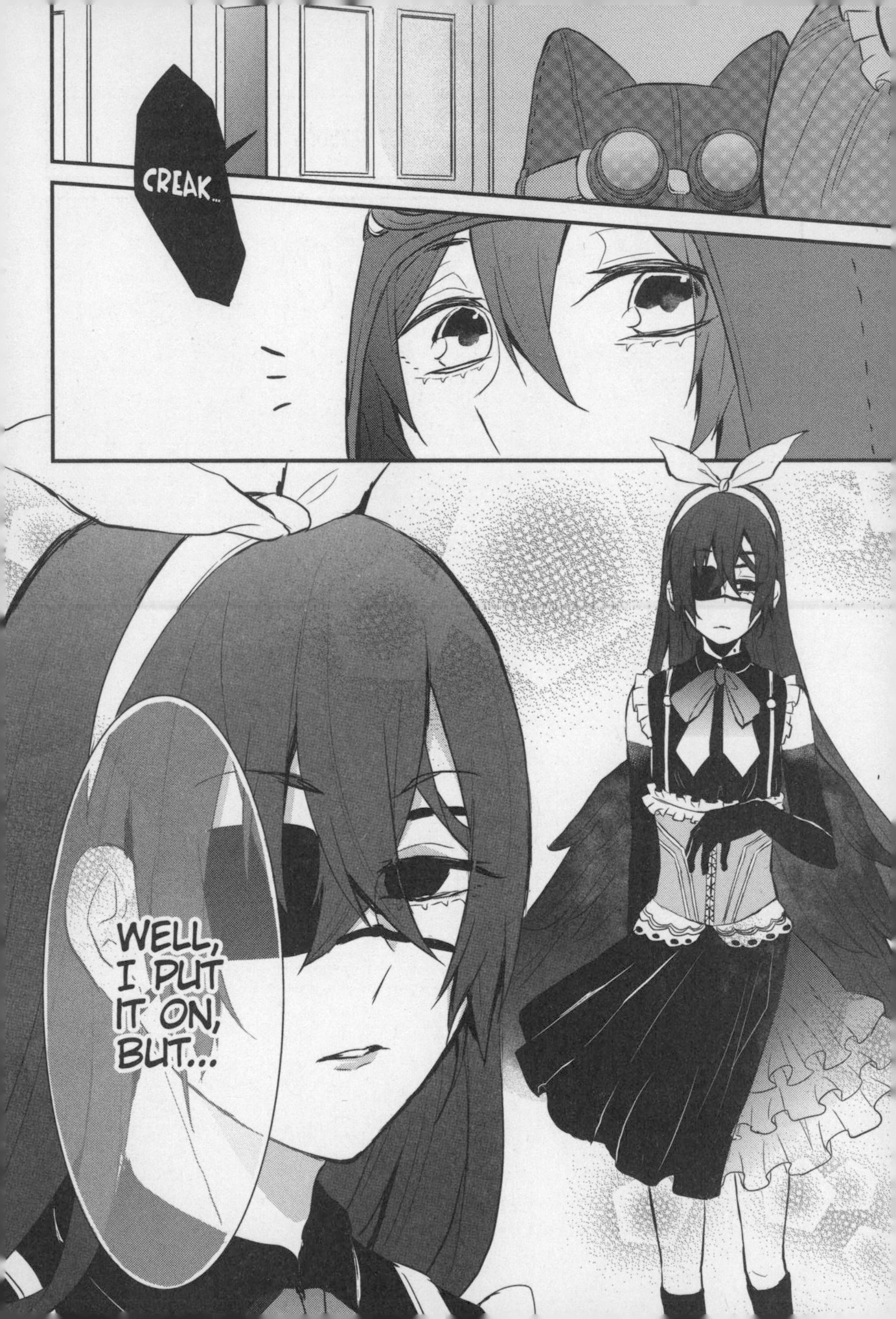
CREAK...
WELL, I PUT IT ON, BUT...

THE FLAMES OF JEALOUSY ARE RED

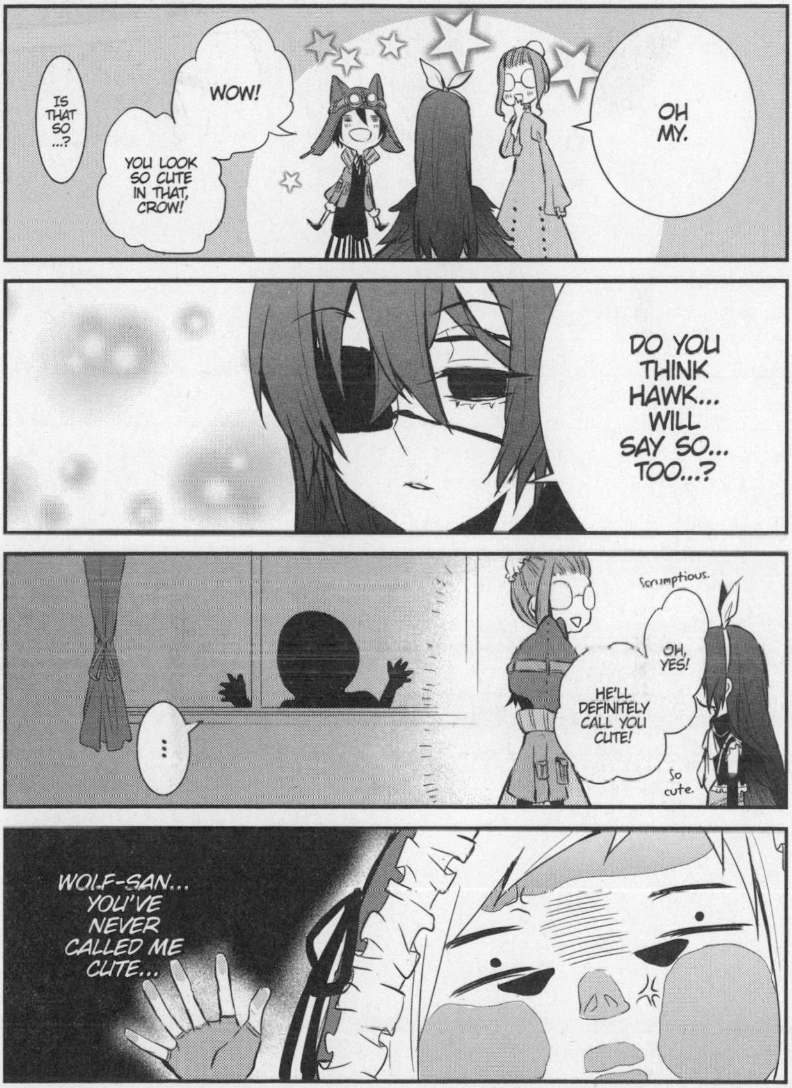
OH MY.
WOW!
YOU LOOK SO CUTE IN THAT, CROW!
IS THAT SO ...?
DO YOU THINK HAWK... WILL SAY SO... TOO...?
Scrumptious.
OH, YES!
HE'LL DEFINITELY CALL YOU CUTE!
So cute.
...
WOLF-SAN... YOU'VE NEVER CALLED ME CUTE...

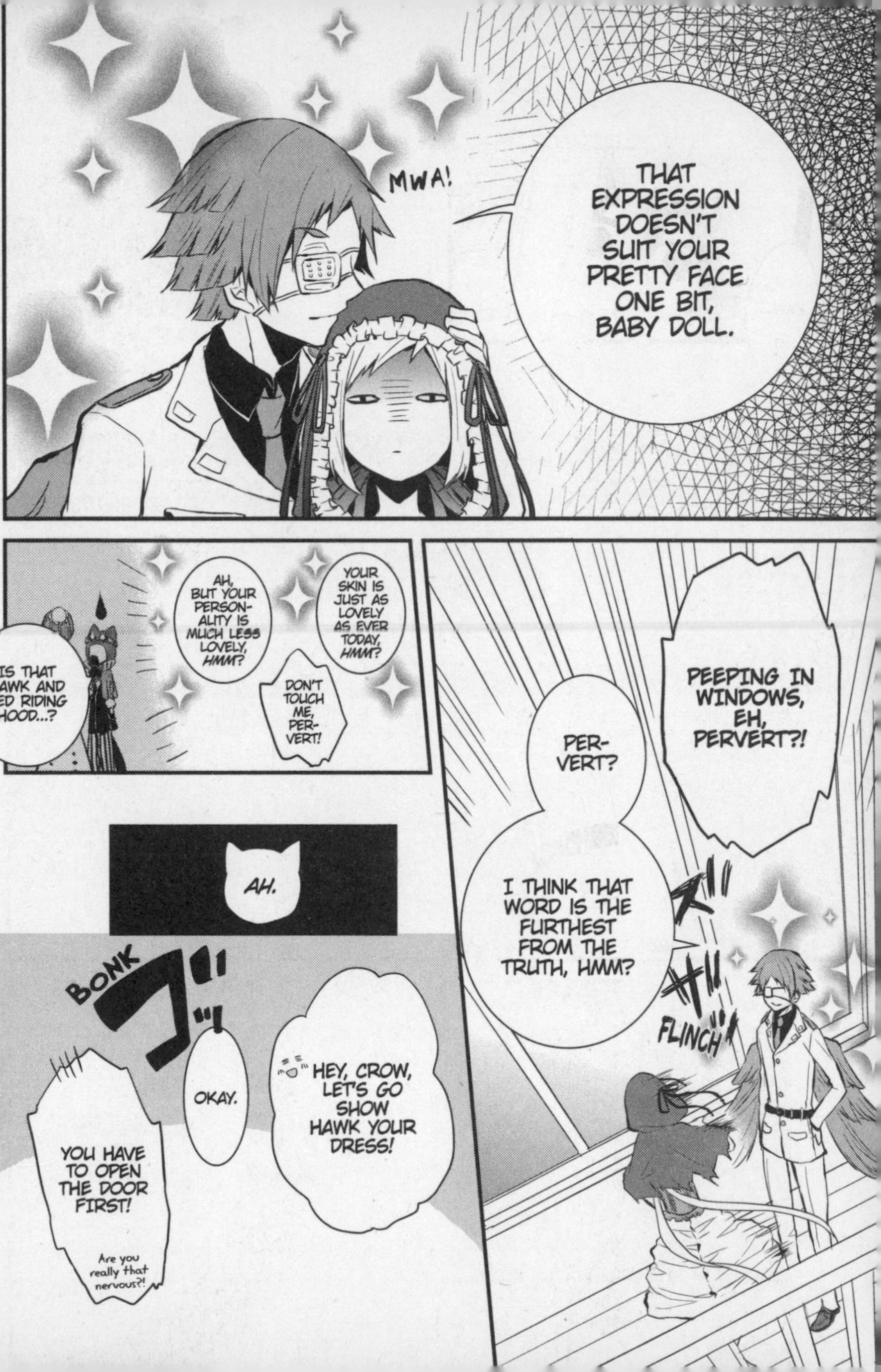
THAT EXPRESSION DOESN'T SUIT YOUR PRETTY FACE ONE BIT, BABY DOLL.
MWA!
PEEPING IN WINDOWS, EH, PERVERT?!
PER-VERT?
I THINK THAT WORD IS THE FURTHEST FROM THE TRUTH, HMM?
FLINCH
YOUR SKIN IS JUST AS LOVELY AS EVER TODAY, HMM?
AH, BUT YOUR PERSON-ALITY IS MUCH LESS LOVELY, HMM?
DON'T TOUCH ME, PER-VERT!
IS THAT HAWK AND RED RIDING HOOD...?
AH.
HEY, CROW, LET'S GO SHOW HAWK YOUR DRESS!
OKAY.
BONK
YOU HAVE TO OPEN THE DOOR FIRST!
Are you really that nervous?!

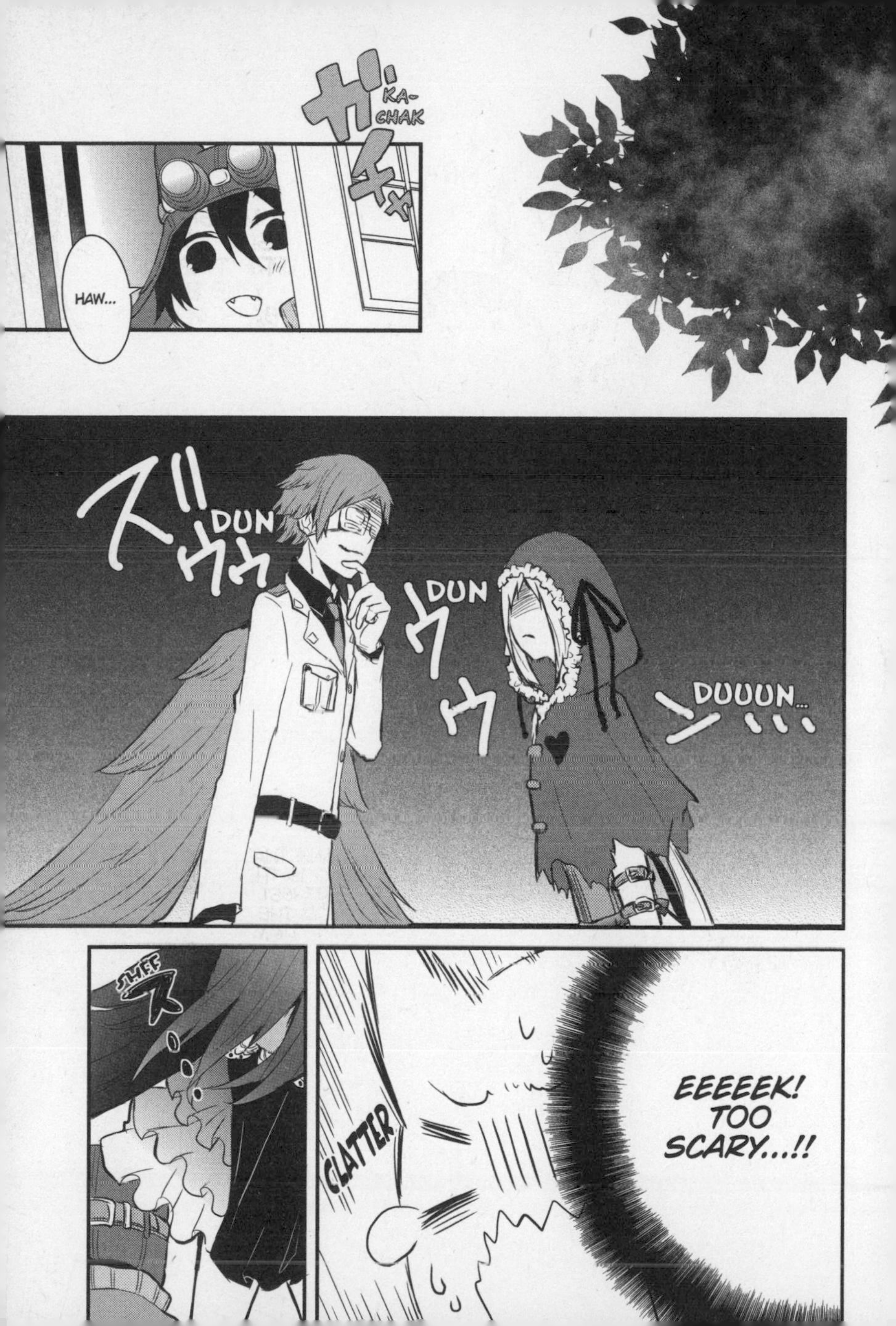
KA-CHAK
HAW...
DUN
DUN
DUUUN...
EEEEEK! TOO SCARY...!!
CLATTER
SHFF

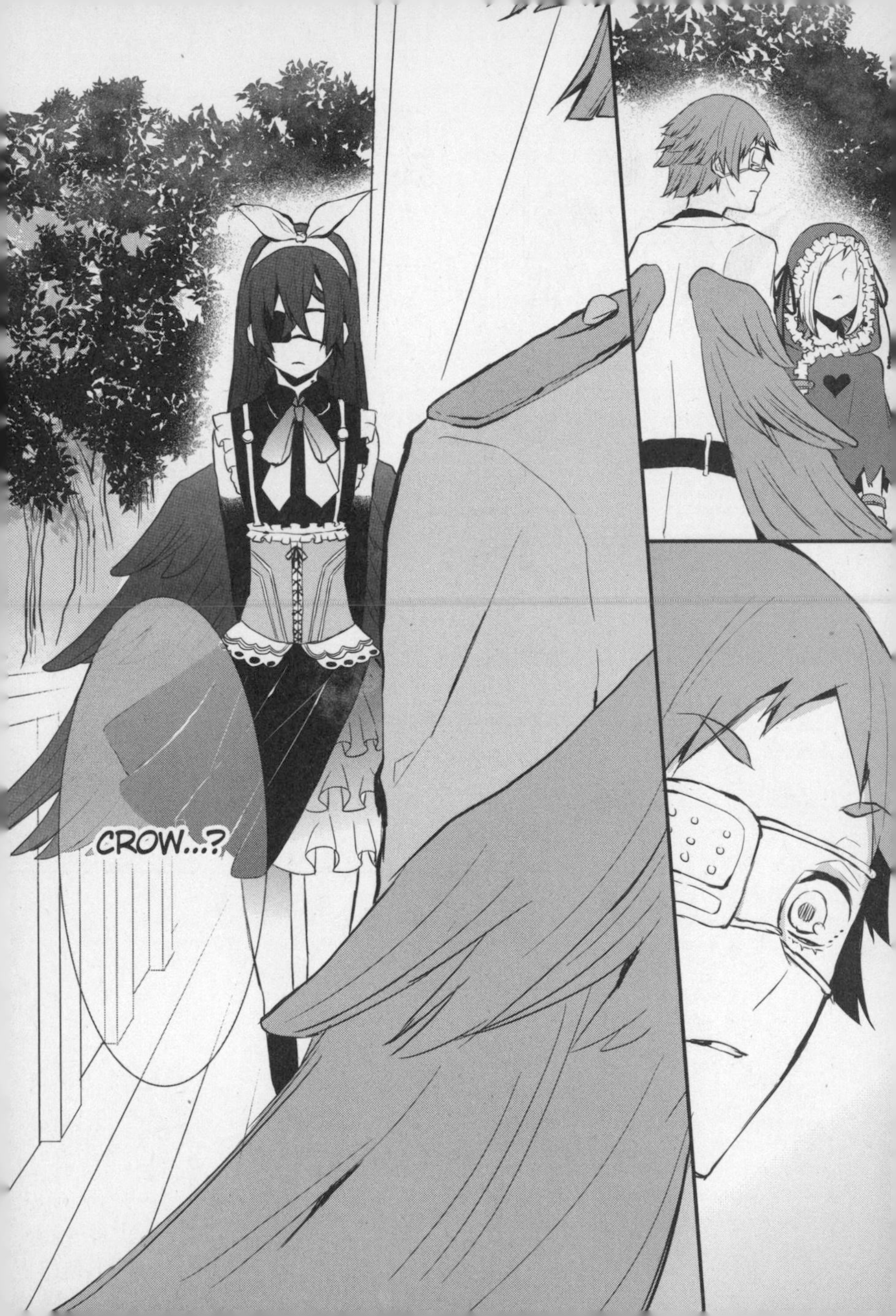
CROW...?

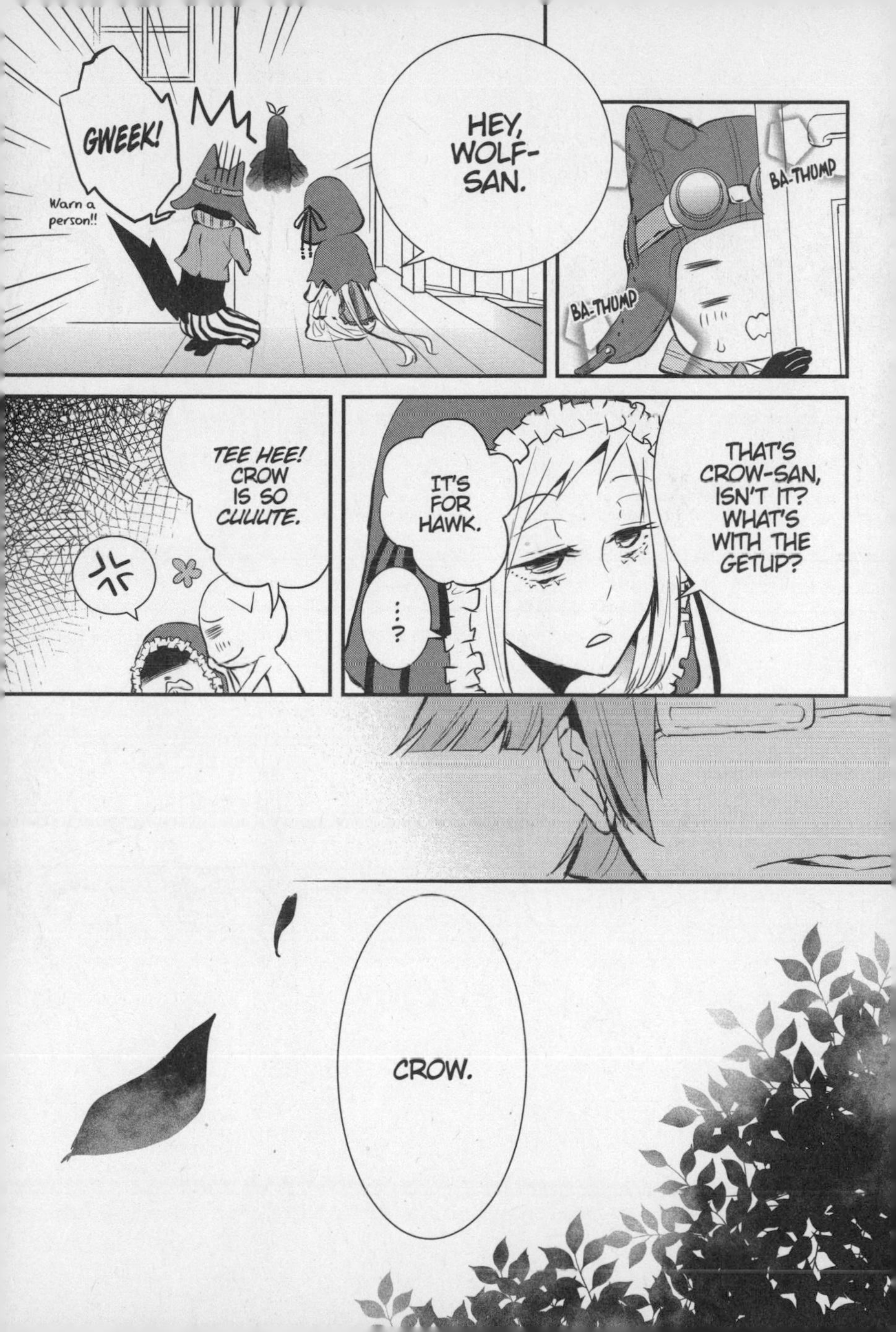
BA-THUMP
BA-THUMP
HEY, WOLF-SAN.
GWEEK!
Warn a person!!
THAT'S CROW-SAN, ISN'T IT? WHAT'S WITH THE GETUP?
IT'S FOR HAWK.
...?
TEE HEE! CROW IS SO CUUUTE.
CROW.

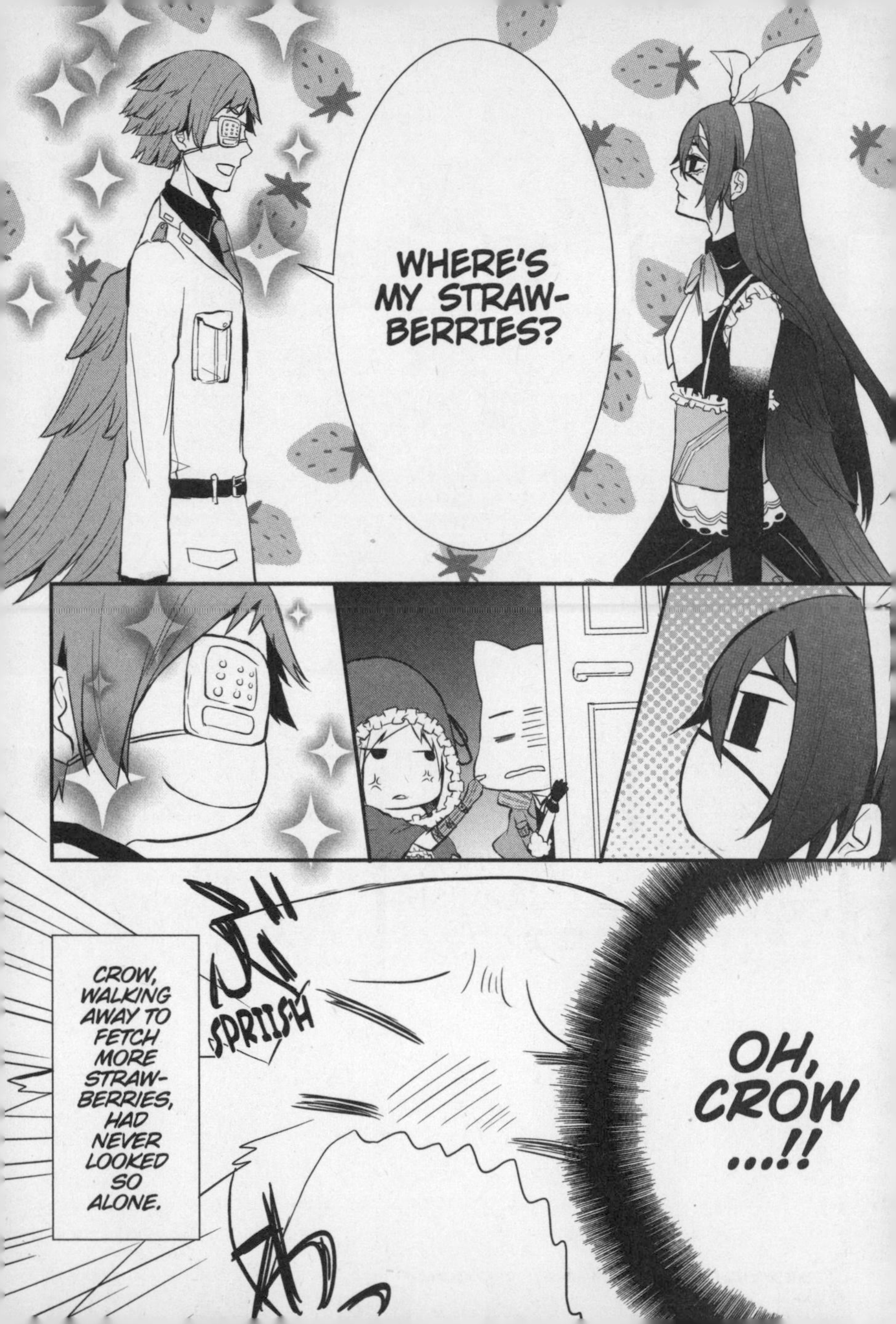

WHERE'S MY STRAW-BERRIES?
CROW, WALKING AWAY TO FETCH MORE STRAW-BERRIES, HAD NEVER LOOKED SO ALONE.
SPRIIISH
OH, CROW ...!!

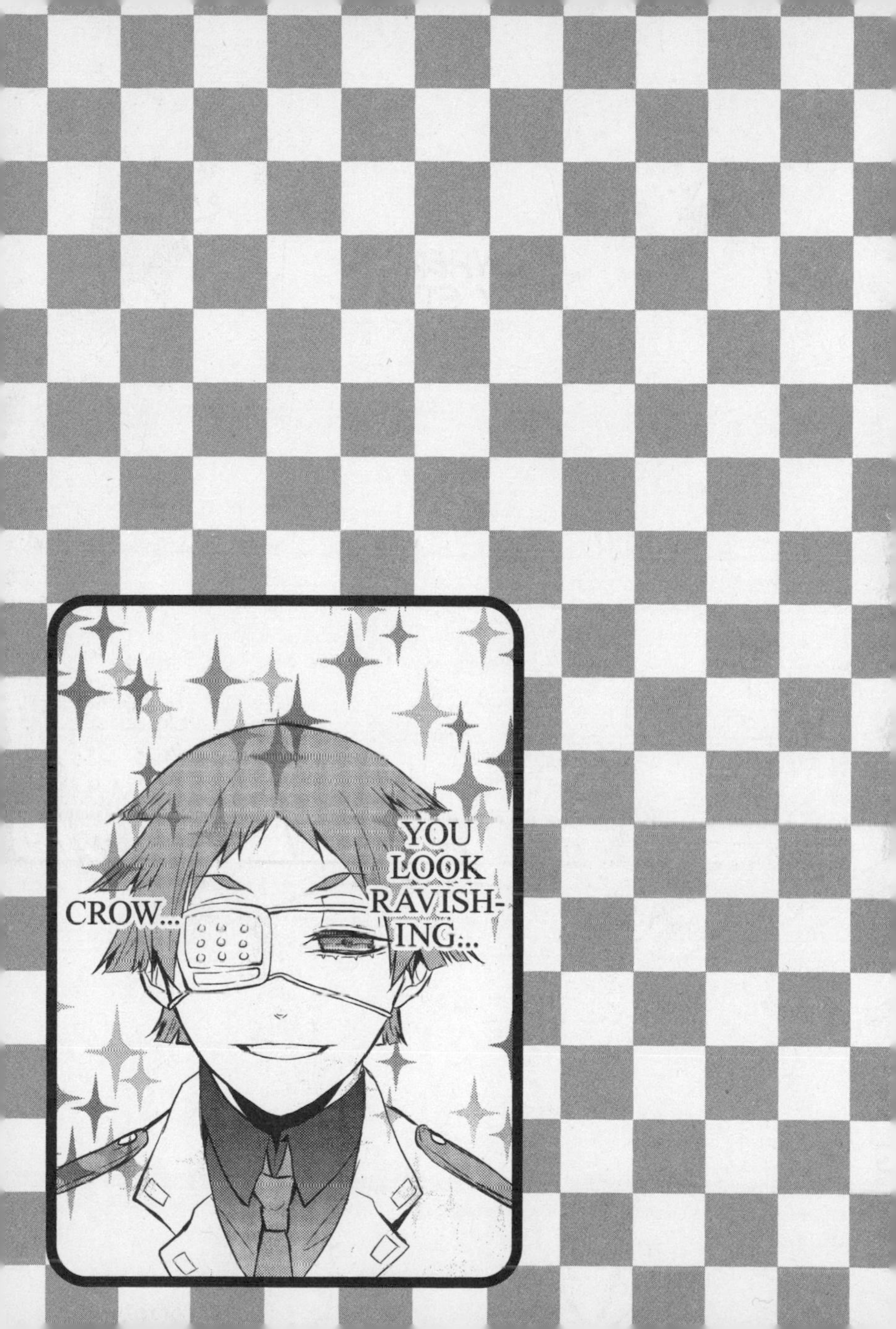
YOU LOOK RAVISH-ING...
CROW...

RED RIDING HOOD AND the BIG·SAD·WOLF

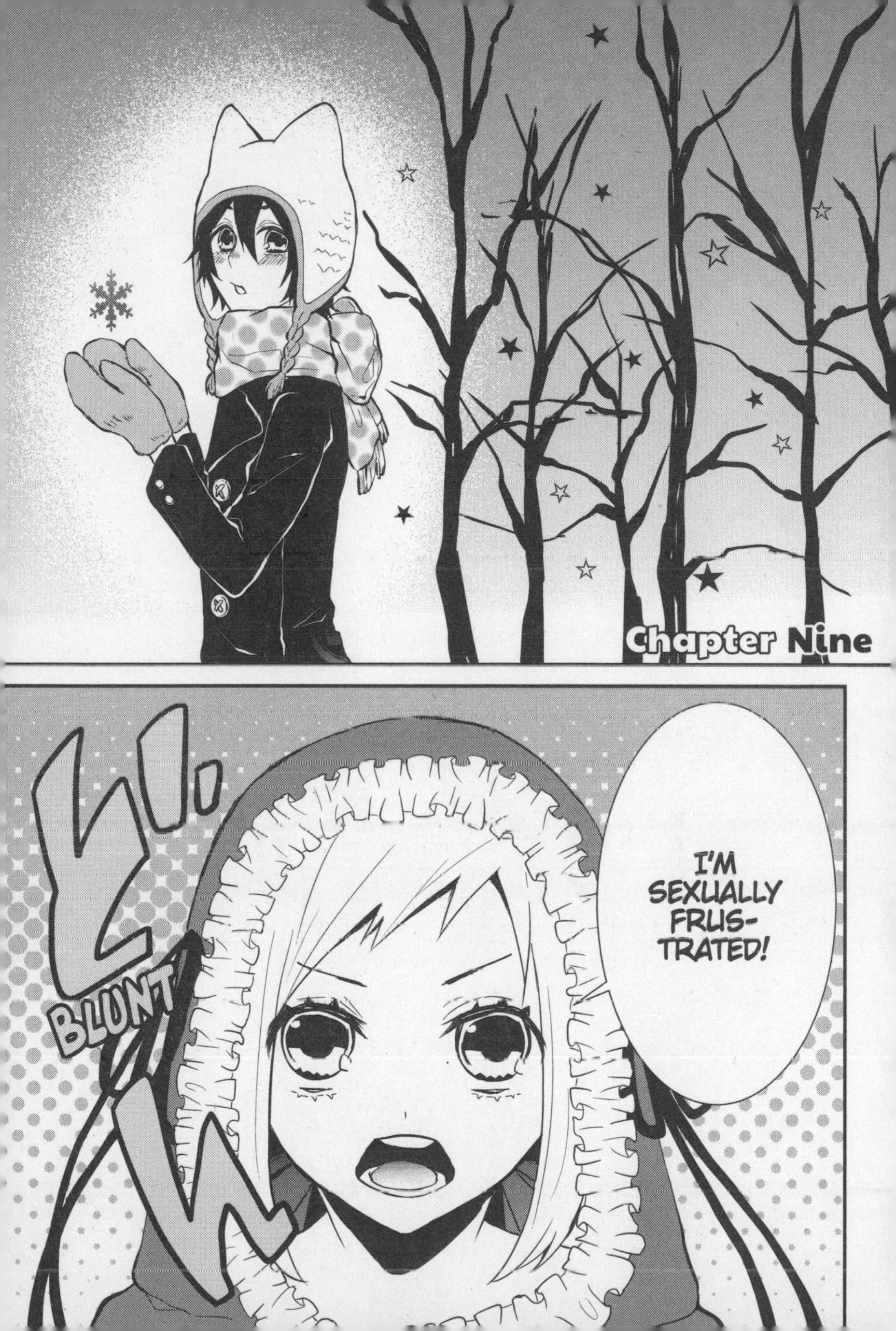
Chapter Nine
I'M SEXUALLY FRUS-TRATED!
BLUNT

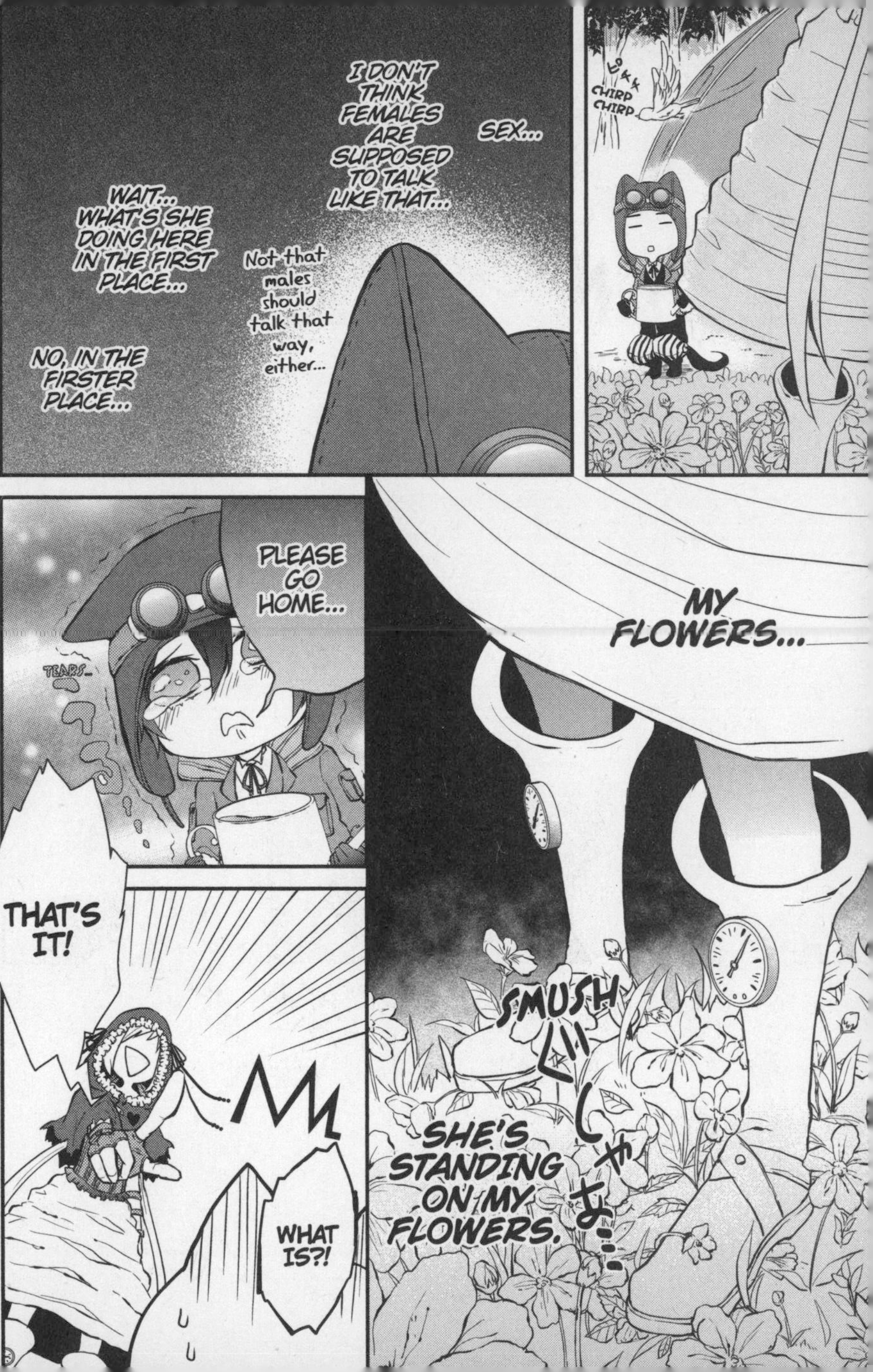
CHIRP CHIRP
SEX...
I DON'T THINK FEMALES ARE SUPPOSED TO TALK LIKE THAT...
Not that males should talk that way, either...
WAIT... WHAT'S SHE DOING HERE IN THE FIRST PLACE...
NO, IN THE FIRSTER PLACE...
MY FLOWERS...
SMUSH
SHE'S STANDING ON MY FLOWERS.
PLEASE GO HOME...
TEARS...
THAT'S IT!
WHAT IS?!

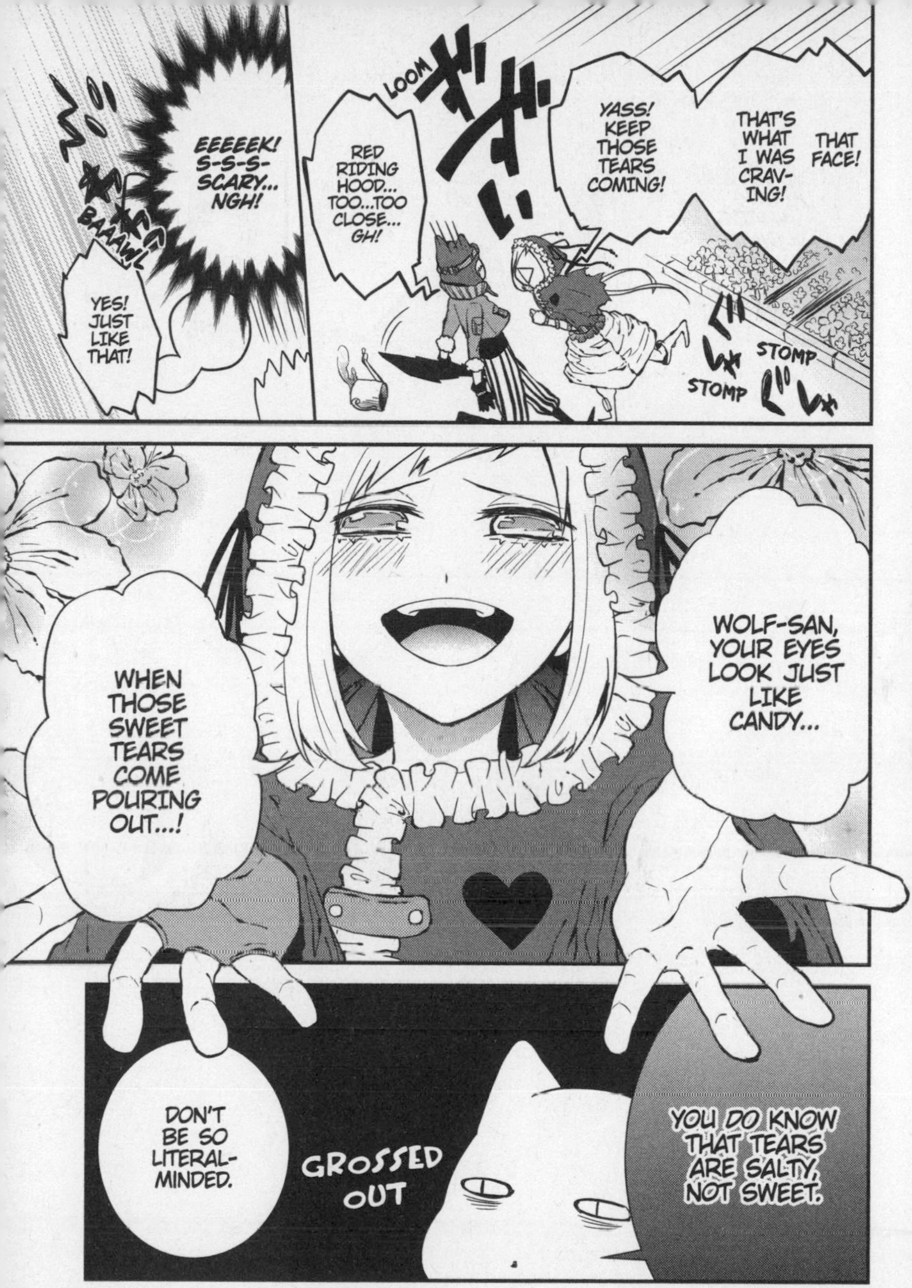
THAT FACE!
THAT'S WHAT I WAS CRAV-ING!
YASS! KEEP THOSE TEARS COMING!
LOOM
RED RIDING HOOD... TOO...TOO CLOSE... GH!
STOMP
STOMP
EEEEEK! S-S-S-SCARY... NGH!
BAAAWL
YES! JUST LIKE THAT!
WOLF-SAN, YOUR EYES LOOK JUST LIKE CANDY...
WHEN THOSE SWEET TEARS COME POURING OUT...!
YOU DO KNOW THAT TEARS ARE SALTY, NOT SWEET.
GROSSED OUT
DON'T BE SO LITERAL-MINDED.

BY WHATEVER MEANS NECESSARY

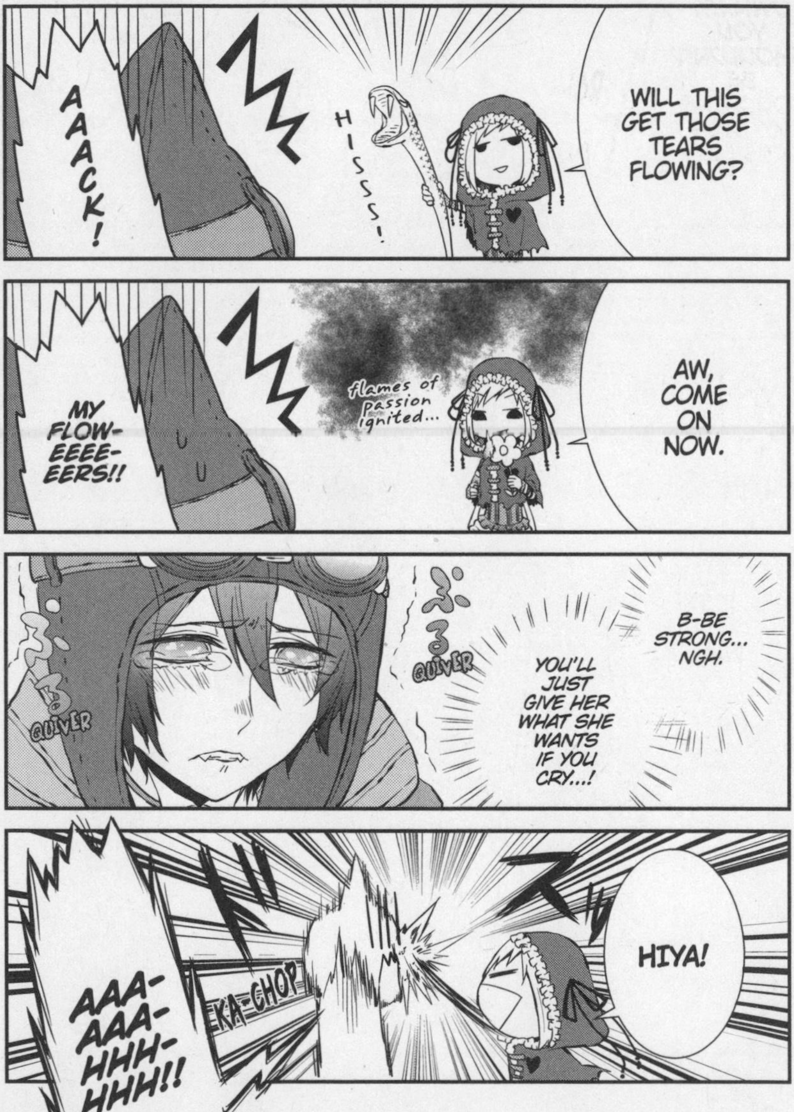
WILL THIS GET THOSE TEARS FLOWING?
HISSS!
AAACK!
AW, COME ON NOW.
flames of passion ignited...
MY FLOW-EEEE-EERS!!
B-BE STRONG... NGH.
YOU'LL JUST GIVE HER WHAT SHE WANTS IF YOU CRY...!
QUIVER
QUIVER
HIYA!
KA-CHOP
AAA-AAA-HHH-HHH!!

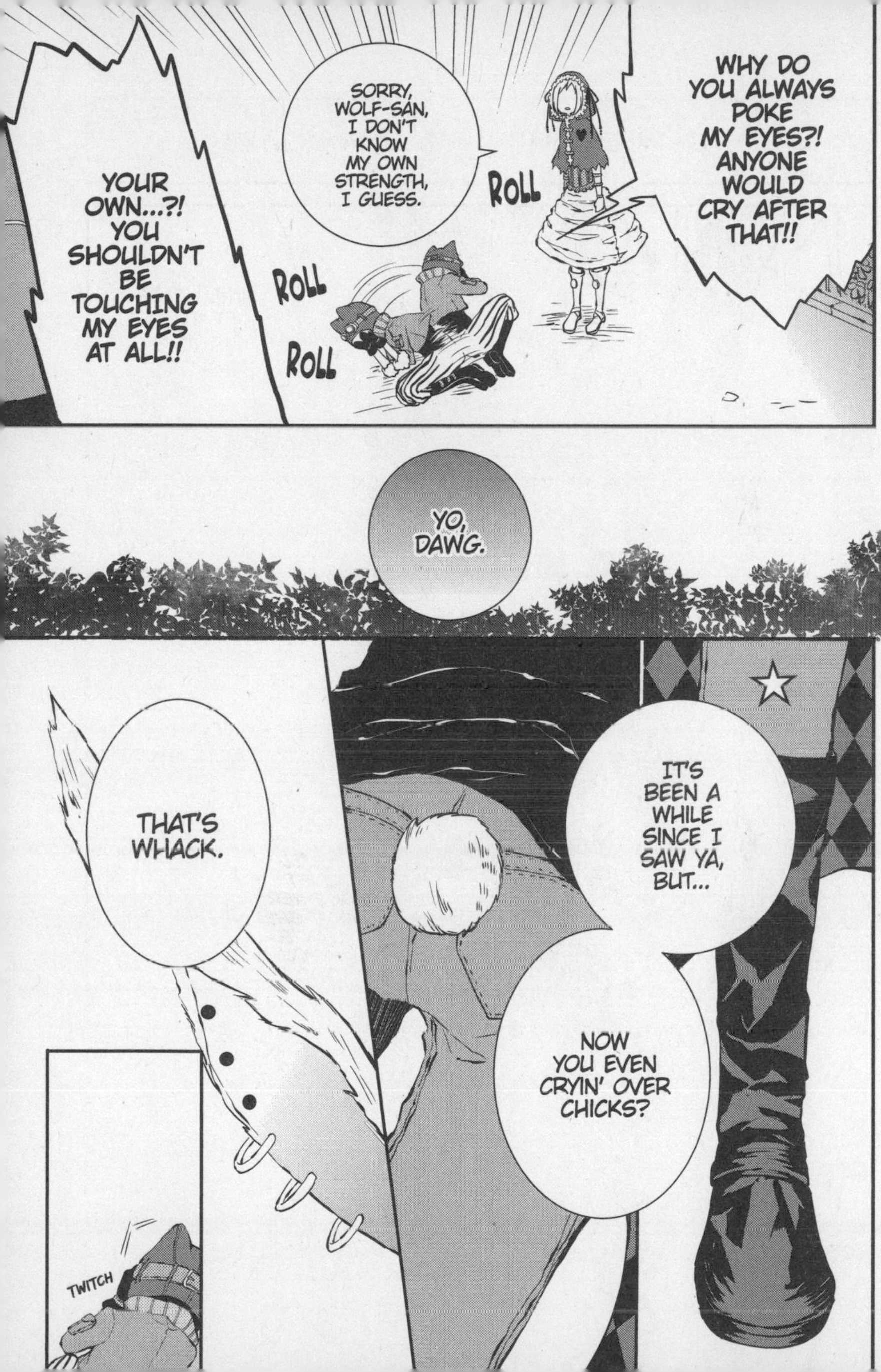

WHY DO YOU ALWAYS POKE MY EYES?! ANYONE WOULD CRY AFTER THAT!!
SORRY, WOLF-SAN, I DON'T KNOW MY OWN STRENGTH, I GUESS.
ROLL
ROLL
ROLL
YOUR OWN...?! YOU SHOULDN'T BE TOUCHING MY EYES AT ALL!!
YO, DAWG.
IT'S BEEN A WHILE SINCE I SAW YA, BUT...
NOW YOU EVEN CRYIN' OVER CHICKS?
THAT'S WHACK.
TWITCH

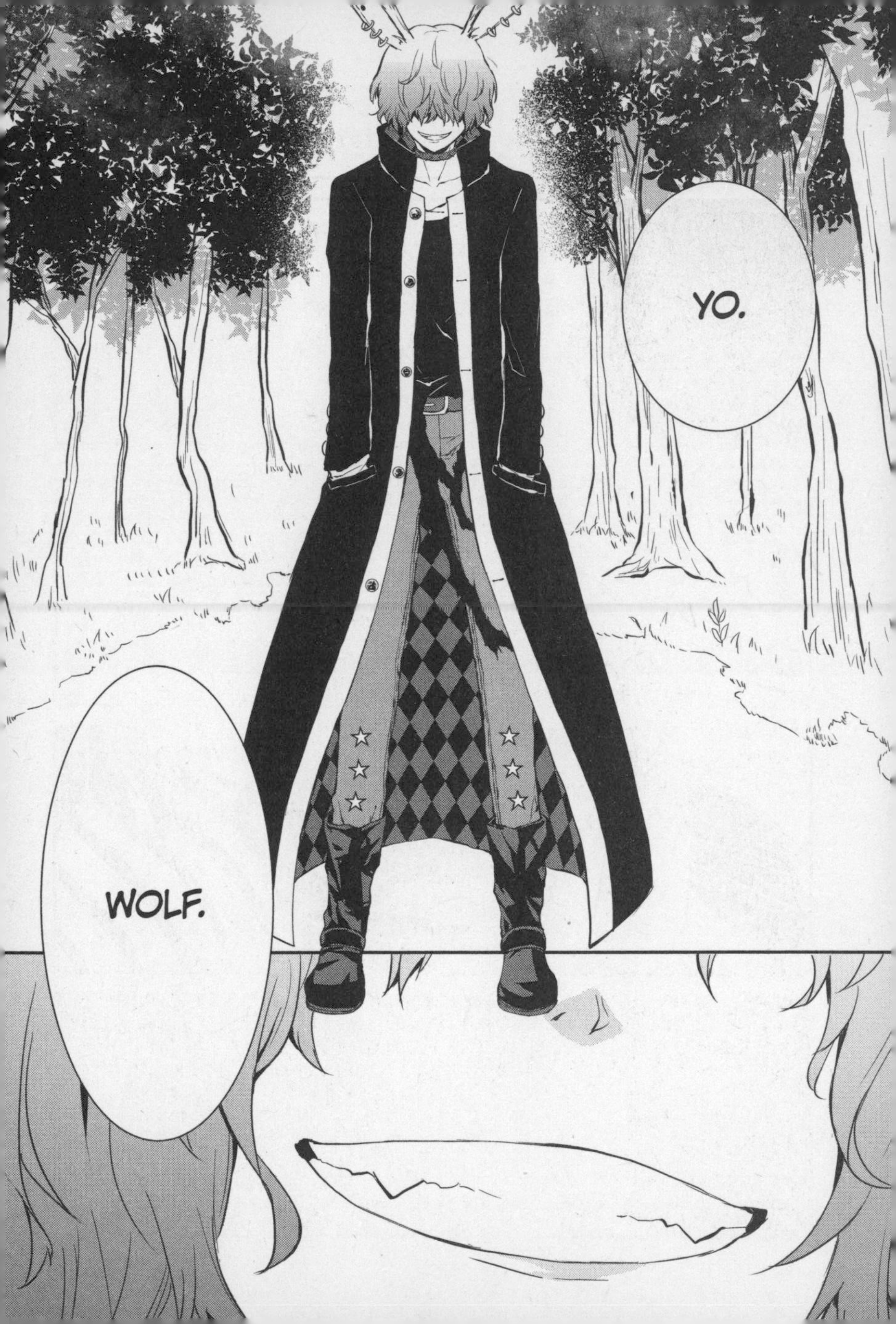
YO.
WOLF.

PRAY FOR OBLIVION

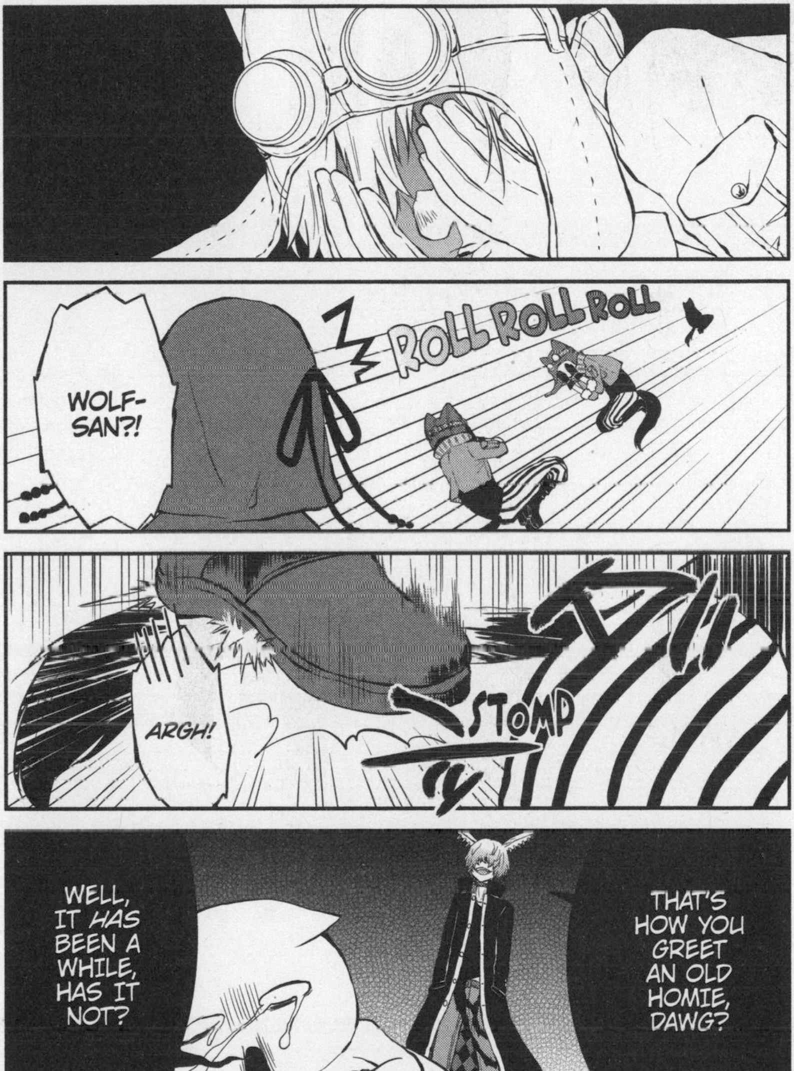
ROLL ROLL ROLL
WOLF-SAN?!
STOMP
ARGH!
THAT'S HOW YOU GREET AN OLD HOMIE, DAWG?
WELL, IT *HAS* BEEN A WHILE, HAS IT NOT?

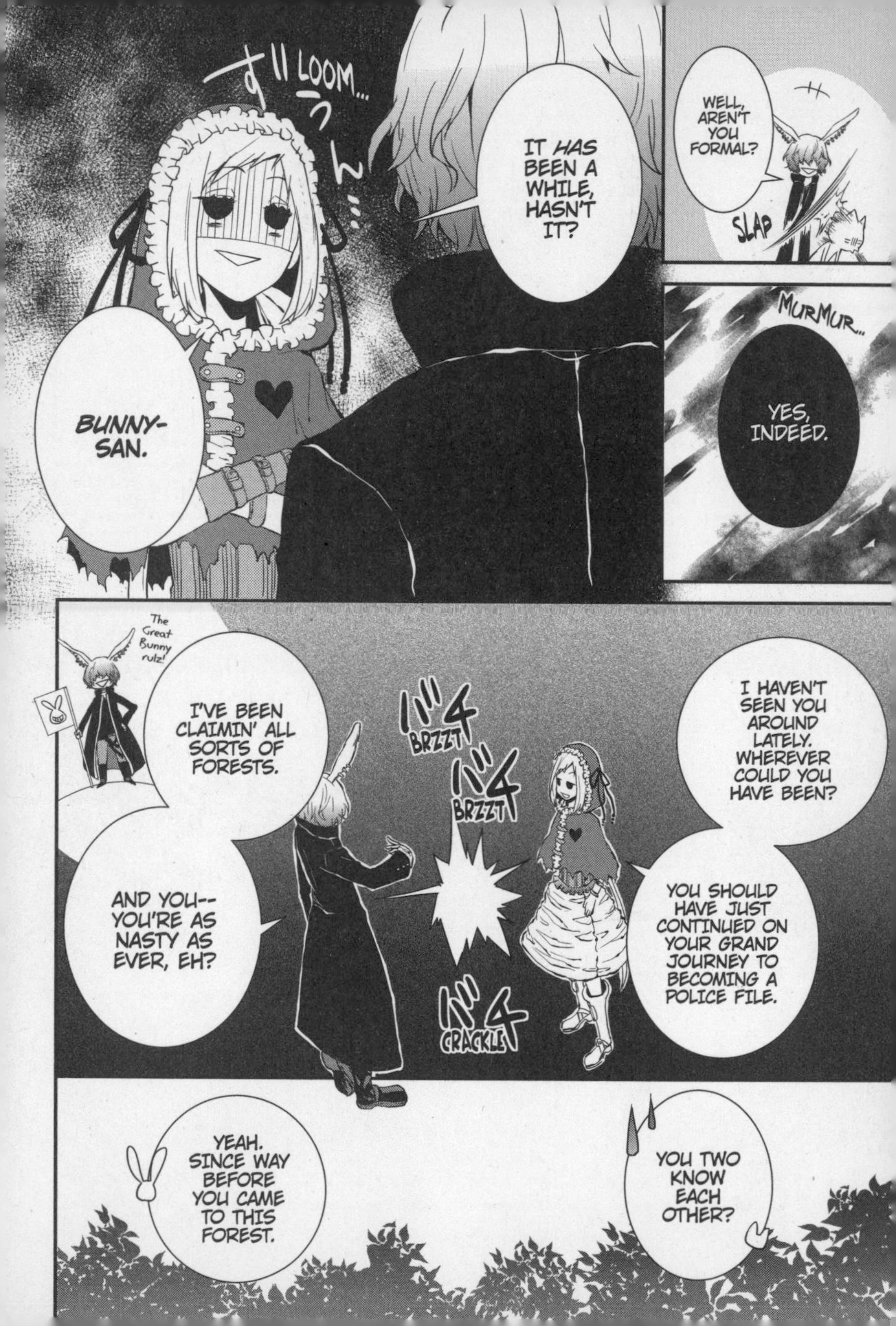
WELL, AREN'T YOU FORMAL?
SLAP
MURMUR...
YES, INDEED.
LOOM...
IT *HAS* BEEN A WHILE, HASN'T IT?
BUNNY-SAN.
I HAVEN'T SEEN YOU AROUND LATELY. WHEREVER COULD YOU HAVE BEEN?
YOU SHOULD HAVE JUST CONTINUED ON YOUR GRAND JOURNEY TO BECOMING A POLICE FILE.
BRZZT
BRZZT
CRACKLE
I'VE BEEN CLAIMIN' ALL SORTS OF FORESTS.
AND YOU-- YOU'RE AS NASTY AS EVER, EH?
The Great Bunny rulz!
YOU TWO KNOW EACH OTHER?
YEAH. SINCE WAY BEFORE YOU CAME TO THIS FOREST.

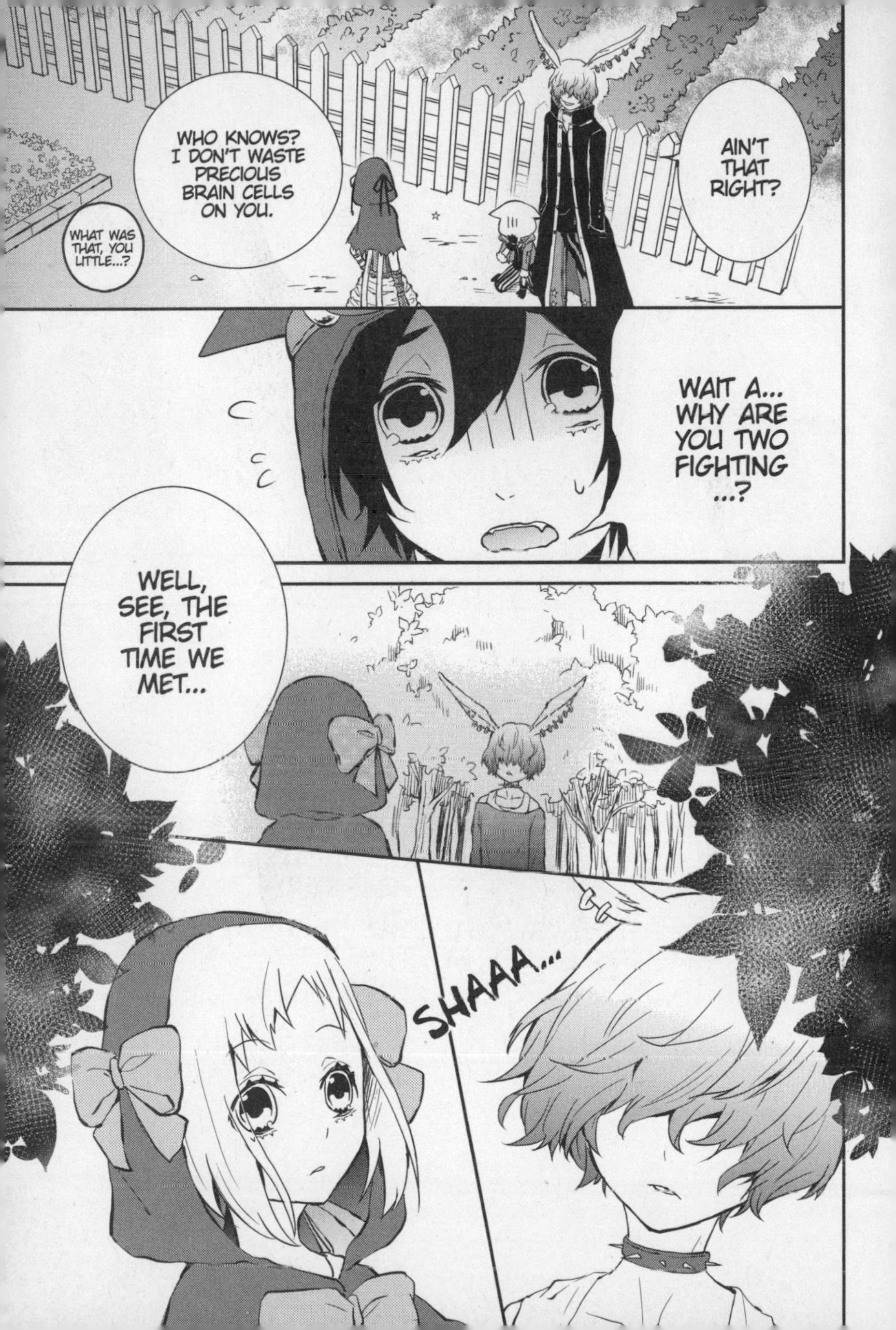
AIN'T THAT RIGHT?
WHO KNOWS? I DON'T WASTE PRECIOUS BRAIN CELLS ON YOU.
WHAT WAS THAT, YOU LITTLE...?
WAIT A... WHY ARE YOU TWO FIGHTING ...?
WELL, SEE, THE FIRST TIME WE MET...
SHAAA...

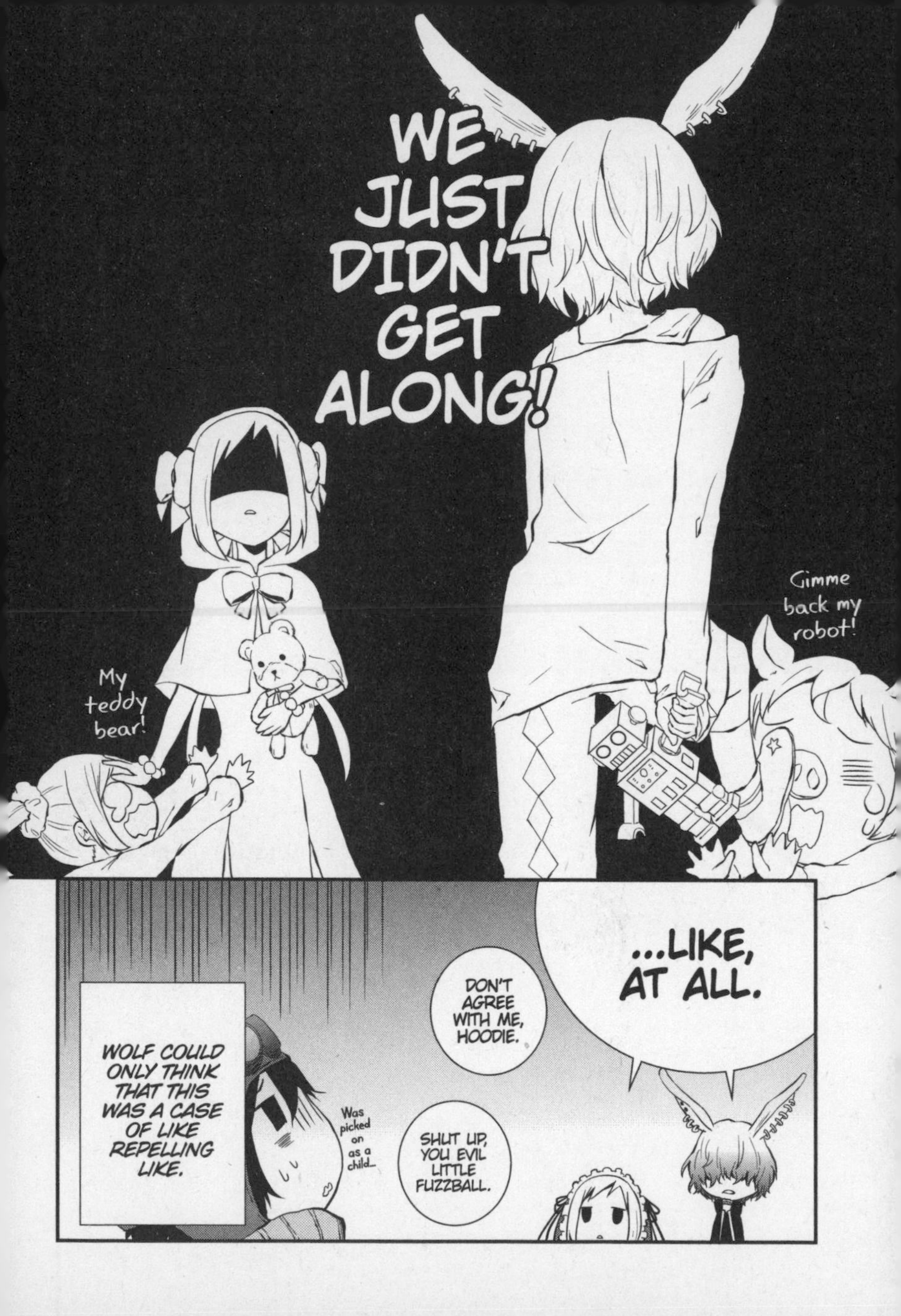
WE JUST DIDN'T GET ALONG!
Gimme back my robot!
My teddy bear!
...LIKE, AT ALL.
DON'T AGREE WITH ME, HOODIE.
SHUT UP, YOU EVIL LITTLE FUZZBALL.
Was picked on as a child...
WOLF COULD ONLY THINK THAT THIS WAS A CASE OF LIKE REPELLING LIKE.

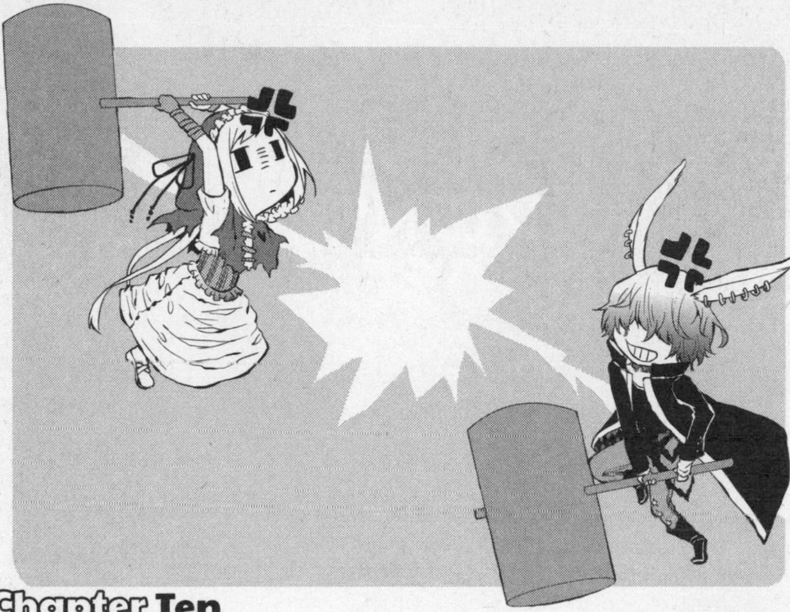

Chapter Ten

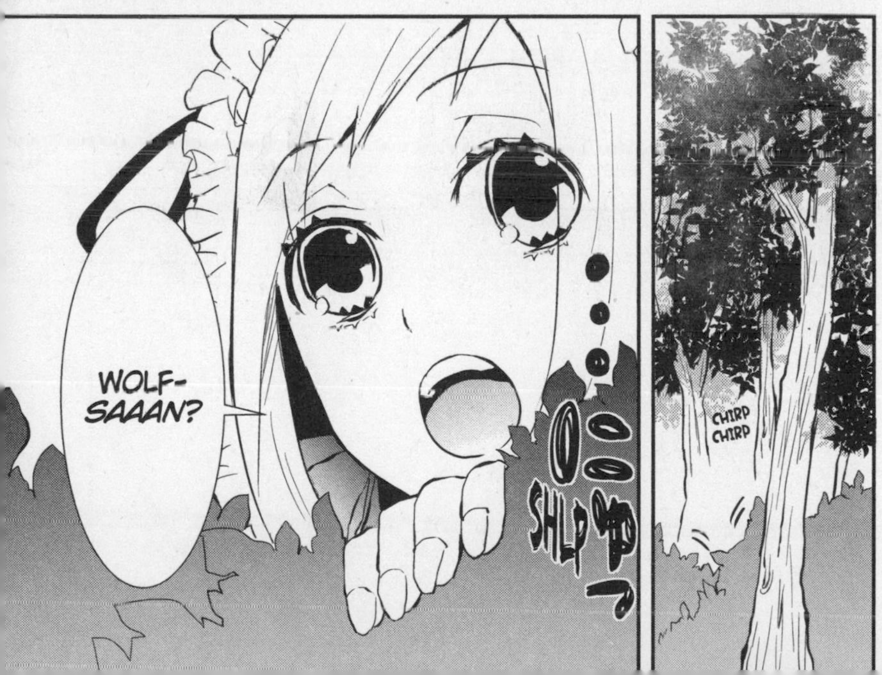
CHIRP
CHIRP
WOLF-SAAAN?
SHLP

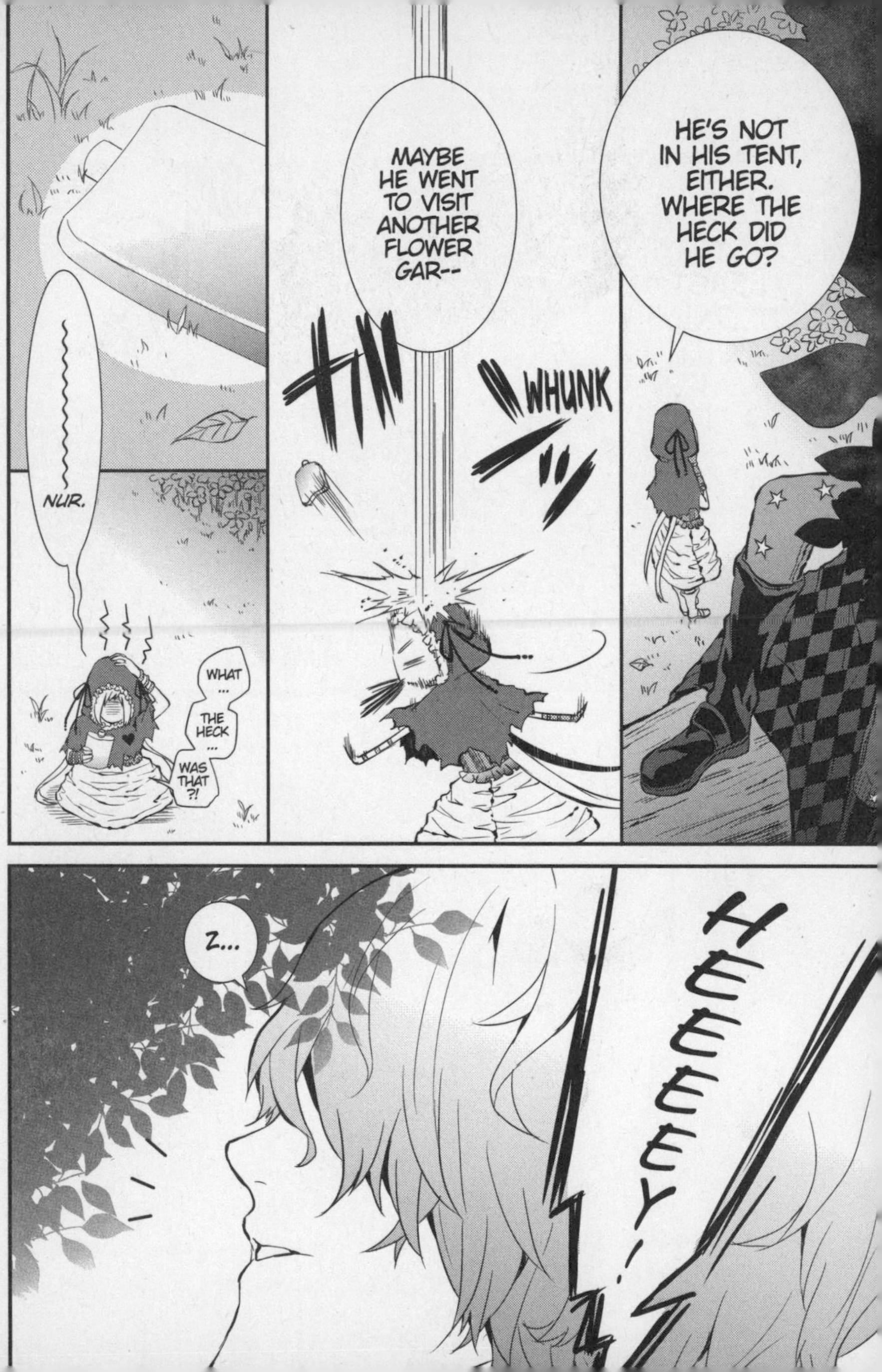
HE'S NOT IN HIS TENT, EITHER. WHERE THE HECK DID HE GO?
MAYBE HE WENT TO VISIT ANOTHER FLOWER GAR--
WHUNK
NUR.
WHAT ... THE HECK ... WAS THAT ?!
HEEEEEY...!
Z...

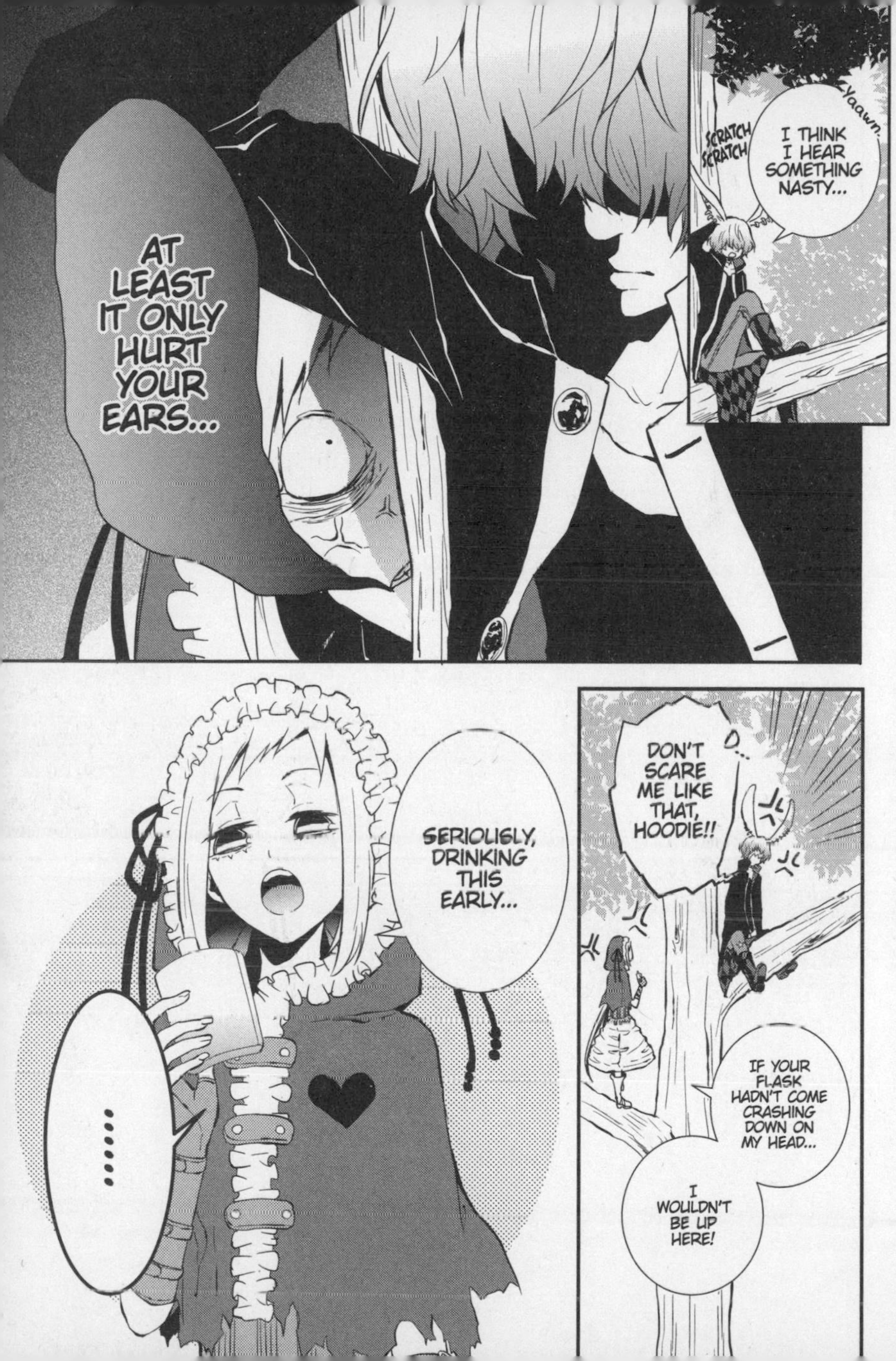
Yaawn.
I THINK I HEAR SOMETHING NASTY...
SCRATCH SCRATCH
AT LEAST IT ONLY HURT YOUR EARS...
DON'T SCARE ME LIKE THAT, HOODIE!!
IF YOUR FLASK HADN'T COME CRASHING DOWN ON MY HEAD...
I WOULDN'T BE UP HERE!
SERIOUSLY, DRINKING THIS EARLY...
......

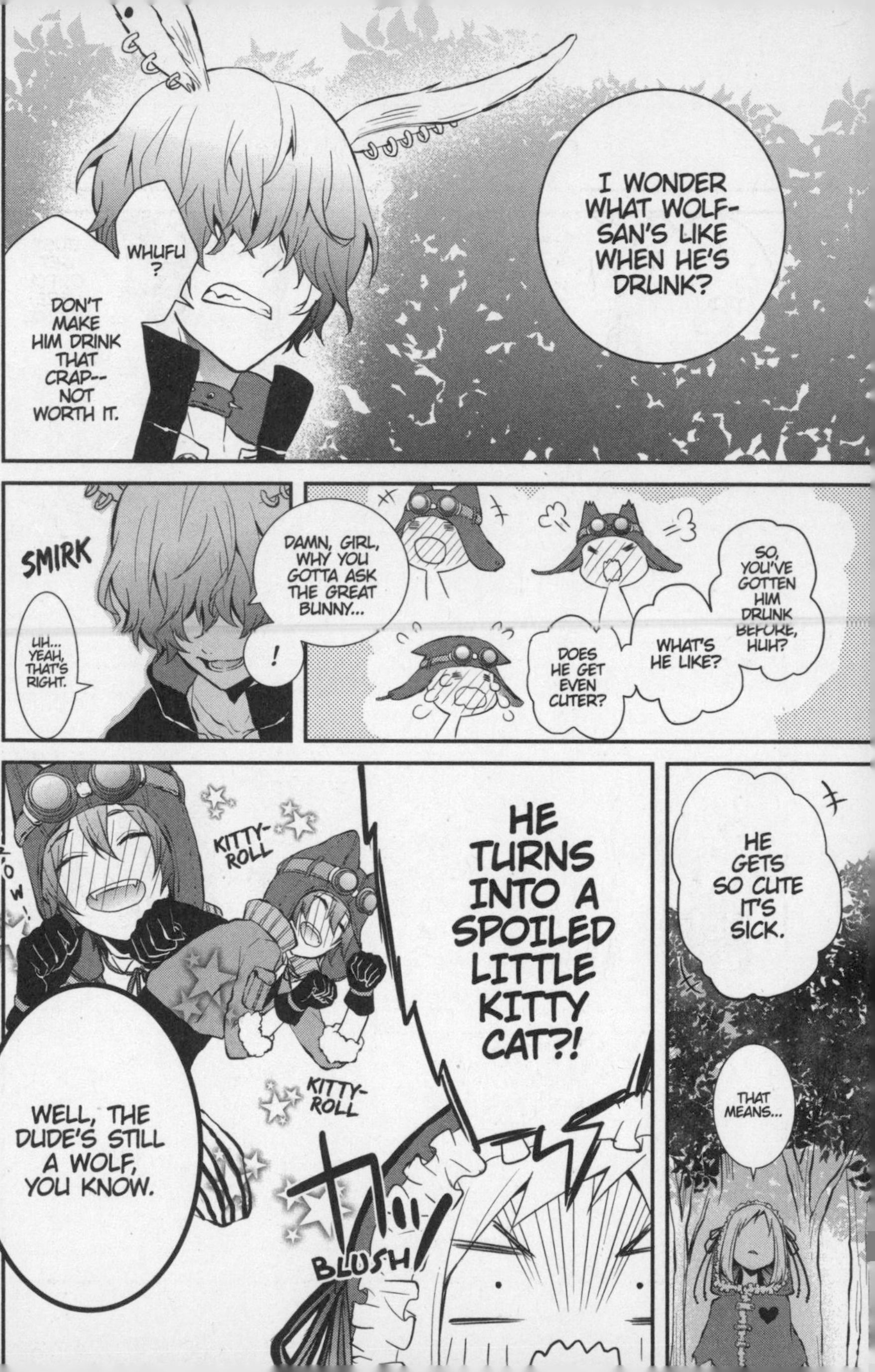
I WONDER WHAT WOLF-SAN'S LIKE WHEN HE'S DRUNK?
WHUFU ?
DON'T MAKE HIM DRINK THAT CRAP-- NOT WORTH IT.
SO, YOU'VE GOTTEN HIM DRUNK BEFORE, HUH?
WHAT'S HE LIKE?
DOES HE GET EVEN CUTER?
DAMN, GIRL, WHY YOU GOTTA ASK THE GREAT BUNNY...
SMIRK
!
UH... YEAH, THAT'S RIGHT.
HE GETS SO CUTE IT'S SICK.
THAT MEANS...
HE TURNS INTO A SPOILED LITTLE KITTY CAT?!
BLUSH
KITTY-ROLL
MROW!
KITTY-ROLL
WELL, THE DUDE'S STILL A WOLF, YOU KNOW.

CURB YOUR ENTHUSIASM

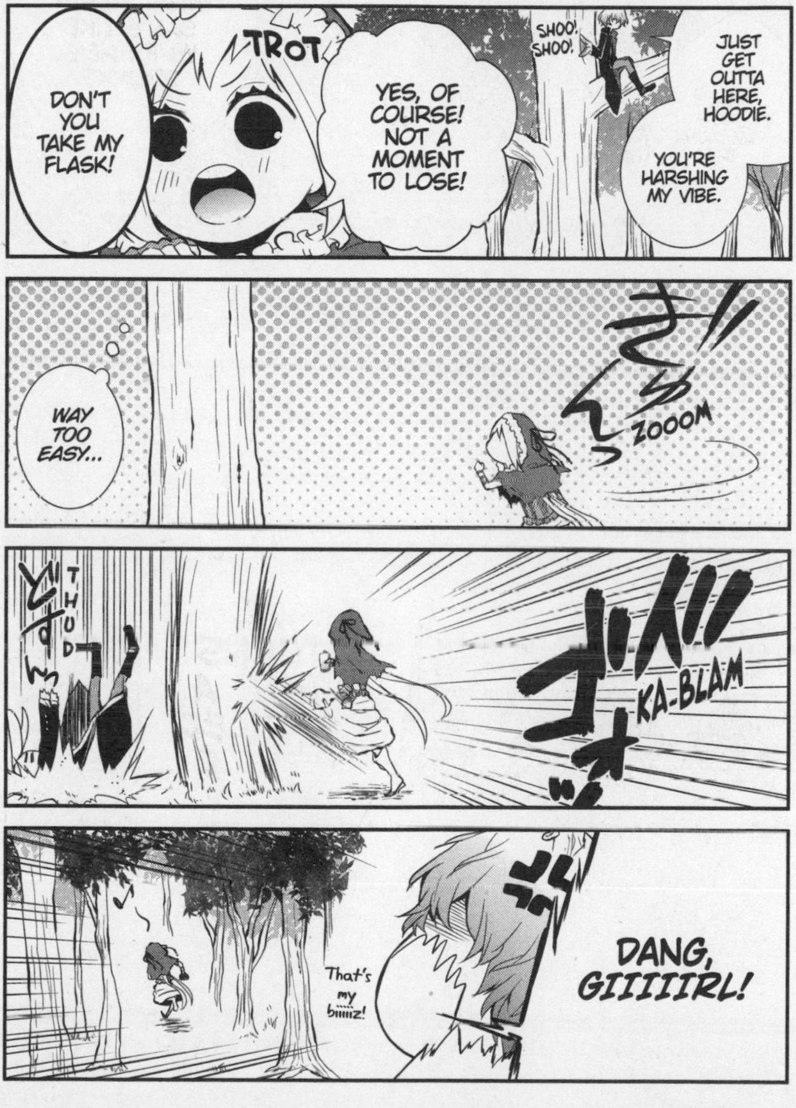

JUST GET OUTTA HERE, HOODIE.
YOU'RE HARSHING MY VIBE.
SHOO! SHOO!
YES, OF COURSE! NOT A MOMENT TO LOSE!
TROT
DON'T YOU TAKE MY FLASK!
ZOOOM
WAY TOO EASY...
KA-BLAM
THUD
DANG, GIIIIIRL!
That's my biiiiiz!

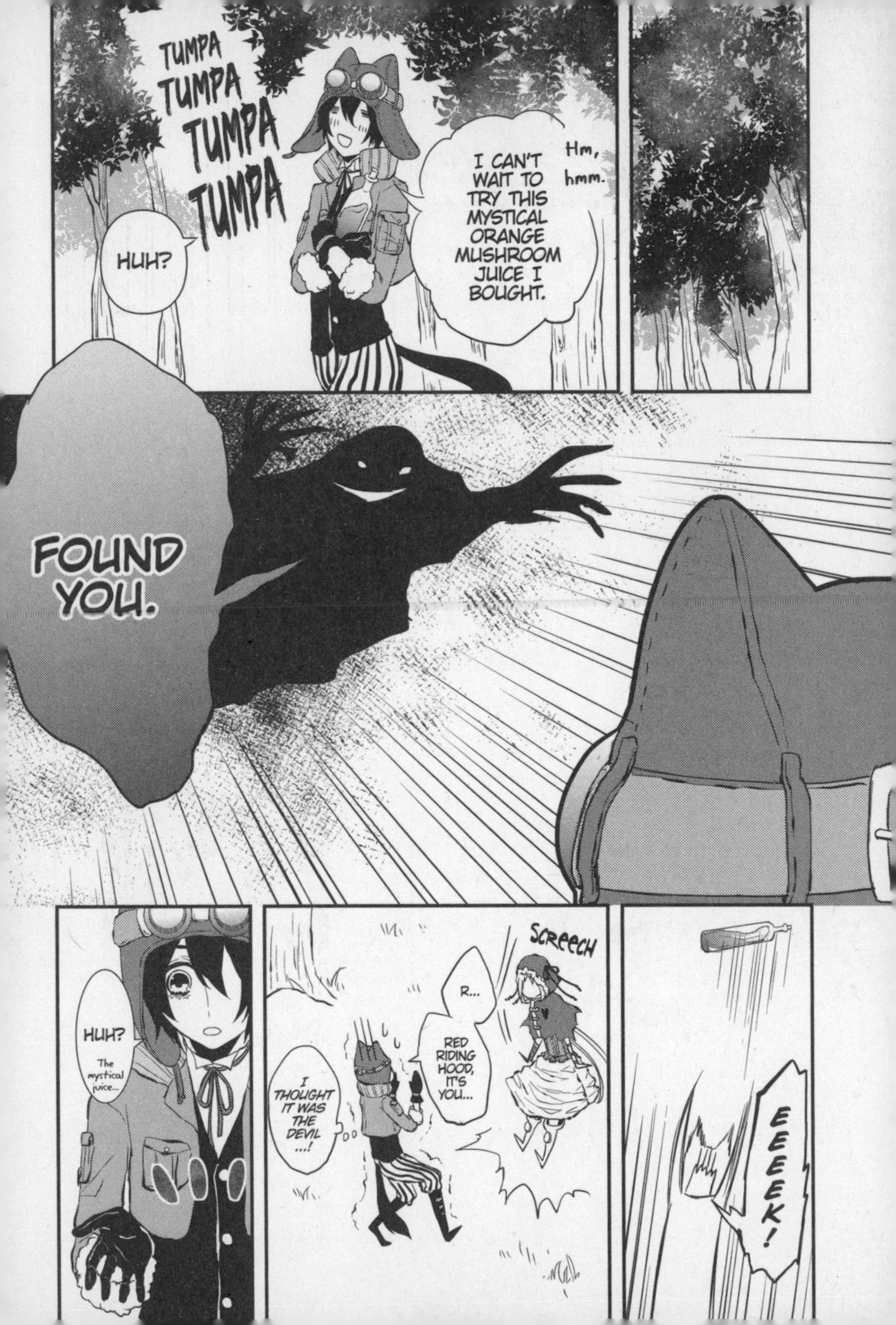
Hm, hmm.
I CAN'T WAIT TO TRY THIS MYSTICAL ORANGE MUSHROOM JUICE I BOUGHT.
TUMPA TUMPA TUMPA TUMPA
HUH?
FOUND YOU.
EEEEK!
SCREECH
R...
RED RIDING HOOD, IT'S YOU...
I THOUGHT IT WAS THE DEVIL ...!
HUH?
The mystical juice...

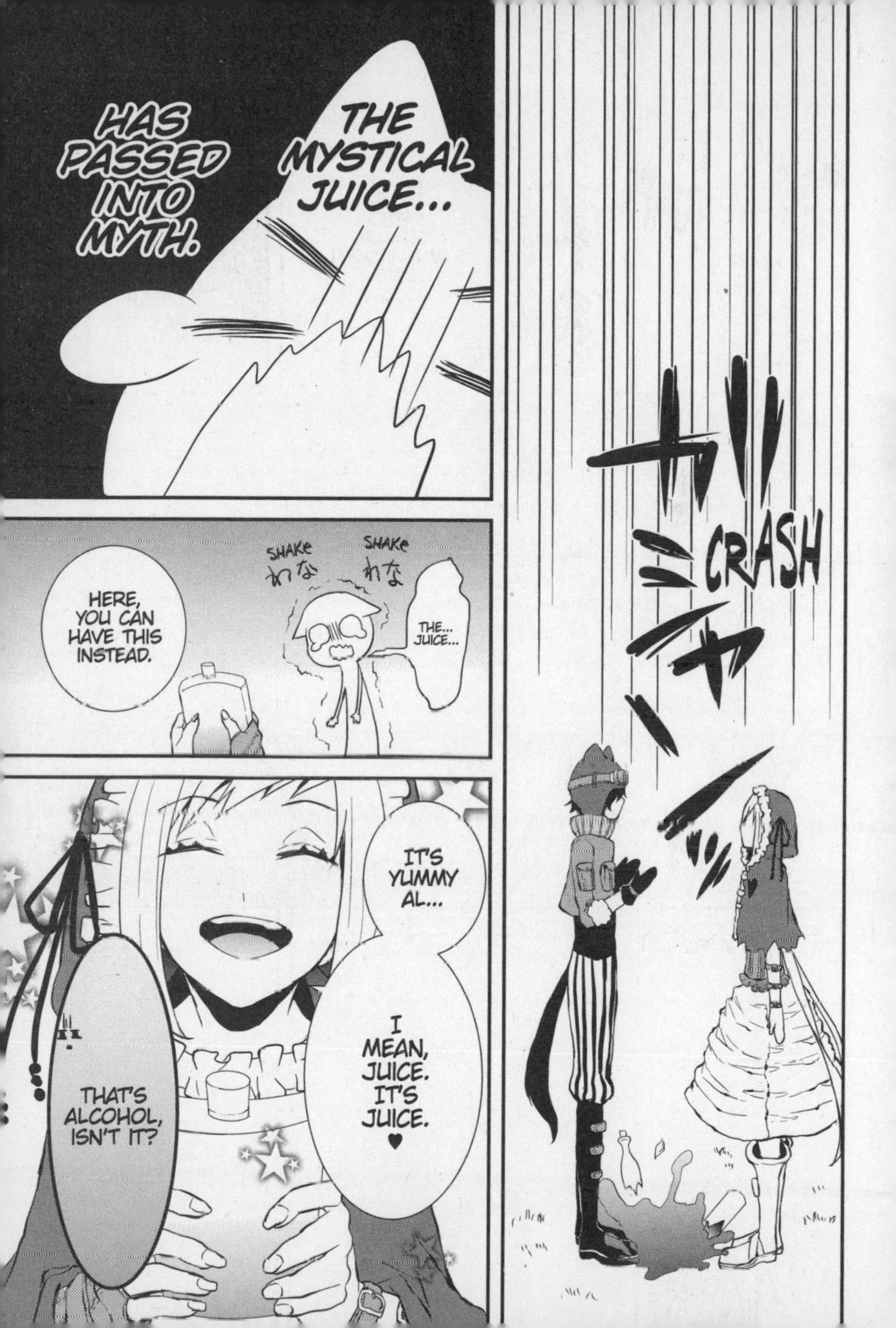
CRASH
THE MYSTICAL JUICE...
HAS PASSED INTO MYTH.
THE... JUICE...
SHAKE わな
SHAKE わな
HERE, YOU CAN HAVE THIS INSTEAD.
IT'S YUMMY AL...
I MEAN, JUICE. IT'S JUICE. ♥
THAT'S ALCOHOL, ISN'T IT?

FAKE EXPECTATIONS

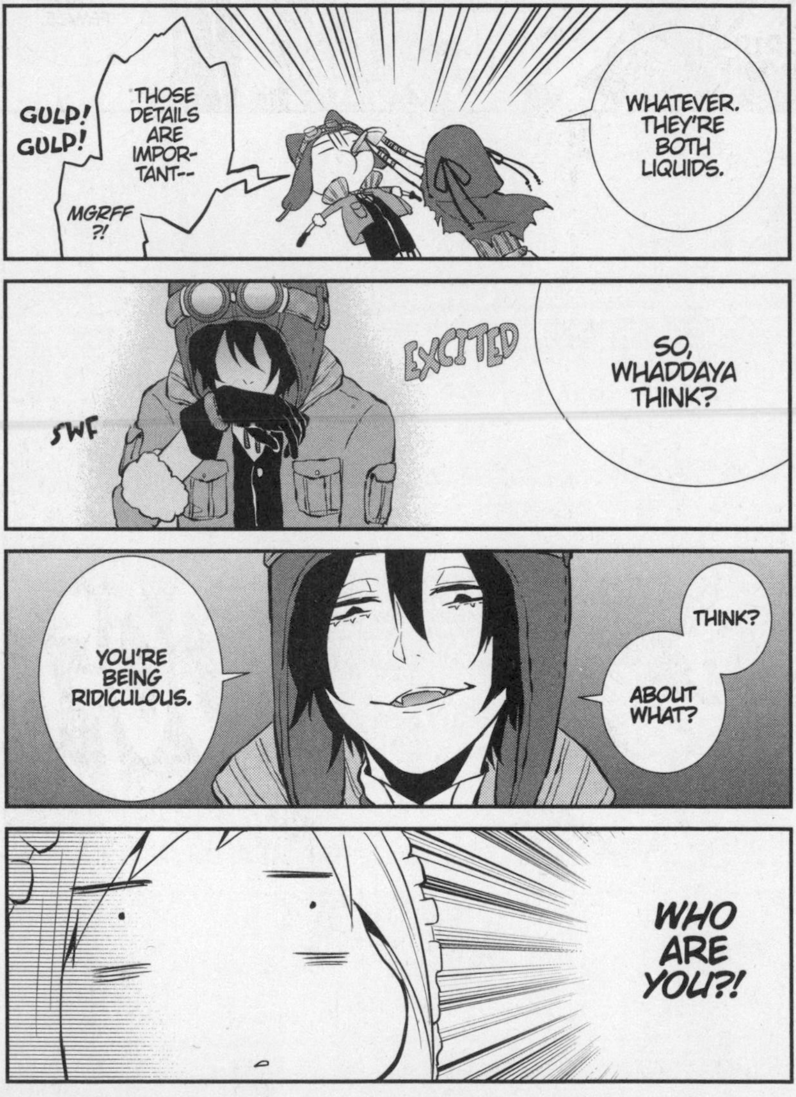
WHATEVER. THEY'RE BOTH LIQUIDS.
THOSE DETAILS ARE IMPOR-TANT--
GULP! GULP!
MGRFF ?!
SO, WHADDAYA THINK?
EXCITED
SWF
THINK? ABOUT WHAT?
YOU'RE BEING RIDICULOUS.
WHO ARE YOU?!

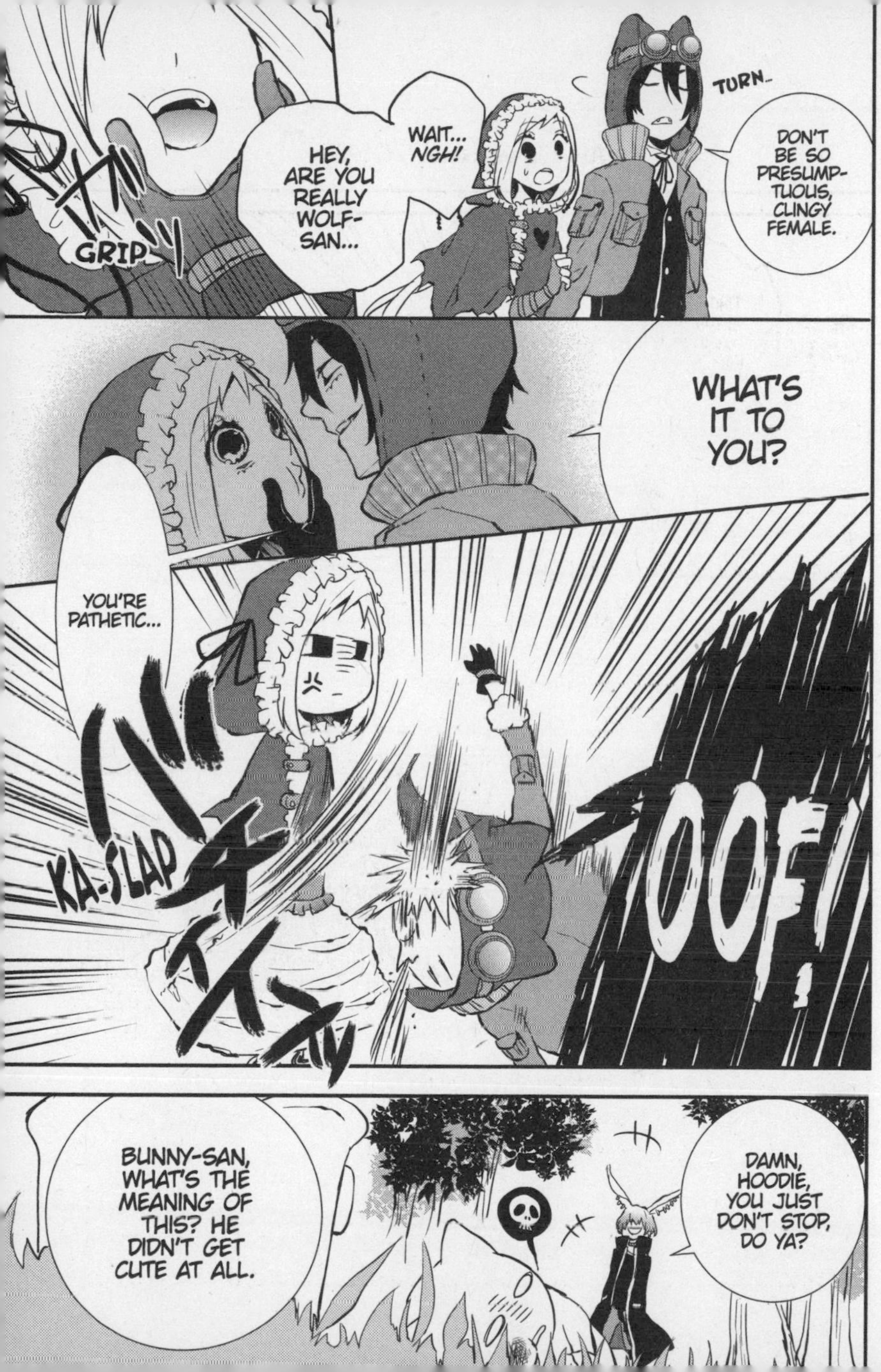
TURN..
DON'T BE SO PRESUMPTUOUS, CLINGY FEMALE.
WAIT... NGH!
HEY, ARE YOU REALLY WOLF-SAN...
GRIP
WHAT'S IT TO YOU?
YOU'RE PATHETIC...
OOF!
KA-SLAP
DAMN, HOODIE, YOU JUST DON'T STOP, DO YA?
BUNNY-SAN, WHAT'S THE MEANING OF THIS? HE DIDN'T GET CUTE AT ALL.

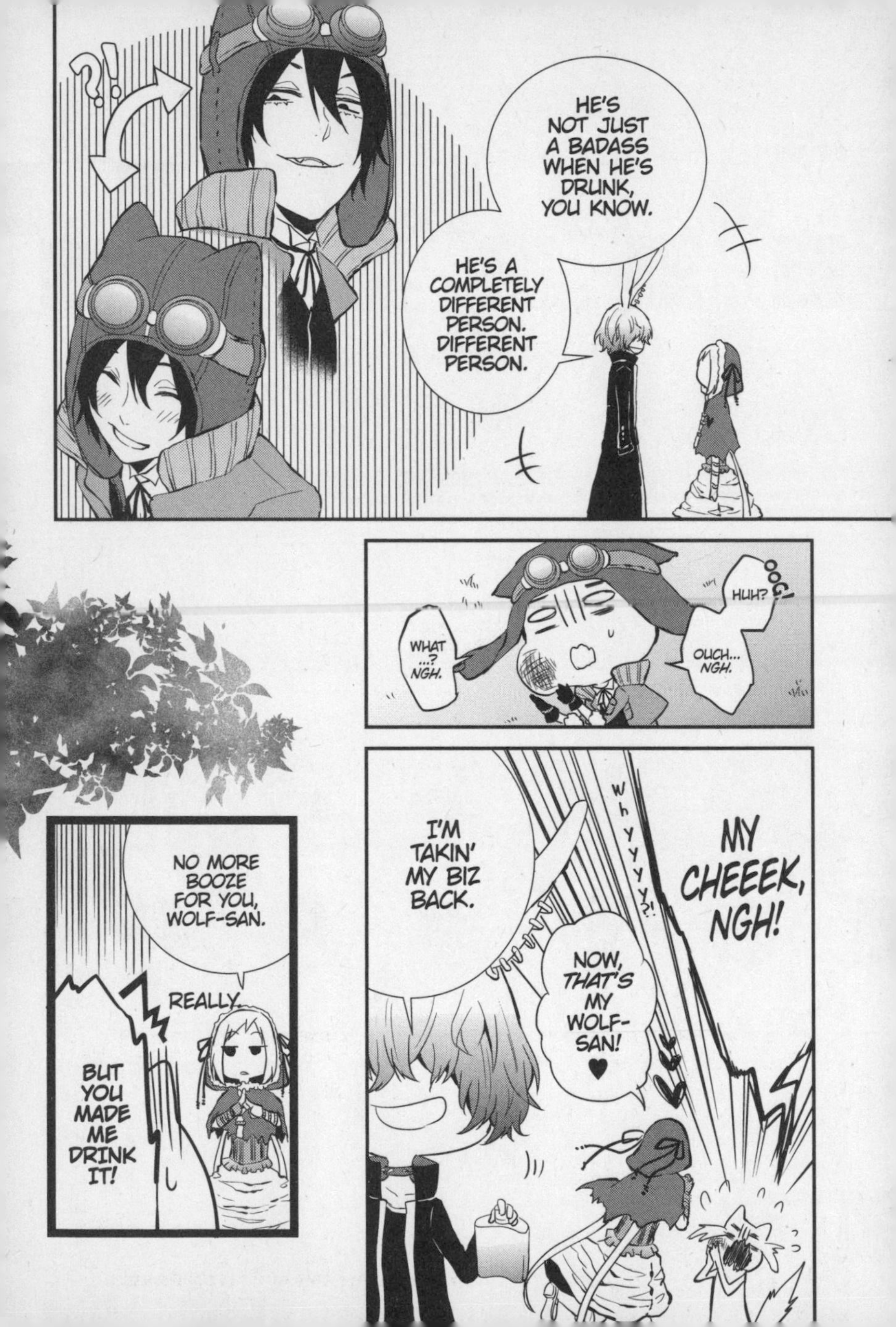
?!
HE'S NOT JUST A BADASS WHEN HE'S DRUNK, YOU KNOW.
HE'S A COMPLETELY DIFFERENT PERSON. DIFFERENT PERSON.
OOG!
HUH?
OUCH... NGH.
WHAT ...? NGH.
MY CHEEEK, NGH!
WhYYYYY?!
NOW, THAT'S MY WOLF-SAN! ♥
I'M TAKIN' MY BIZ BACK.
NO MORE BOOZE FOR YOU, WOLF-SAN.
REALLY.
BUT YOU MADE ME DRINK IT!

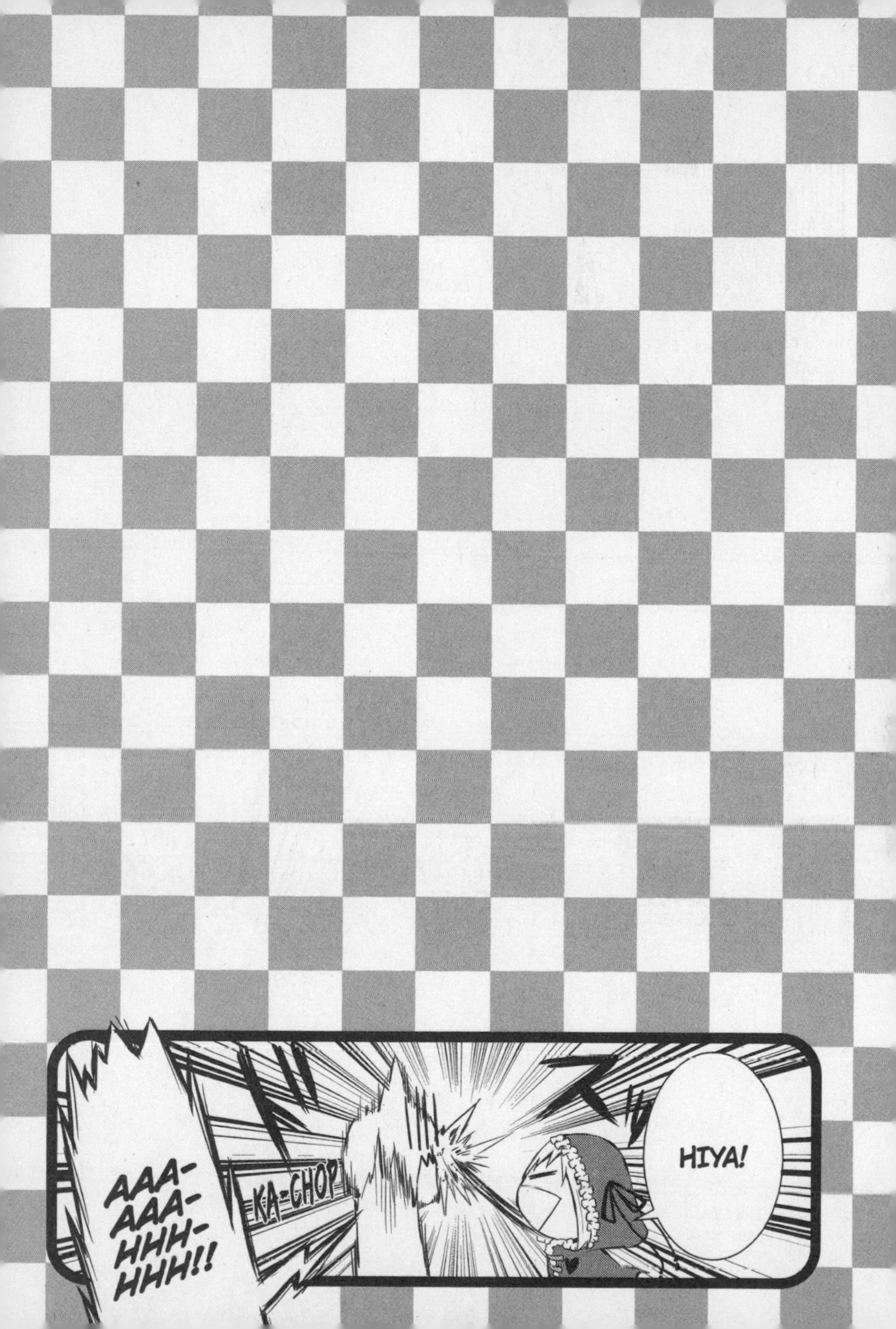
HIYA!
KA-CHOP
AAA-AAA-HHH-HHH!!

RED RIDING HOOD AND THE BIG SAD WOLF

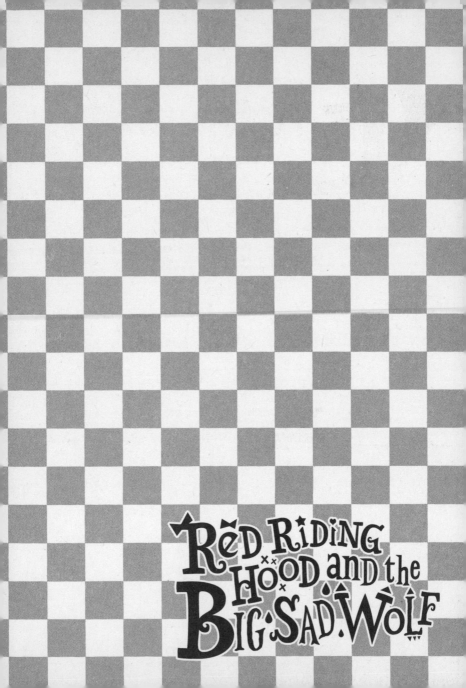

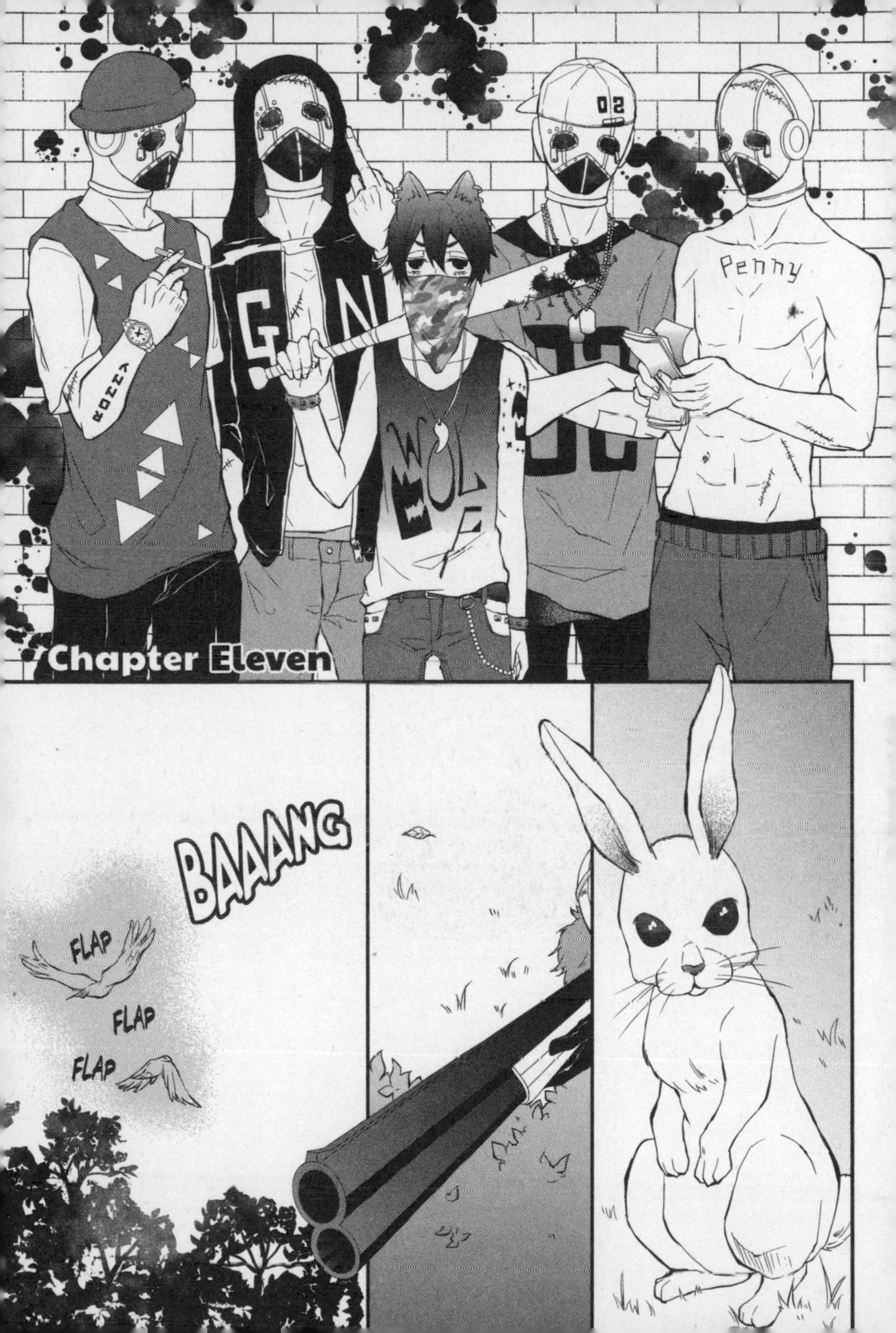
Chapter Eleven
BAAANG
FLAP
FLAP
FLAP

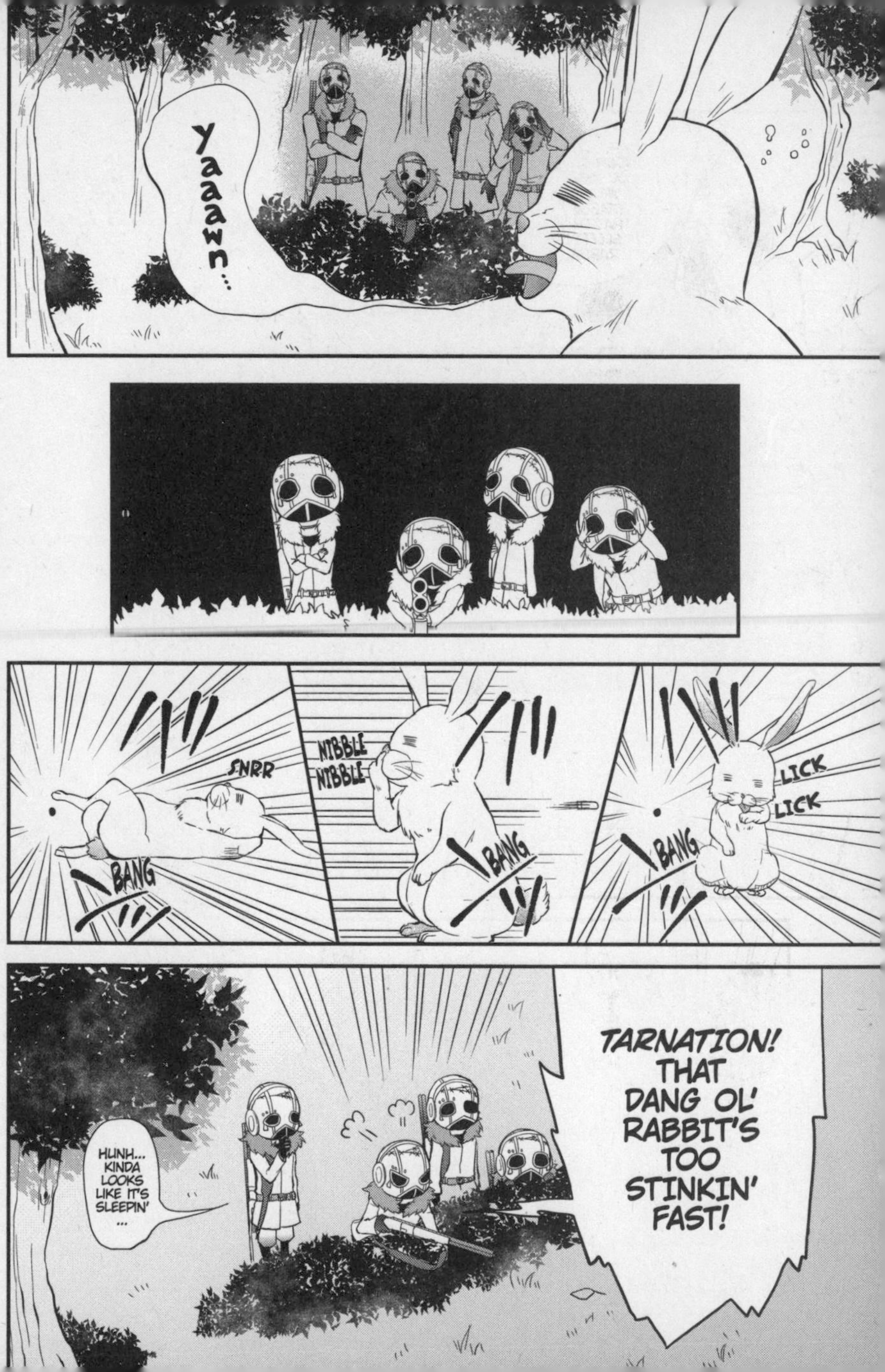
Yaaawn...
LICK
LICK
BANG
NIBBLE
NIBBLE
BANG
SNRR
BANG
TARNATION! THAT DANG OL' RABBIT'S TOO STINKIN' FAST!
HUNH... KINDA LOOKS LIKE IT'S SLEEPIN' ...

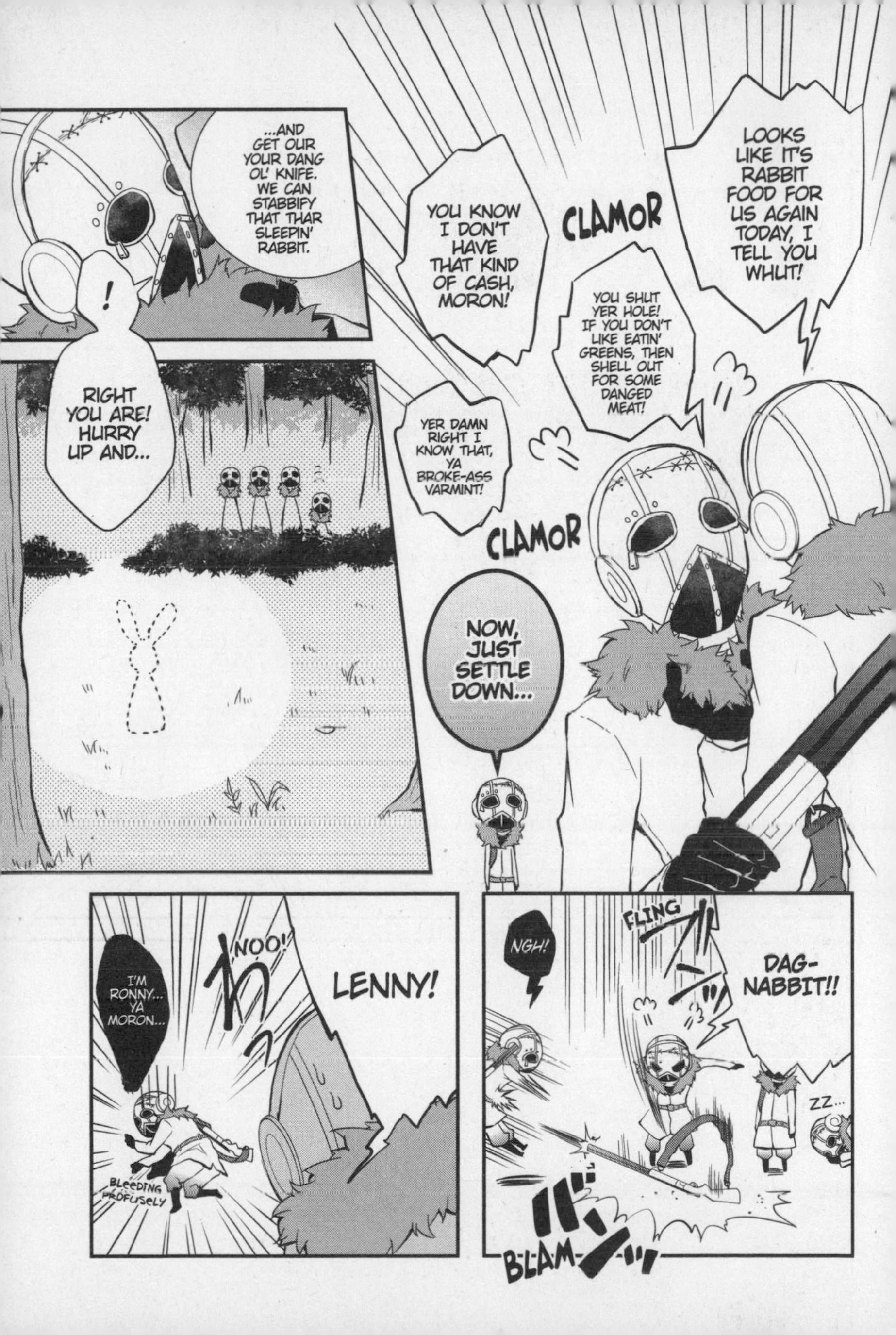
LOOKS LIKE IT'S RABBIT FOOD FOR US AGAIN TODAY, I TELL YOU WHUT!
CLAMOR
YOU KNOW I DON'T HAVE THAT KIND OF CASH, MORON!
YOU SHUT YER HOLE! IF YOU DON'T LIKE EATIN' GREENS, THEN SHELL OUT FOR SOME DANGED MEAT!
YER DAMN RIGHT I KNOW THAT, YA BROKE-ASS VARMINT!
CLAMOR
NOW, JUST SETTLE DOWN...
...AND GET OUR YOUR DANG OL' KNIFE. WE CAN STABBIFY THAT THAR SLEEPIN' RABBIT.
!
RIGHT YOU ARE! HURRY UP AND...
FLING
NGH!
DAG-NABBIT!!
ZZ...
BLAM
LENNY!
NOO!
I'M RONNY... YA MORON...
BLEEDING PROFUSELY

OUR HOPE LIES IN THE WOMB

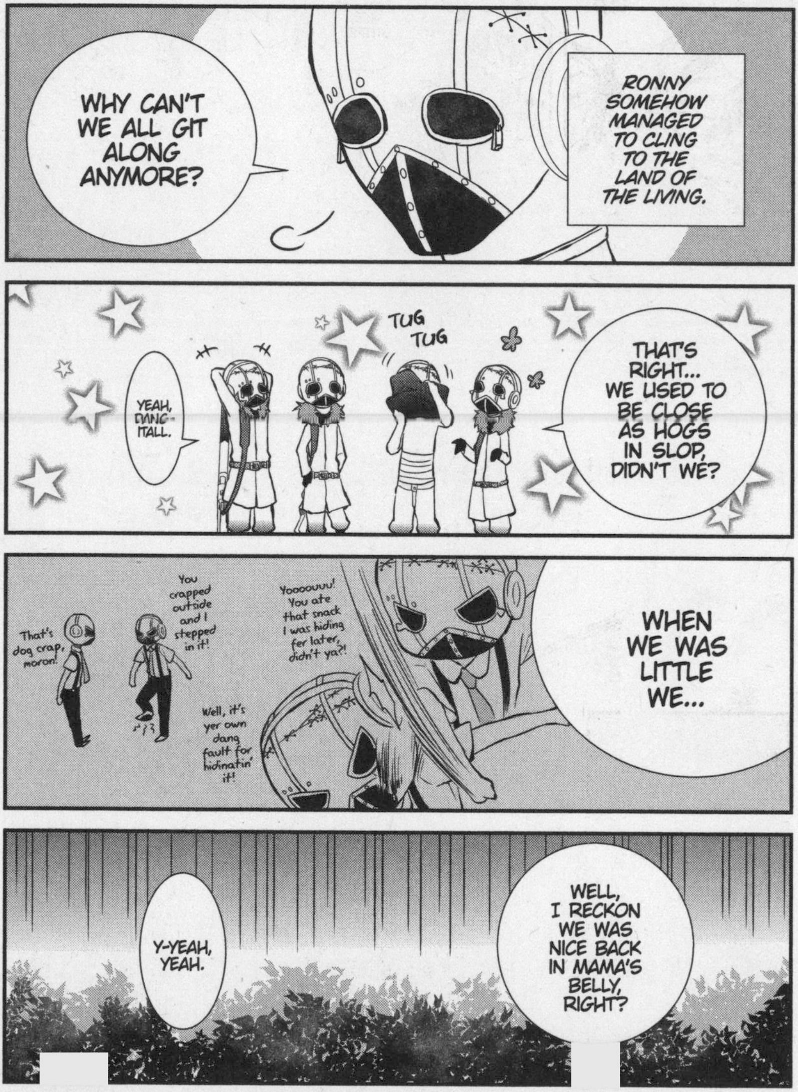
RONNY SOMEHOW MANAGED TO CLING TO THE LAND OF THE LIVING.
WHY CAN'T WE ALL GIT ALONG ANYMORE?
TUG TUG
THAT'S RIGHT... WE USED TO BE CLOSE AS HOGS IN SLOP, DIDN'T WE?
YEAH, DANG-ITALL.
WHEN WE WAS LITTLE WE...
Yoooouuu! You ate that snack I was hiding fer later, didn't ya?!
Well, it's yer own dang fault for hidinatin' it!
You crapped outside and I stepped in it!
That's dog crap, moron!
WELL, I RECKON WE WAS NICE BACK IN MAMA'S BELLY, RIGHT?
Y-YEAH, YEAH.

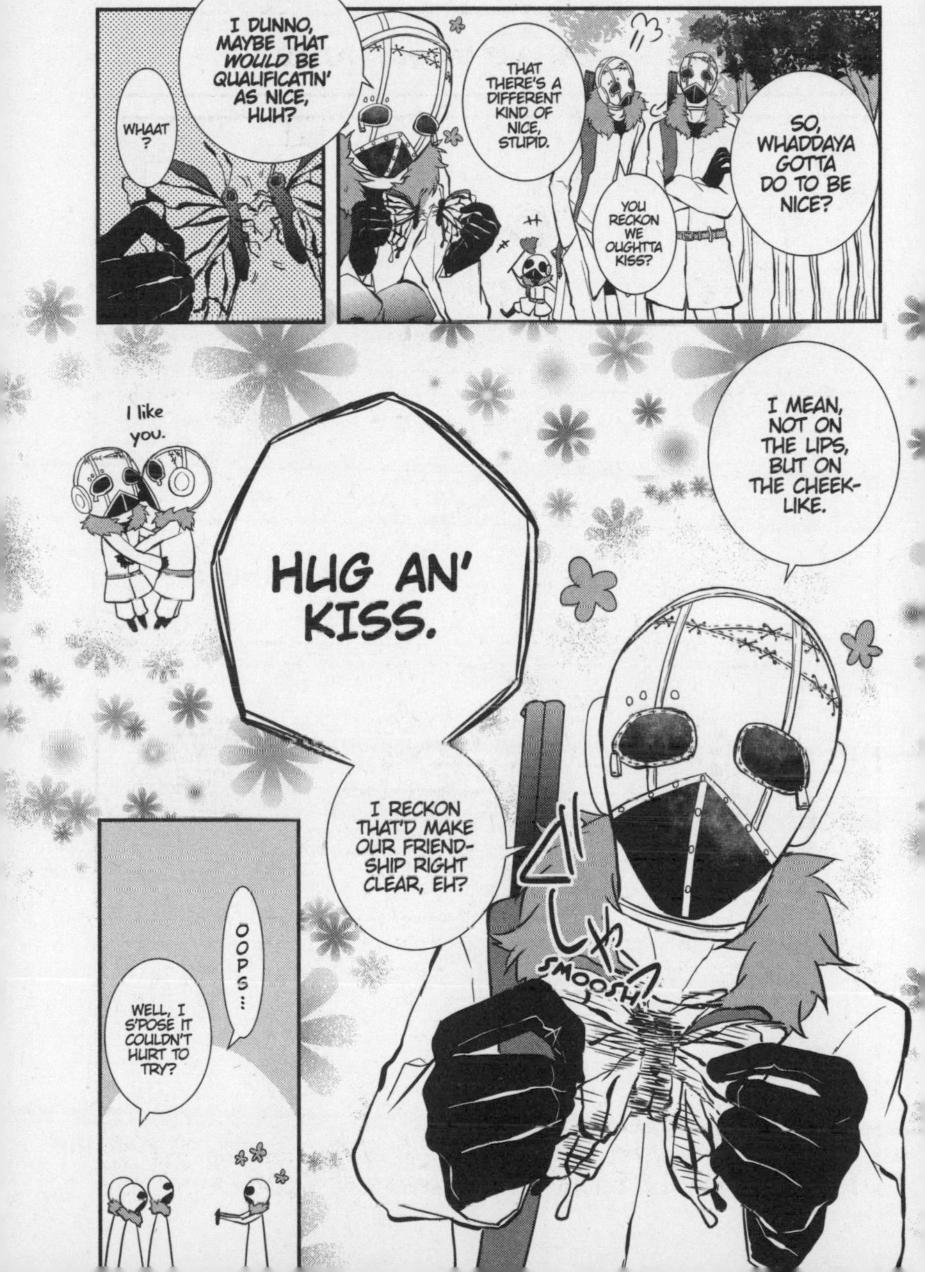
SO, WHADDAYA GOTTA DO TO BE NICE?
YOU RECKON WE OUGHTTA KISS?
THAT THERE'S A DIFFERENT KIND OF NICE, STUPID.
I DUNNO, MAYBE THAT *WOULD* BE QUALIFICATIN' AS NICE, HUH?
WHAAT?
I MEAN, NOT ON THE LIPS, BUT ON THE CHEEK-LIKE.
HUG AN' KISS.
I RECKON THAT'D MAKE OUR FRIENDSHIP RIGHT CLEAR, EH?
SMOOSH
I like you.
OOPS...
WELL, I S'POSE IT COULDN'T HURT TO TRY?

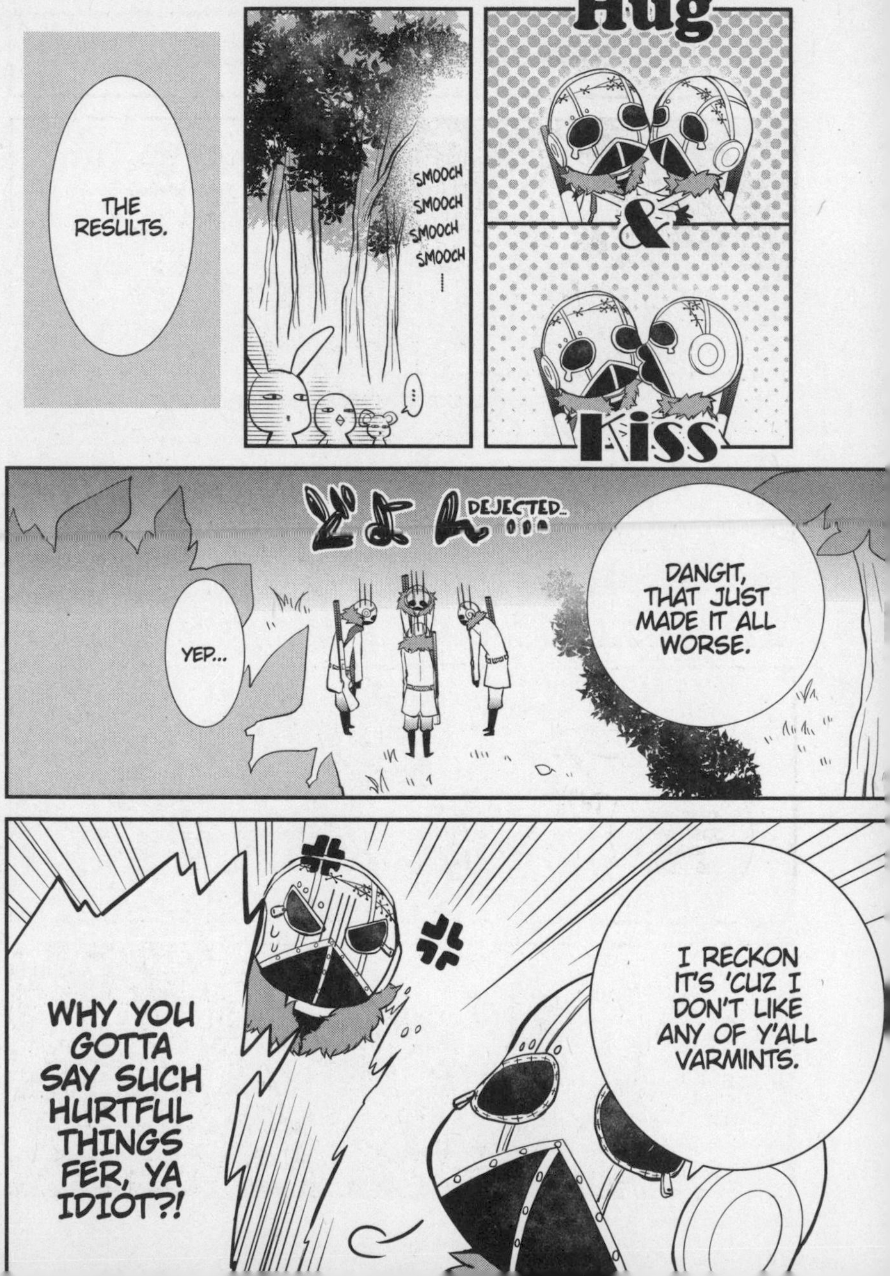
Hug
&
Kiss
SMOOCH
SMOOCH
SMOOCH
SMOOCH
...
...
THE RESULTS.
DEJECTED...
DANGIT, THAT JUST MADE IT ALL WORSE.
YEP...
I RECKON IT'S 'CUZ I DON'T LIKE ANY OF Y'ALL VARMINTS.
WHY YOU GOTTA SAY SUCH HURTFUL THINGS FER, YA IDIOT?!

LOOKING FOR AN ADVANTAGE

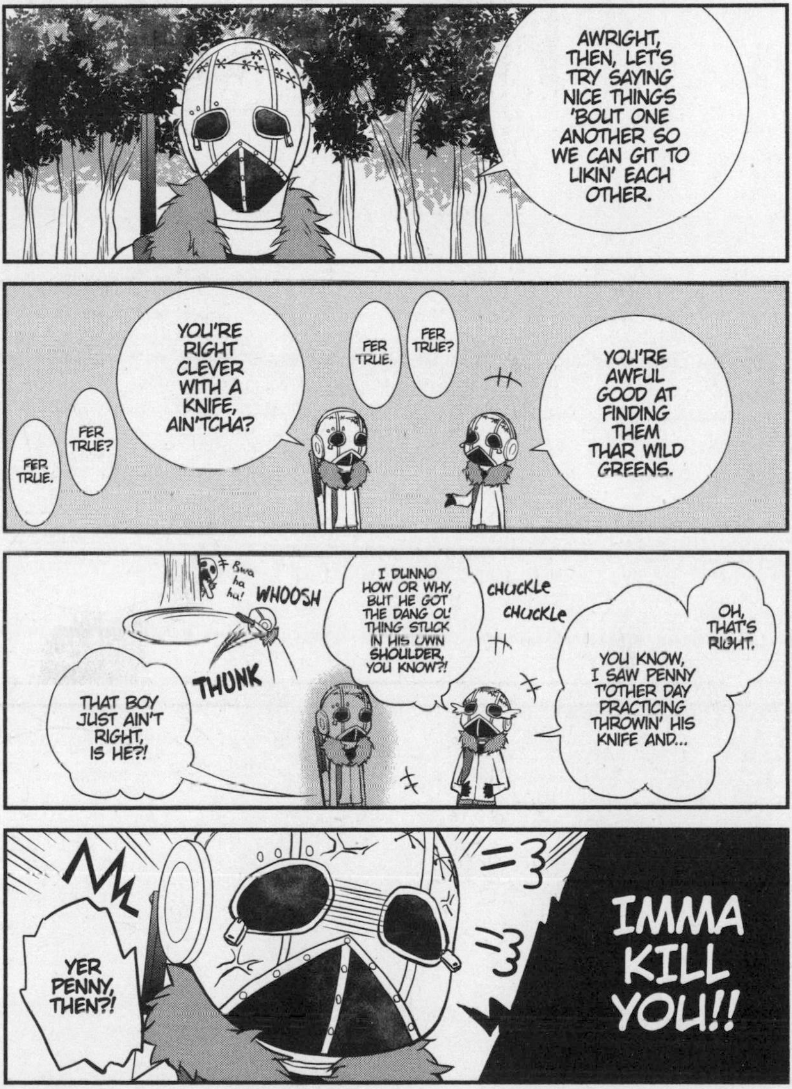
AWRIGHT, THEN, LET'S TRY SAYING NICE THINGS 'BOUT ONE ANOTHER SO WE CAN GIT TO LIKIN' EACH OTHER.
YOU'RE AWFUL GOOD AT FINDING THEM THAR WILD GREENS.
FER TRUE?
FER TRUE.
YOU'RE RIGHT CLEVER WITH A KNIFE, AIN'TCHA?
FER TRUE?
FER TRUE.
OH, THAT'S RIGHT.
YOU KNOW, I SAW PENNY T'OTHER DAY PRACTICING THROWIN' HIS KNIFE AND...
CHUCKLE
CHUCKLE
I DUNNO HOW OR WHY, BUT HE GOT THE DANG OL' THING STUCK IN HIS OWN SHOULDER, YOU KNOW?!
WHOOSH
Bwa ha ha!
THUNK
THAT BOY JUST AIN'T RIGHT, IS HE?!
IMMA KILL YOU!!
YER PENNY, THEN?!

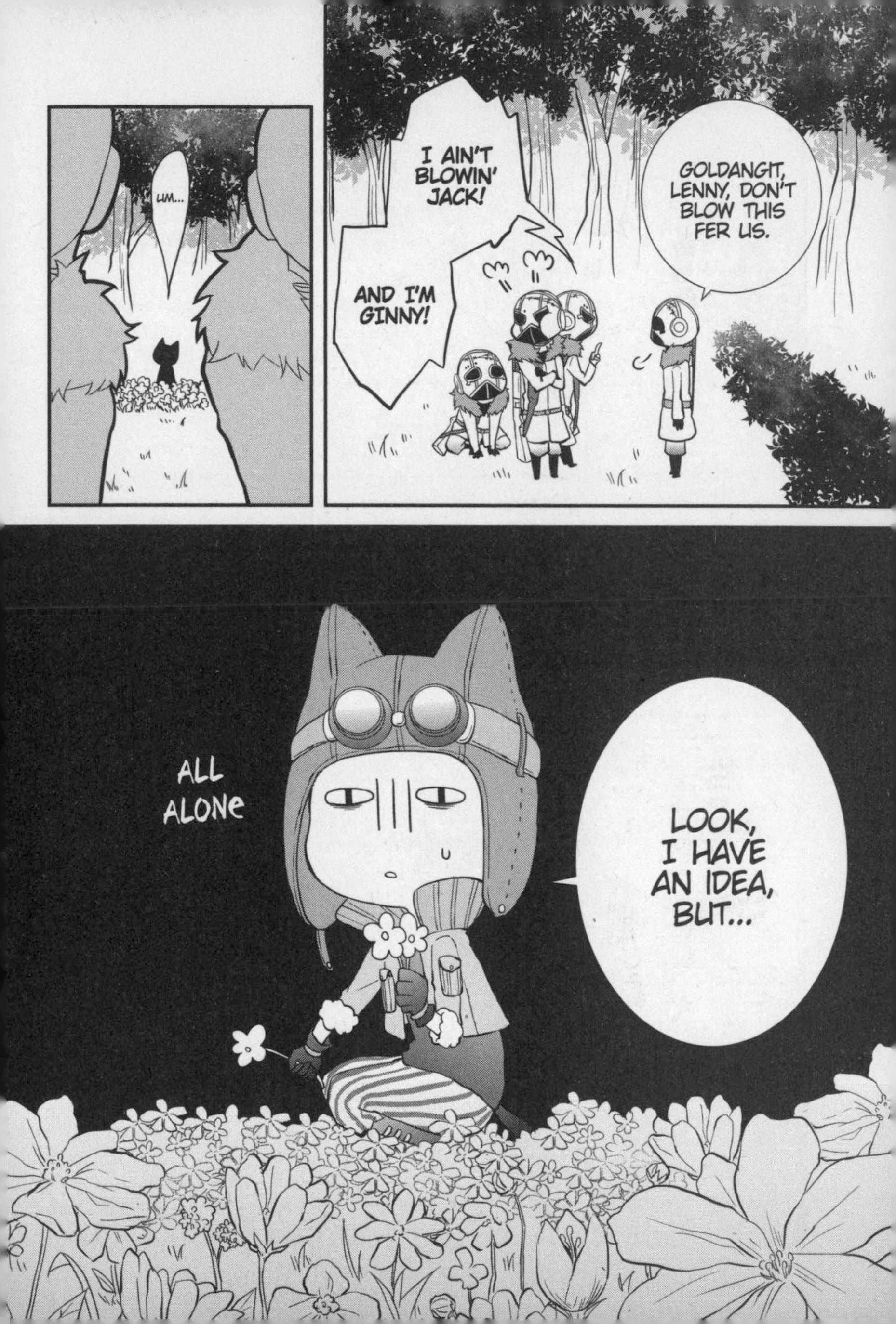
GOLDANGIT, LENNY, DON'T BLOW THIS FER US.
I AIN'T BLOWIN' JACK!
AND I'M GINNY!
UM...
LOOK, I HAVE AN IDEA, BUT...
ALL ALONE

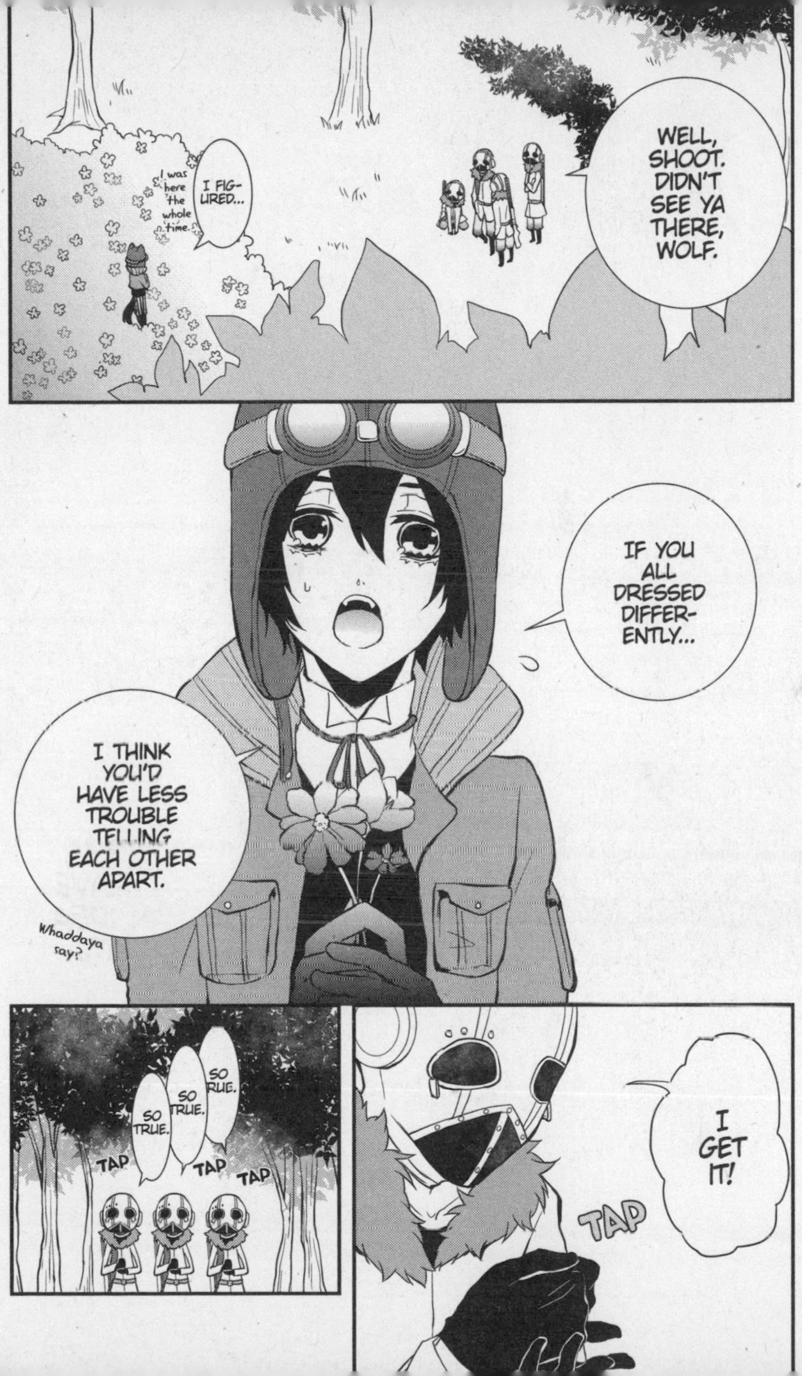
WELL, SHOOT. DIDN'T SEE YA THERE, WOLF.
I FIGURED...
I was here the whole time.
IF YOU ALL DRESSED DIFFERENTLY...
I THINK YOU'D HAVE LESS TROUBLE TELLING EACH OTHER APART.
Whaddaya say?
I GET IT!
TAP
SO TRUE.
SO TRUE.
SO TRUE.
TAP
TAP
TAP

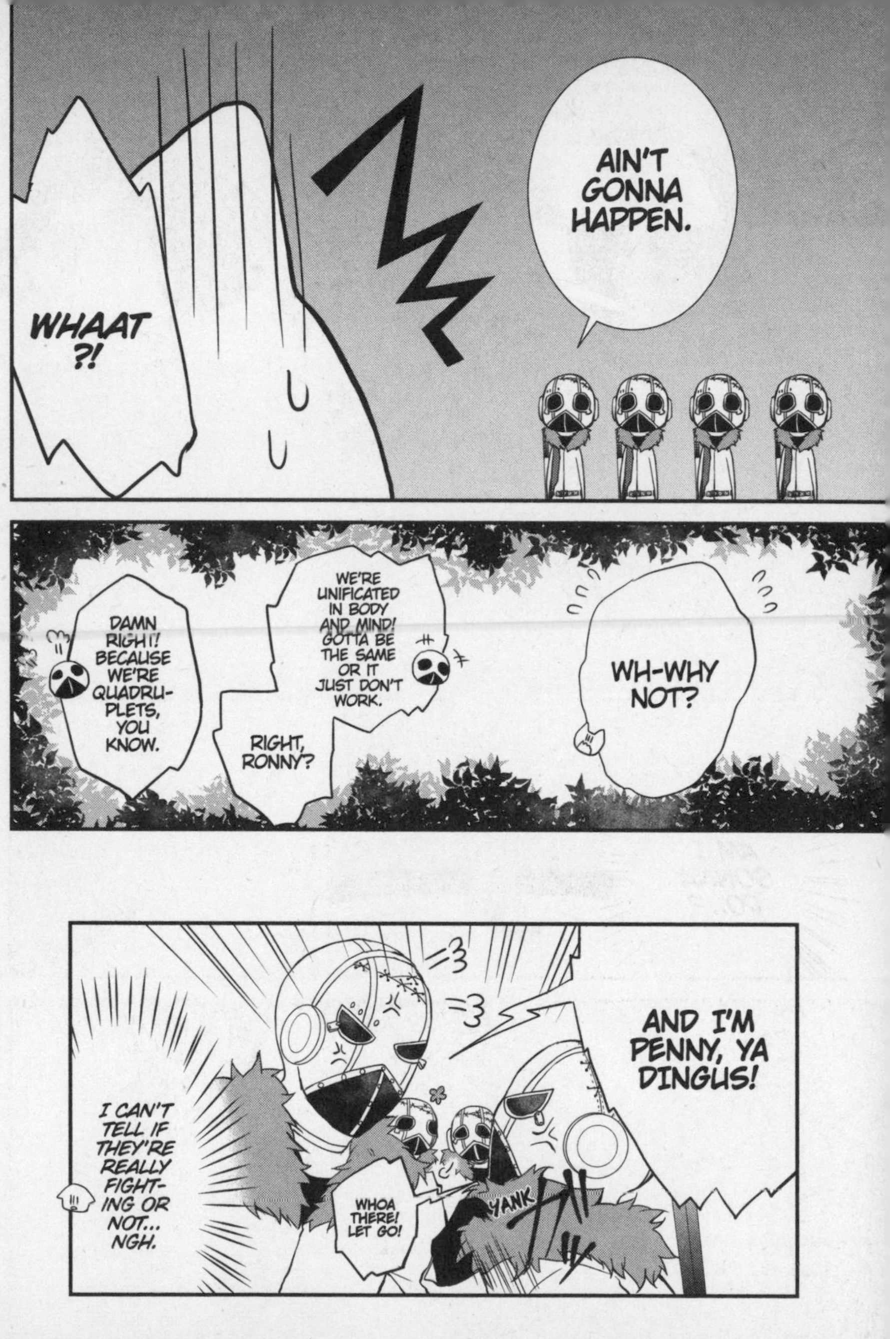
AIN'T GONNA HAPPEN.
WHAAT ?!
WH-WHY NOT?
WE'RE UNIFICATED IN BODY AND MIND! GOTTA BE THE SAME OR IT JUST DON'T WORK.
RIGHT, RONNY?
DAMN RIGHT! BECAUSE WE'RE QUADRU-PLETS, YOU KNOW.
AND I'M PENNY, YA DINGUS!
WHOA THERE! LET GO!
YANK
I CAN'T TELL IF THEY'RE REALLY FIGHT-ING OR NOT... NGH.

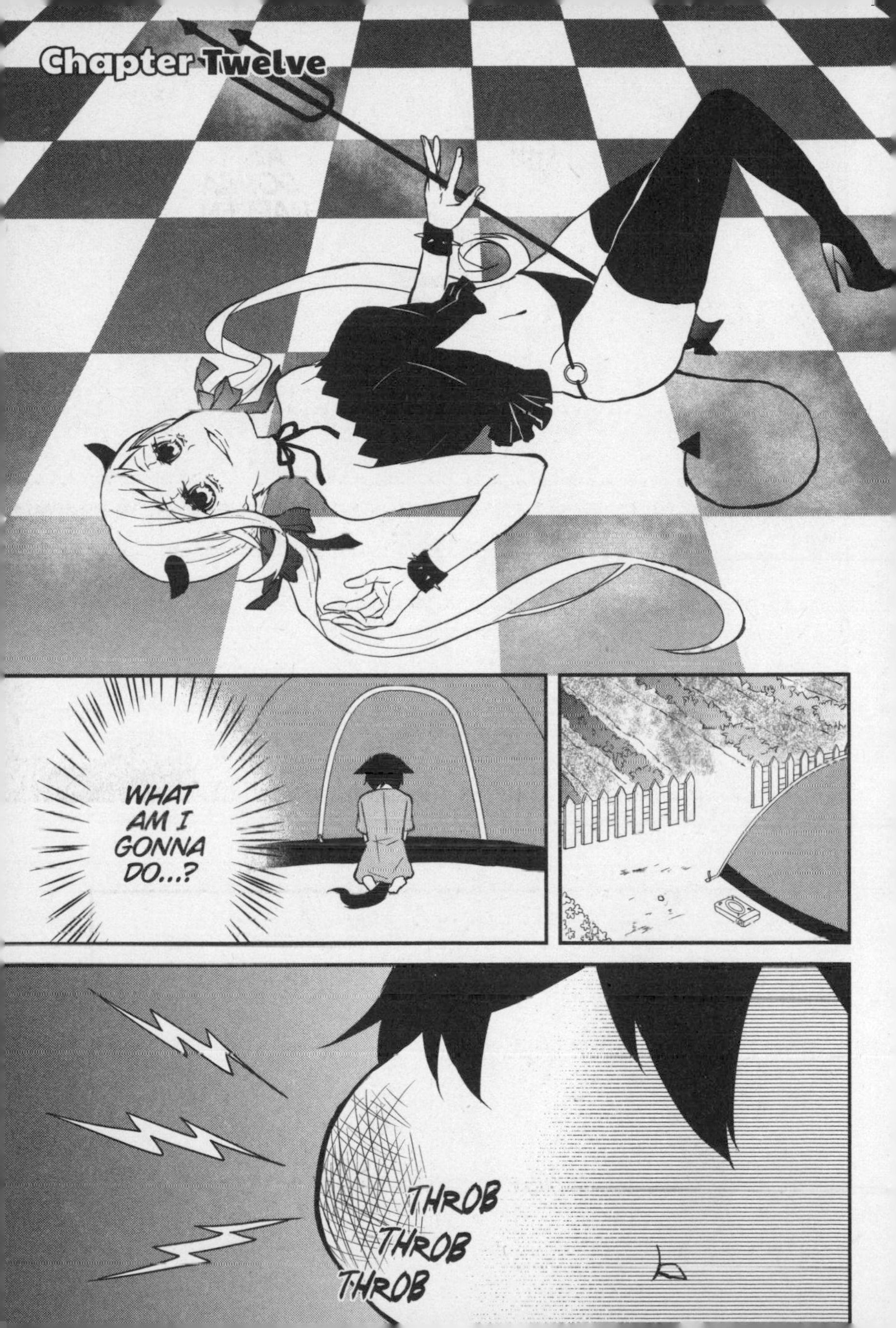
Chapter Twelve
WHAT AM I GONNA DO...?
THROB
THROB
THROB

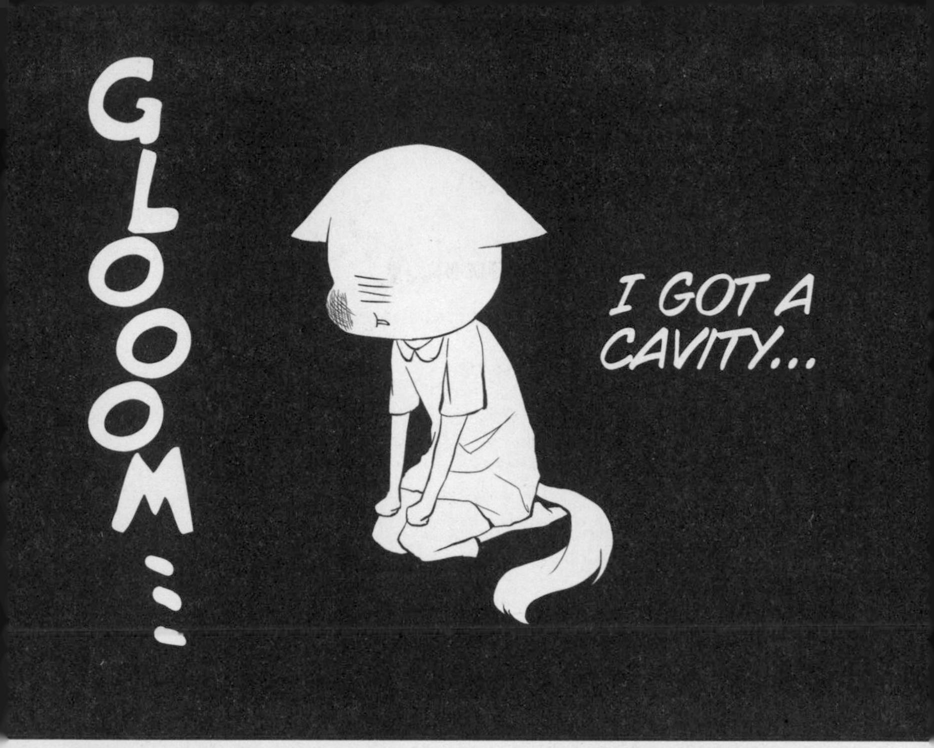
GLOOOM...
I GOT A CAVITY...

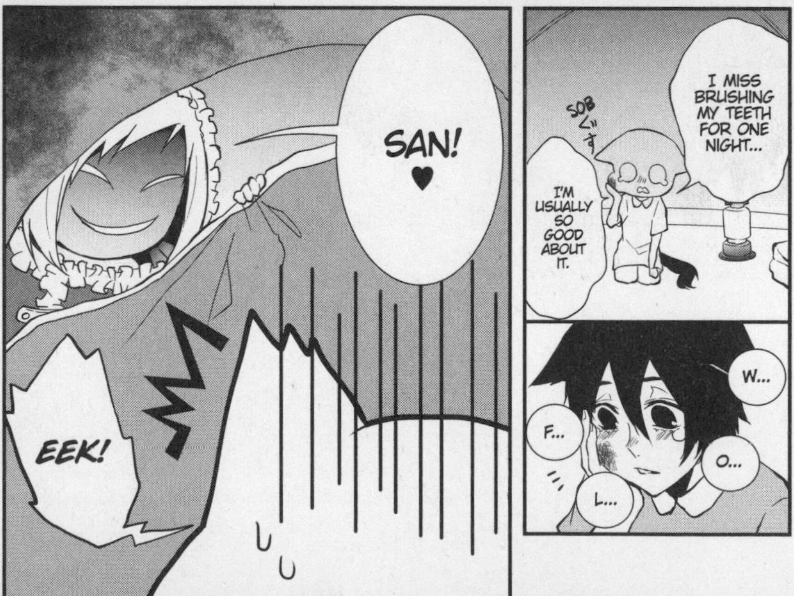
I MISS BRUSHING MY TEETH FOR ONE NIGHT...
SOB ぐす
I'M USUALLY SO GOOD ABOUT IT.
W...
O...
L...
F...
SAN! ♥
EEK!

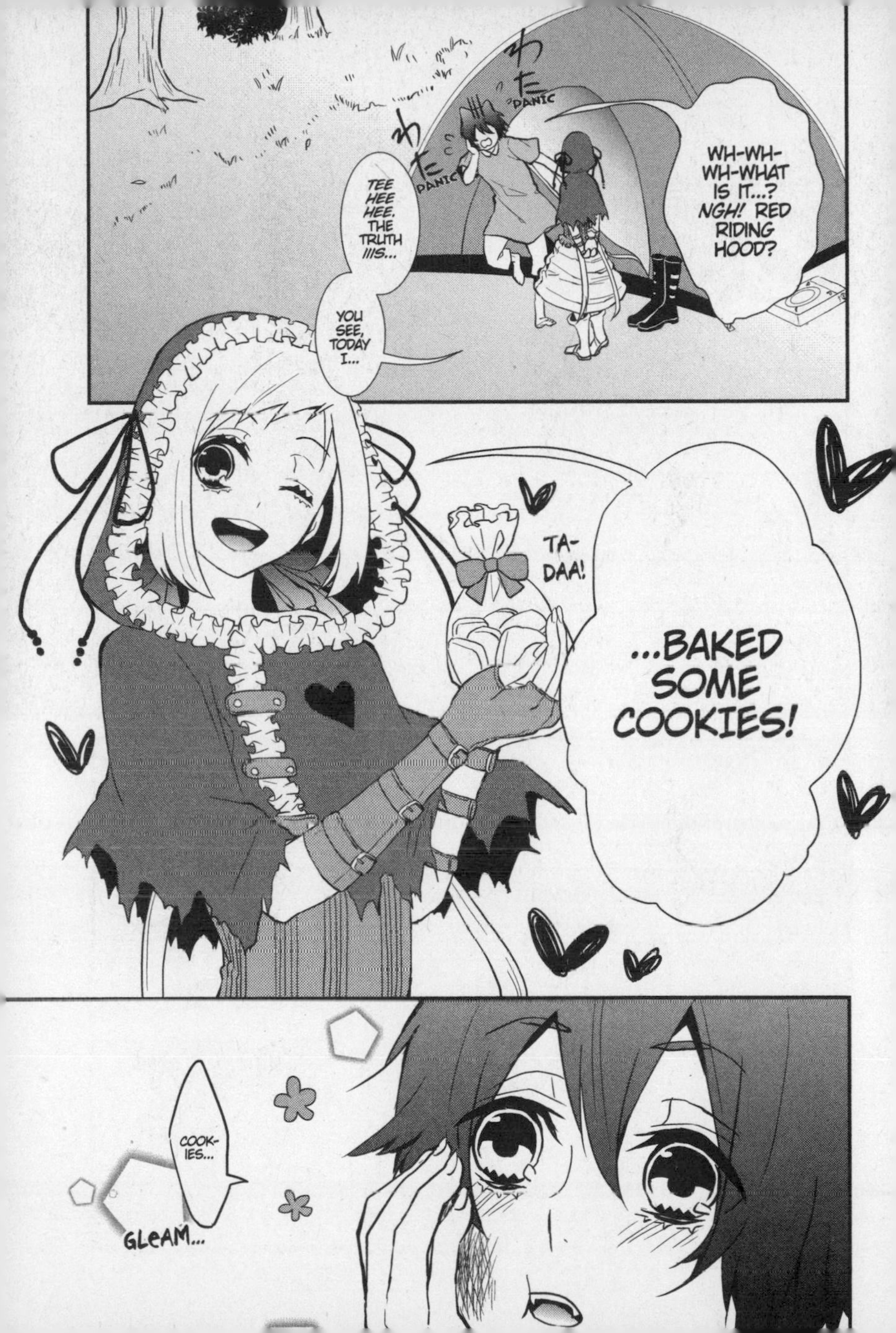

わた
PANIC
わた
PANIC
WH-WH-WH-WHAT IS IT...? NGH! RED RIDING HOOD?
TEE HEE HEE. THE TRUTH IIIS...
YOU SEE, TODAY I...
...BAKED SOME COOKIES!
TA-DAA!
COOK-IES...
GLEAM...

I DON'T TRUST YOU

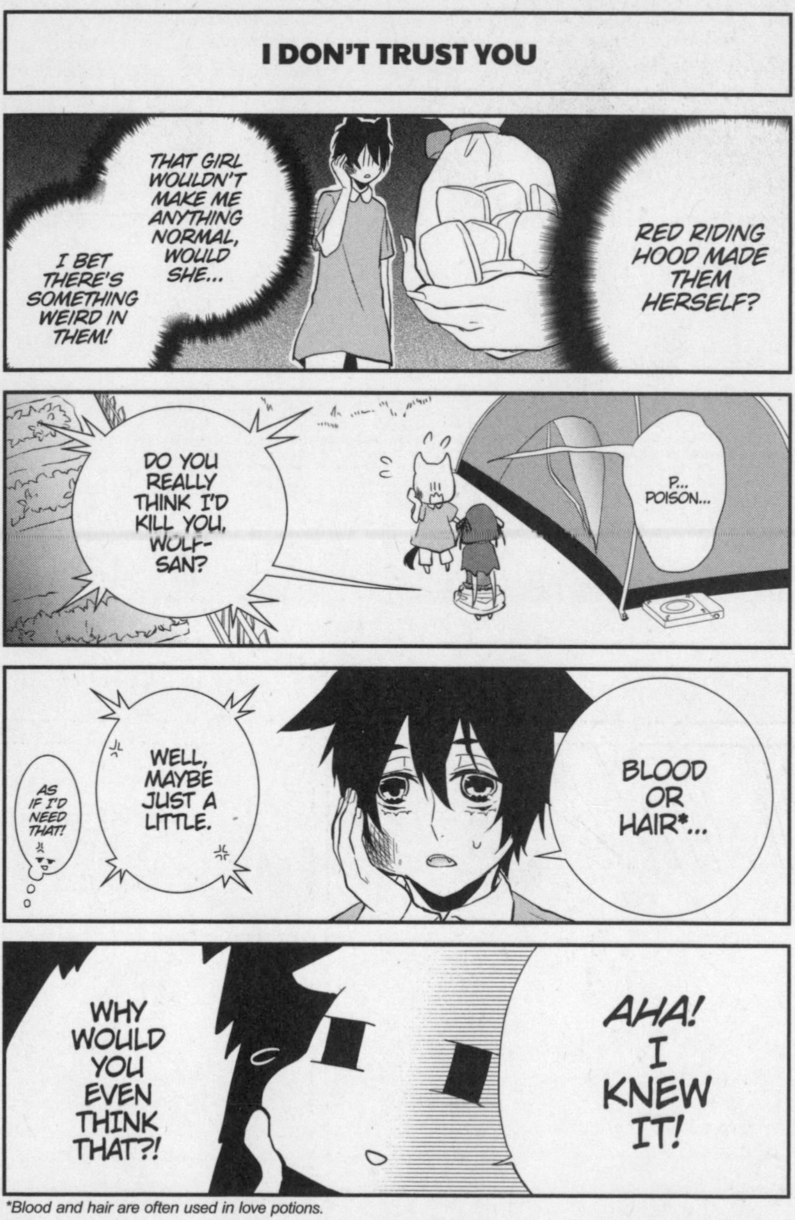
RED RIDING HOOD MADE THEM HERSELF?
THAT GIRL WOULDN'T MAKE ME ANYTHING NORMAL, WOULD SHE...
I BET THERE'S SOMETHING WEIRD IN THEM!
P... POISON...
DO YOU REALLY THINK I'D KILL YOU, WOLF-SAN?
BLOOD OR HAIR*...
WELL, MAYBE JUST A LITTLE.
AS IF I'D NEED THAT!
AHA! I KNEW IT!
WHY WOULD YOU EVEN THINK THAT?!

*Blood and hair are often used in love potions.

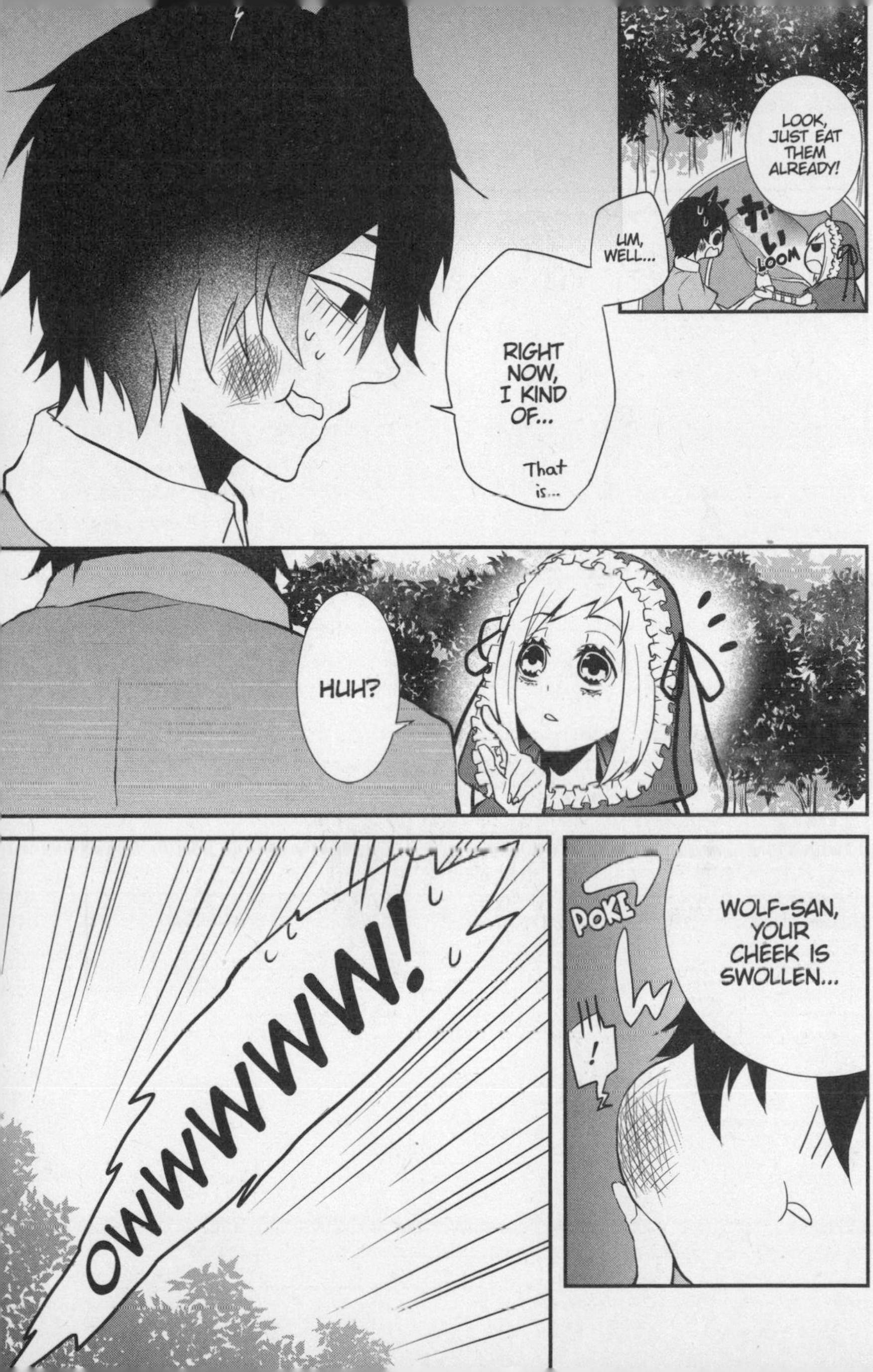
LOOK, JUST EAT THEM ALREADY!
LOOM
UM, WELL...
RIGHT NOW, I KIND OF...
That is...
HUH?
POKE
WOLF-SAN, YOUR CHEEK IS SWOLLEN...
!
OWWWWW!

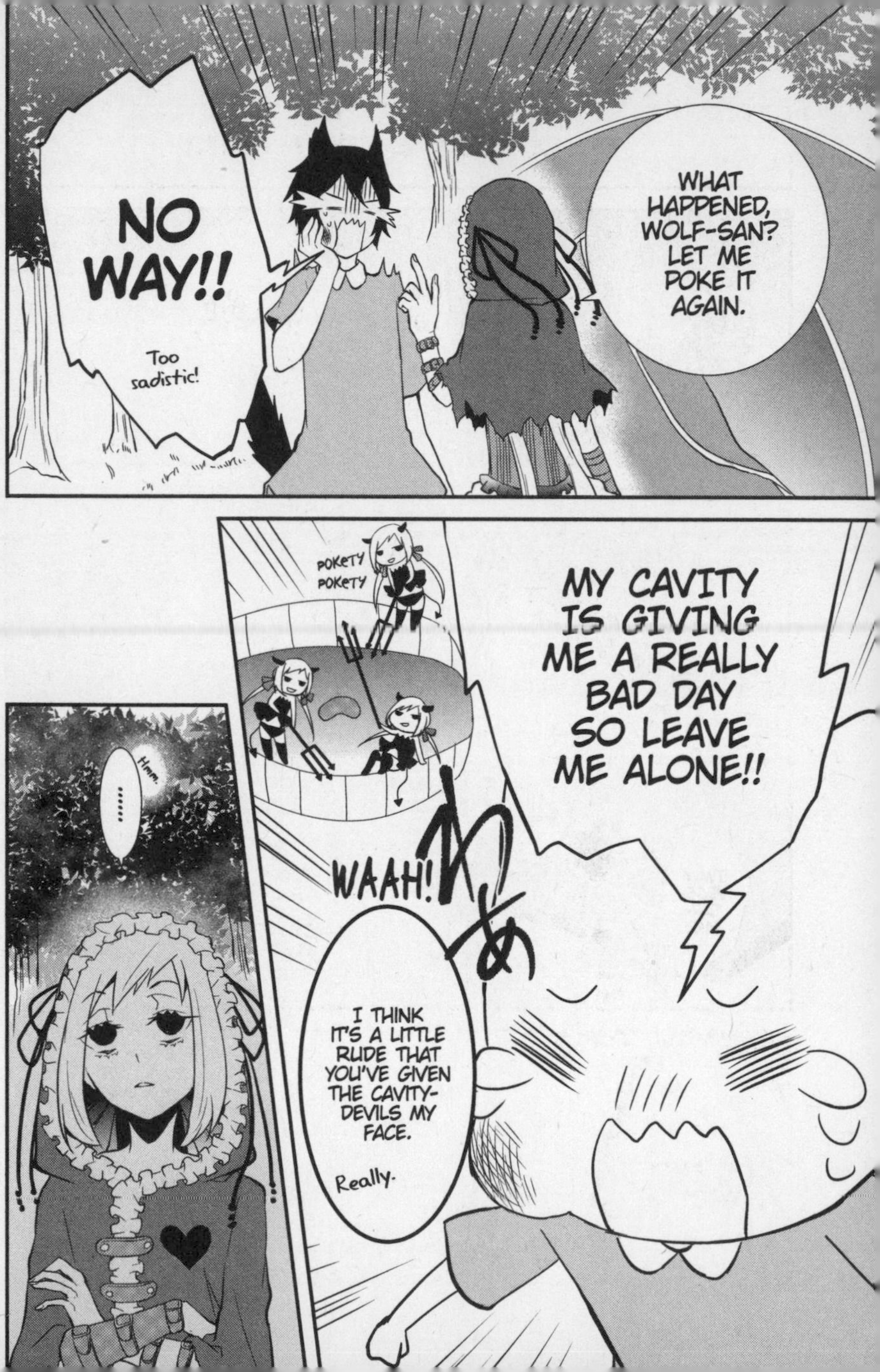
WHAT HAPPENED, WOLF-SAN? LET ME POKE IT AGAIN.
NO WAY!!
Too sadistic!
MY CAVITY IS GIVING ME A REALLY BAD DAY SO LEAVE ME ALONE!!
POKETY POKETY
WAAH!
......
Hmm.
I THINK IT'S A LITTLE RUDE THAT YOU'VE GIVEN THE CAVITY-DEVILS MY FACE.
Really.

THE CONSEQUENCES OF DELAY

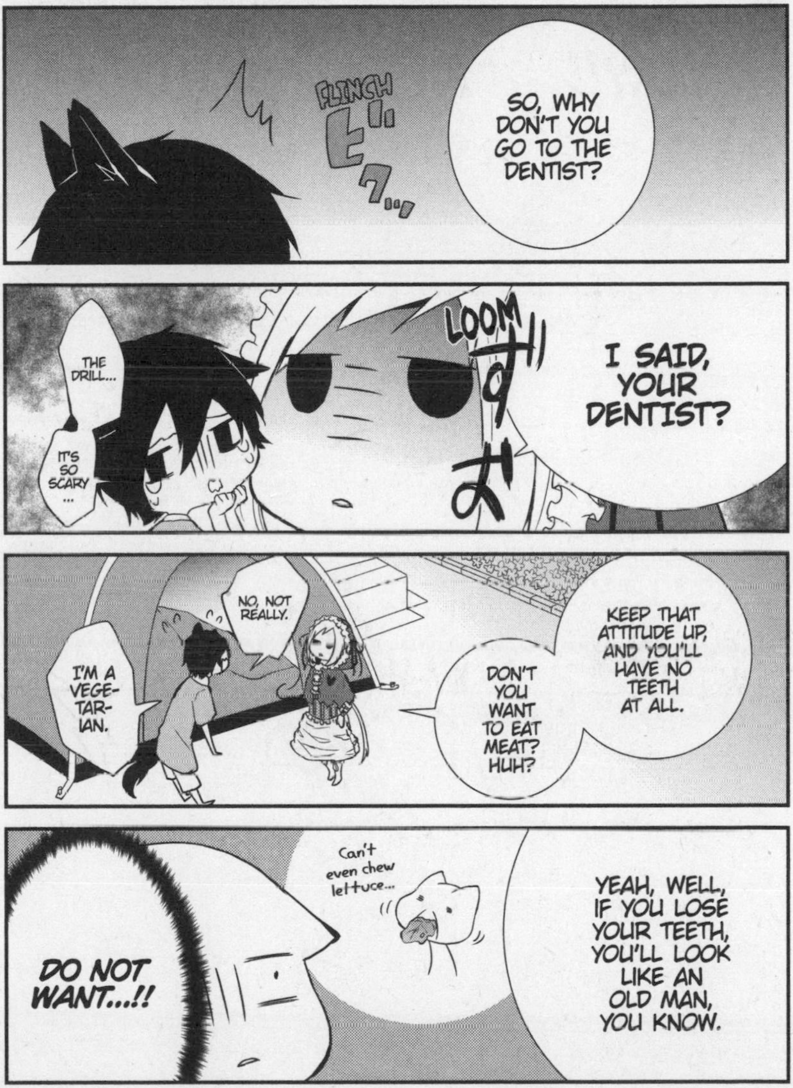
SO, WHY DON'T YOU GO TO THE DENTIST?
FLINCH
I SAID, YOUR DENTIST?
LOOM
THE DRILL...
IT'S SO SCARY ...
KEEP THAT ATTITUDE UP, AND YOU'LL HAVE NO TEETH AT ALL.
DON'T YOU WANT TO EAT MEAT? HUH?
NO, NOT REALLY.
I'M A VEGE-TAR-IAN.
YEAH, WELL, IF YOU LOSE YOUR TEETH, YOU'LL LOOK LIKE AN OLD MAN, YOU KNOW.
Can't even chew lettuce...
DO NOT WANT...!!

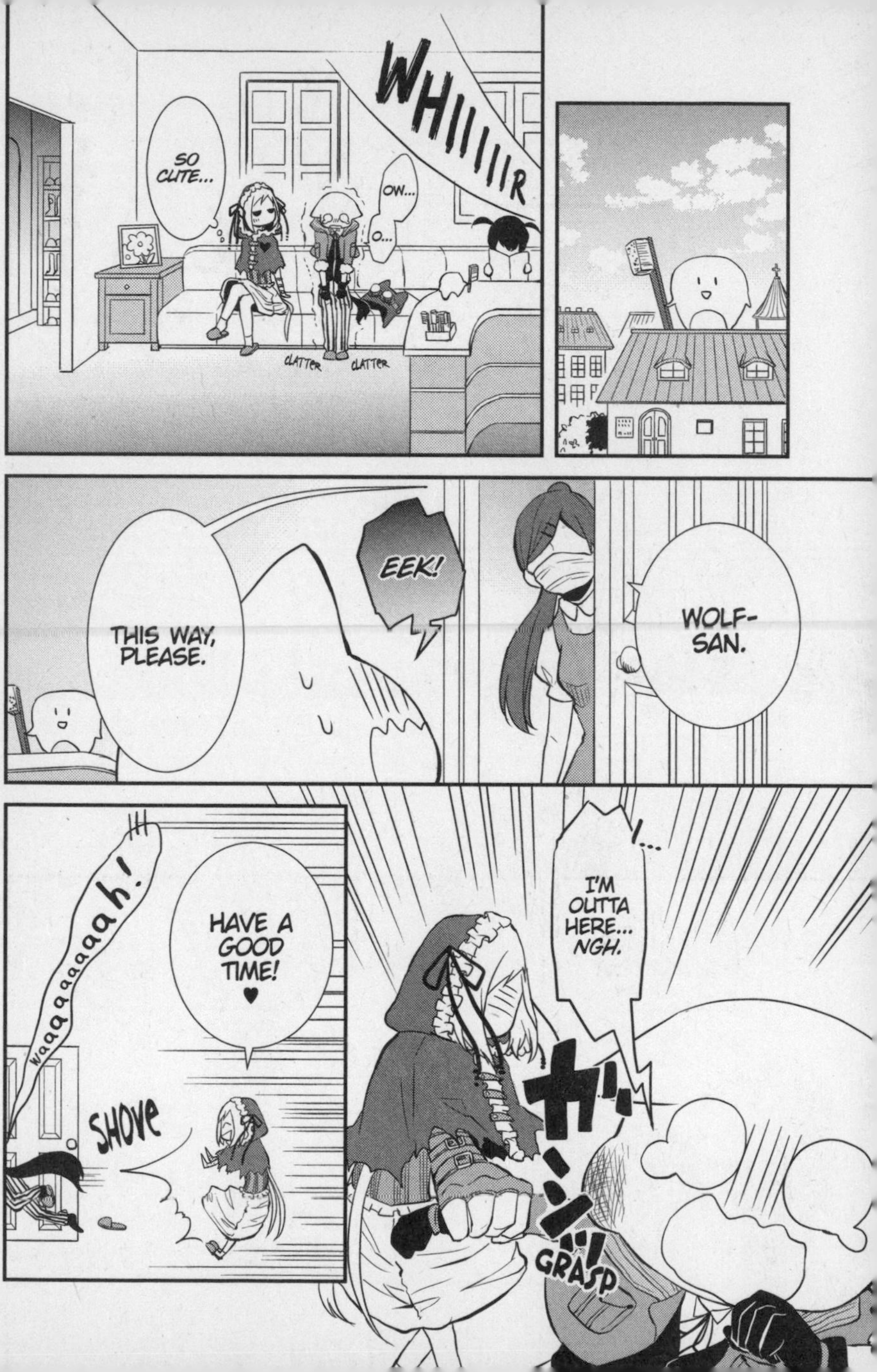
WHIIIIIR
OW... O...
SO CUTE...
CLATTER CLATTER
WOLF-SAN.
EEK!
THIS WAY, PLEASE.
I... I'M OUTTA HERE... NGH.
ガッ
GRASP
waaaaaaaah!
HAVE A GOOD TIME! ♥
SHOVE

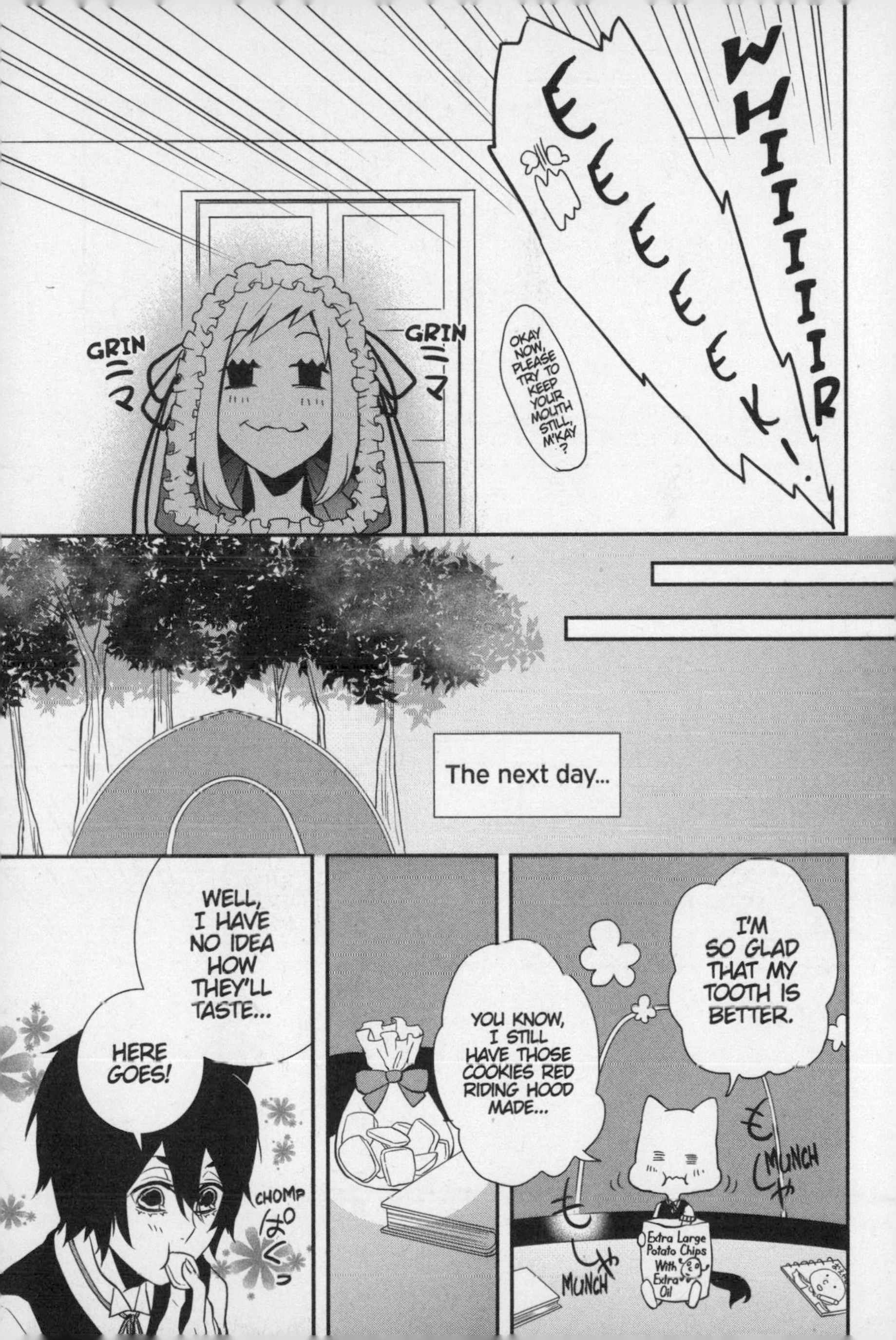
WHIIIIR
EEEEEEK!
OKAY NOW, PLEASE TRY TO KEEP YOUR MOUTH STILL, M'KAY?
GRIN
GRIN
The next day...
I'M SO GLAD THAT MY TOOTH IS BETTER.
MUNCH
MUNCH
Extra Large Potato Chips With Extra Oil
YOU KNOW, I STILL HAVE THOSE COOKIES RED RIDING HOOD MADE...
WELL, I HAVE NO IDEA HOW THEY'LL TASTE...
HERE GOES!
CHOMP

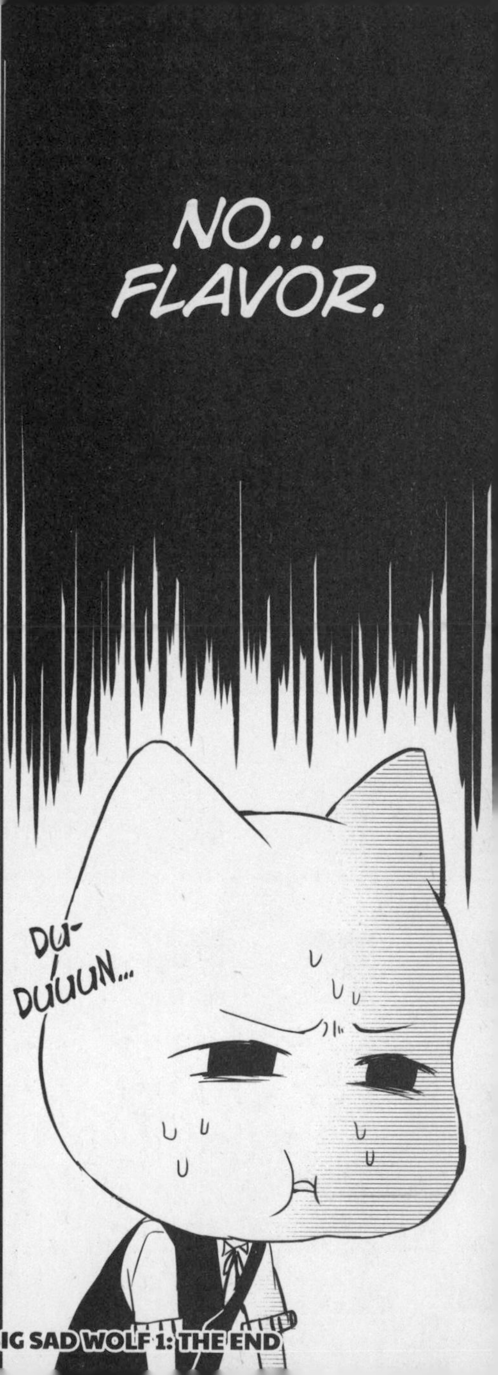
NO... FLAVOR.
DU-DUUUN...
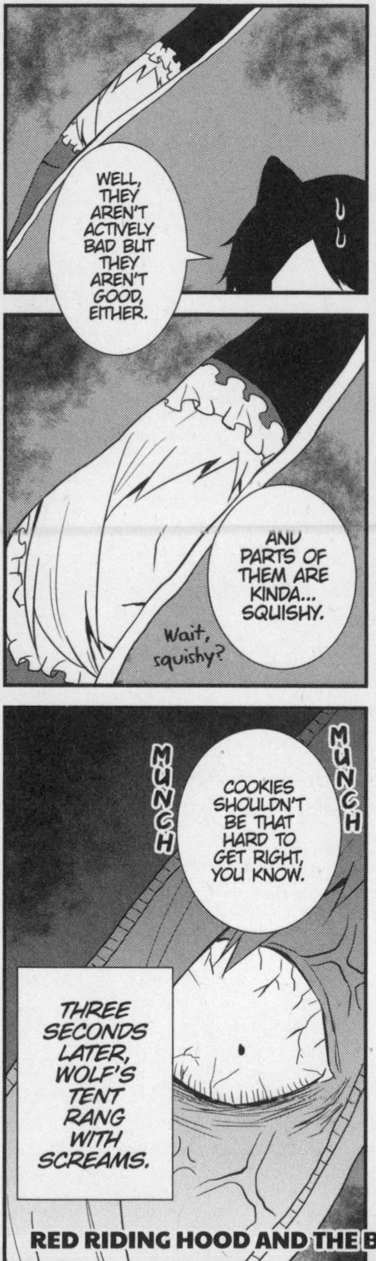
WELL, THEY AREN'T ACTIVELY BAD BUT THEY AREN'T GOOD, EITHER.
AND PARTS OF THEM ARE KINDA... SQUISHY.
Wait, squishy?
MUNCH
MUNCH
COOKIES SHOULDN'T BE THAT HARD TO GET RIGHT, YOU KNOW.
THREE SECONDS LATER, WOLF'S TENT RANG WITH SCREAMS.
RED RIDING HOOD AND THE BIG SAD WOLF 1: THE END

RED RIDING HOOD and the BIG SAD WOLF

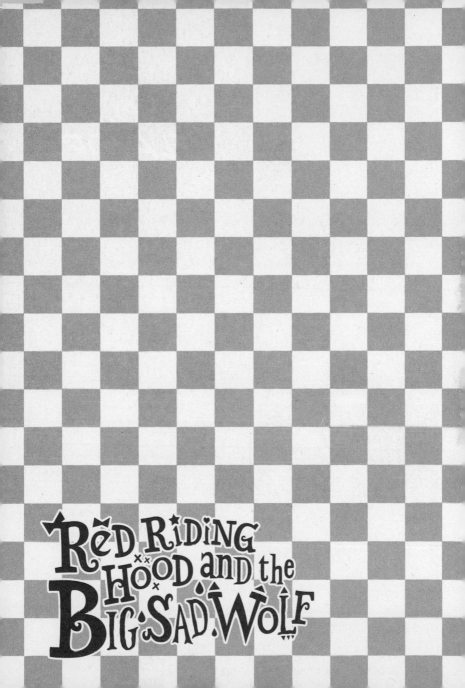

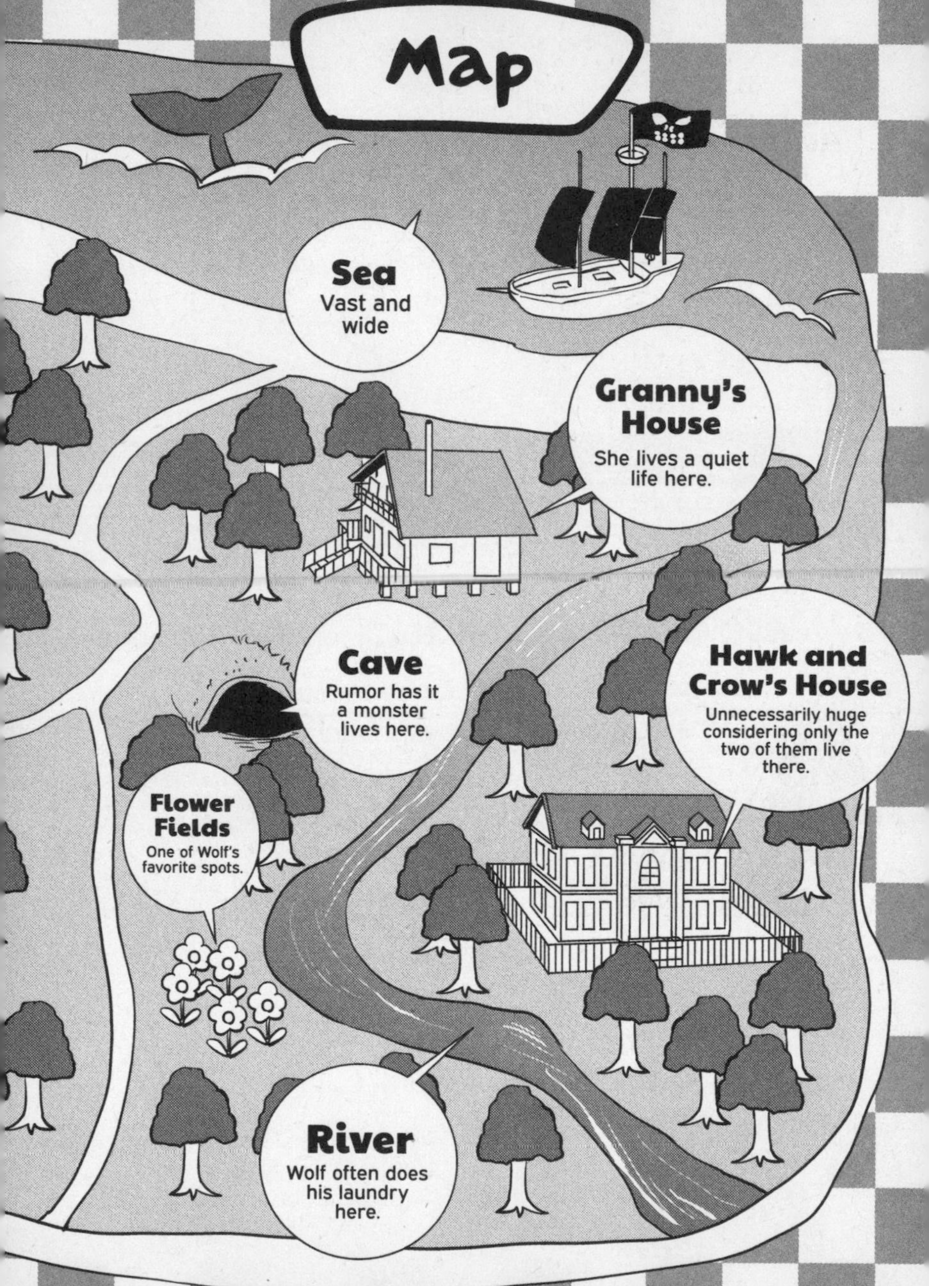
Map
Sea
Vast and wide
Granny's House
She lives a quiet life here.
Cave
Rumor has it a monster lives here.
Hawk and Crow's House
Unnecessarily huge considering only the two of them live there.
Flower Fields
One of Wolf's favorite spots.
River
Wolf often does his laundry here.

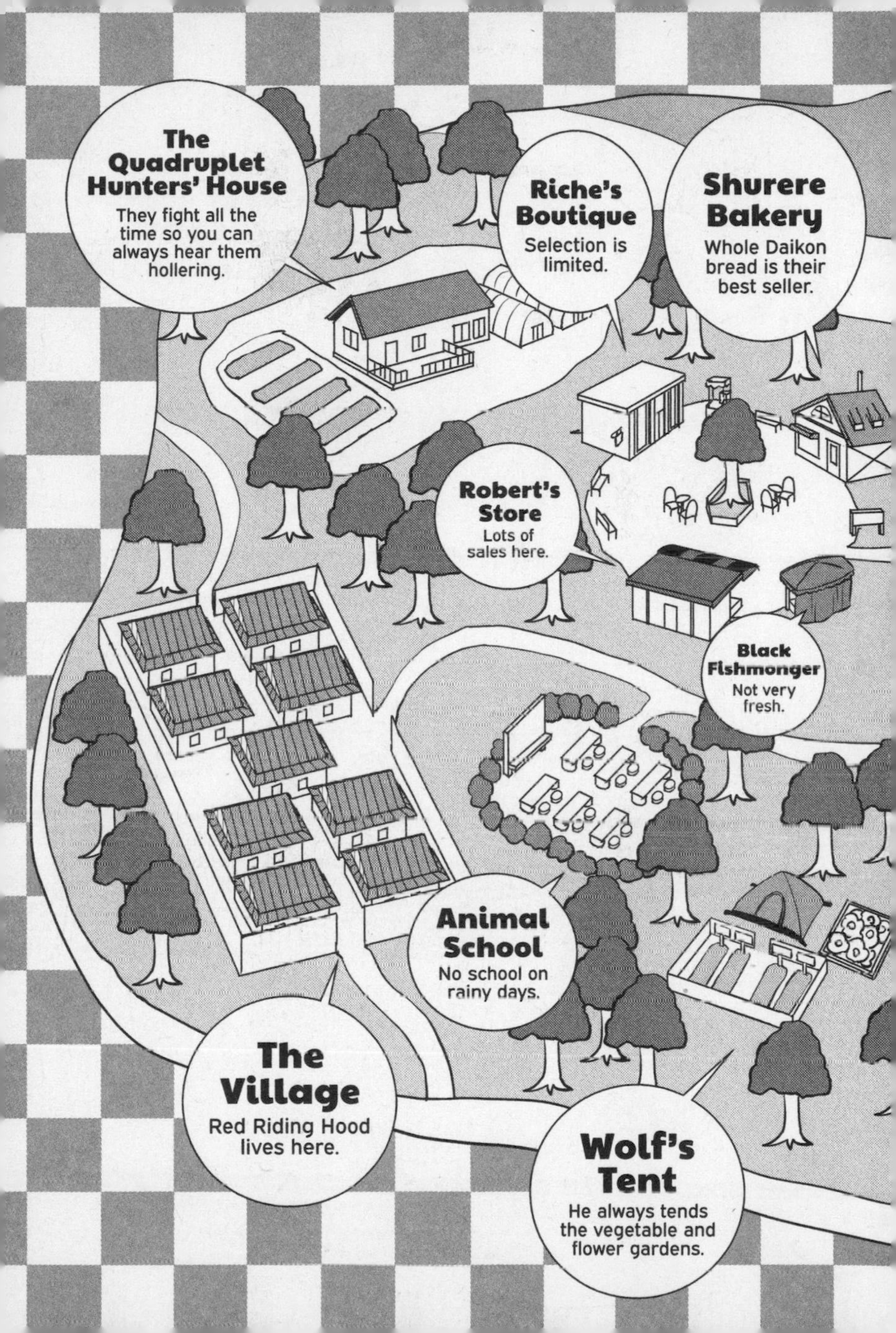
The Quadruplet Hunters' House
They fight all the time so you can always hear them hollering.
Riche's Boutique
Selection is limited.
Shurere Bakery
Whole Daikon bread is their best seller.
Robert's Store
Lots of sales here.
Black Fishmonger
Not very fresh.
Animal School
No school on rainy days.
The Village
Red Riding Hood lives here.
Wolf's Tent
He always tends the vegetable and flower gardens.

A TIMID CRYBABY

- **LIKES**
  FLOWERS, VEGETABLES, SWEET STUFF
- **DISLIKES**
  MEAT, GHOSTS, STRONG-WILLED PEOPLE
- **FAMILY MEMBERS**
  FATHER, MOTHER, YOUNGER BROTHER

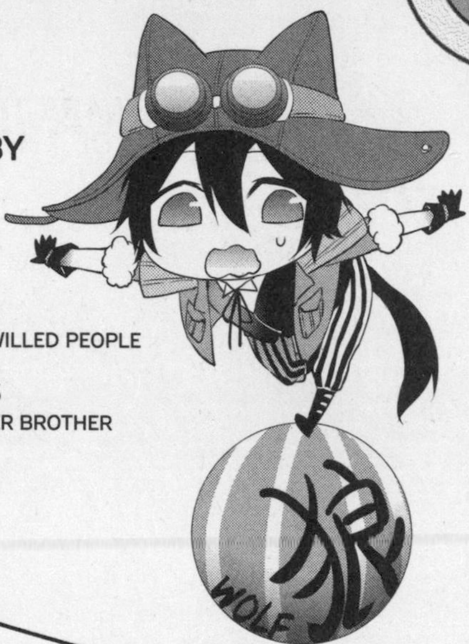
狼
WOLF

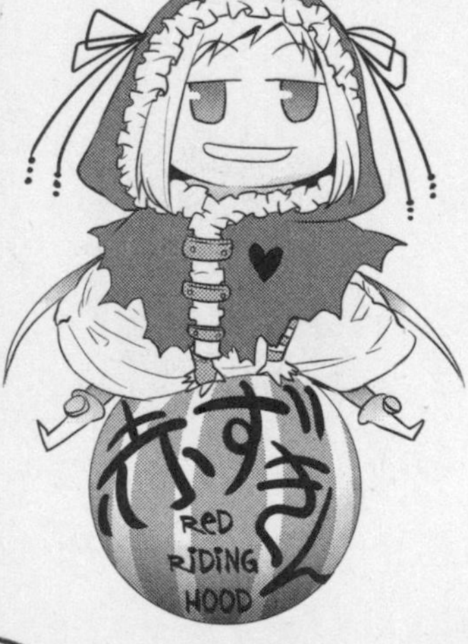
RED RIDING HOOD

A STRONG-WILLED GIRL

- **LIKES**
  WOLF, FIRE, MEAT
- **DISLIKES**
  HAWK, ARRANGED MARRIAGES, CELERY
- **FAMILY MEMBERS**
  FATHER, MOTHER

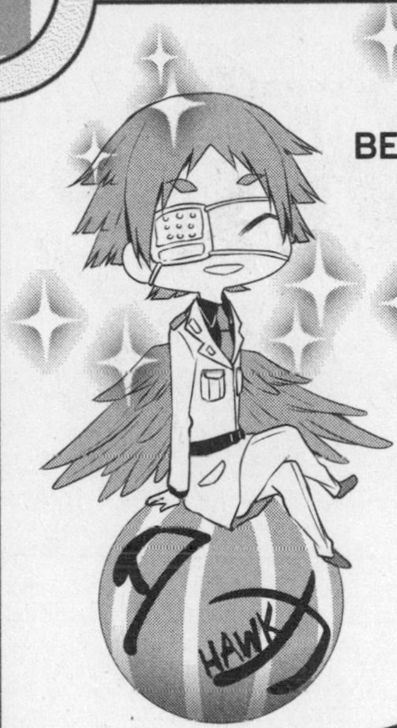
HAWK

BEWARE THE DISAPPEARANCE OF THE SPARKLY AURA!

- **LIKES**
  STRAWBERRIES, SUPERFICIAL BEAUTY
- **DISLIKES**
  [REDACTED]
- **FAMILY MEMBERS**
  FATHER, MOTHER, BIG BROTHER, LITTLE SISTER

HAS EYES ONLY FOR HAWK

- **LIKES**
  HAWK
- **DISLIKES**
  ANYTHING HAWK DOESN'T LIKE
- **FAMILY MEMBERS**
  FATHER, MOTHER

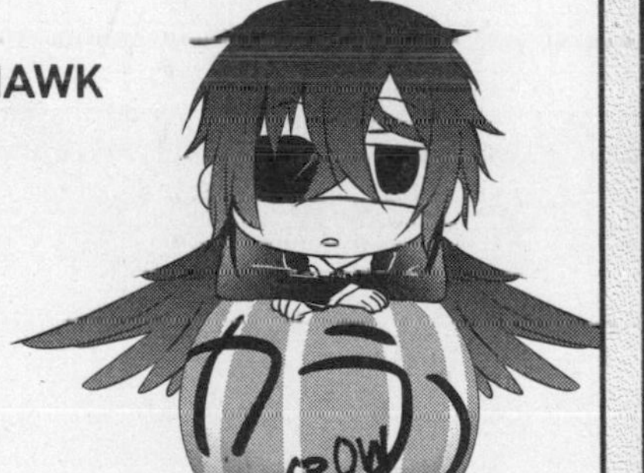
CROW

THE ETERNAL ROVING LAD

- **LIKES**
  RAW CARROTS, TRAVEL
- **DISLIKES**
  COOKING, SWEET SAUTÉED CARROTS
- **FAMILY MEMBERS**
  FATHER, MOTHER, BIG SISTER

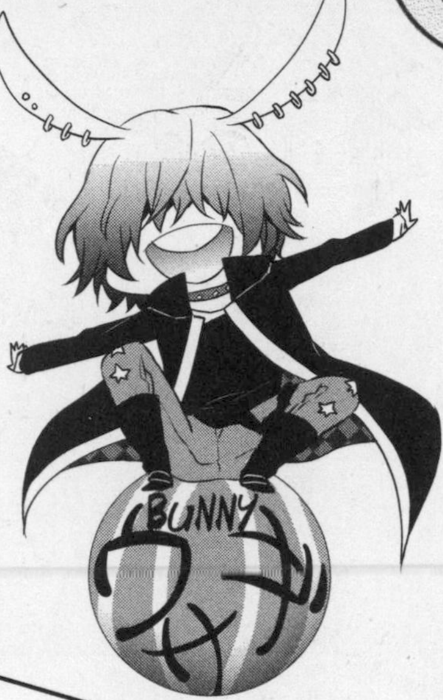
BUNNY

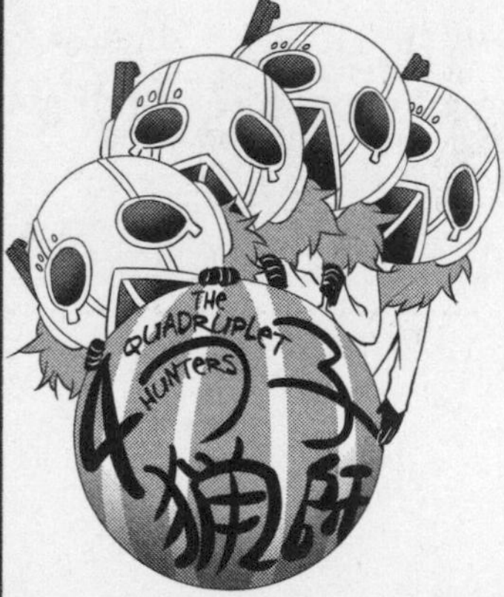
THE QUADRUPLET HUNTERS

THE FIGHTING FOURSOME

- **LIKES**
  HUNTING
- **DISLIKES**
  EACH OTHER'S UNMASKED FACES
- **FAMILY MEMBERS**
  MOTHER

Extras One

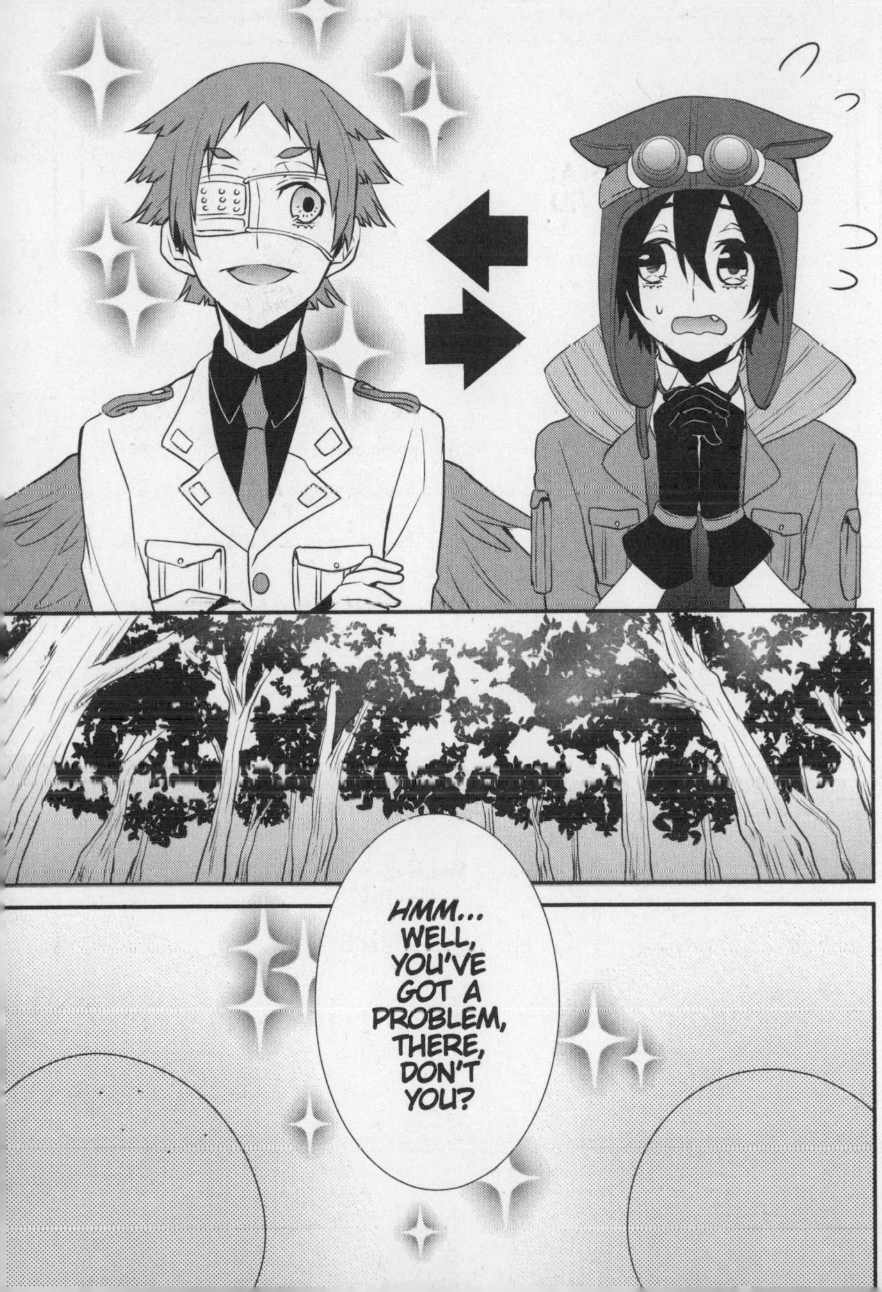
HMM... WELL, YOU'VE GOT A PROBLEM, THERE, DON'T YOU?

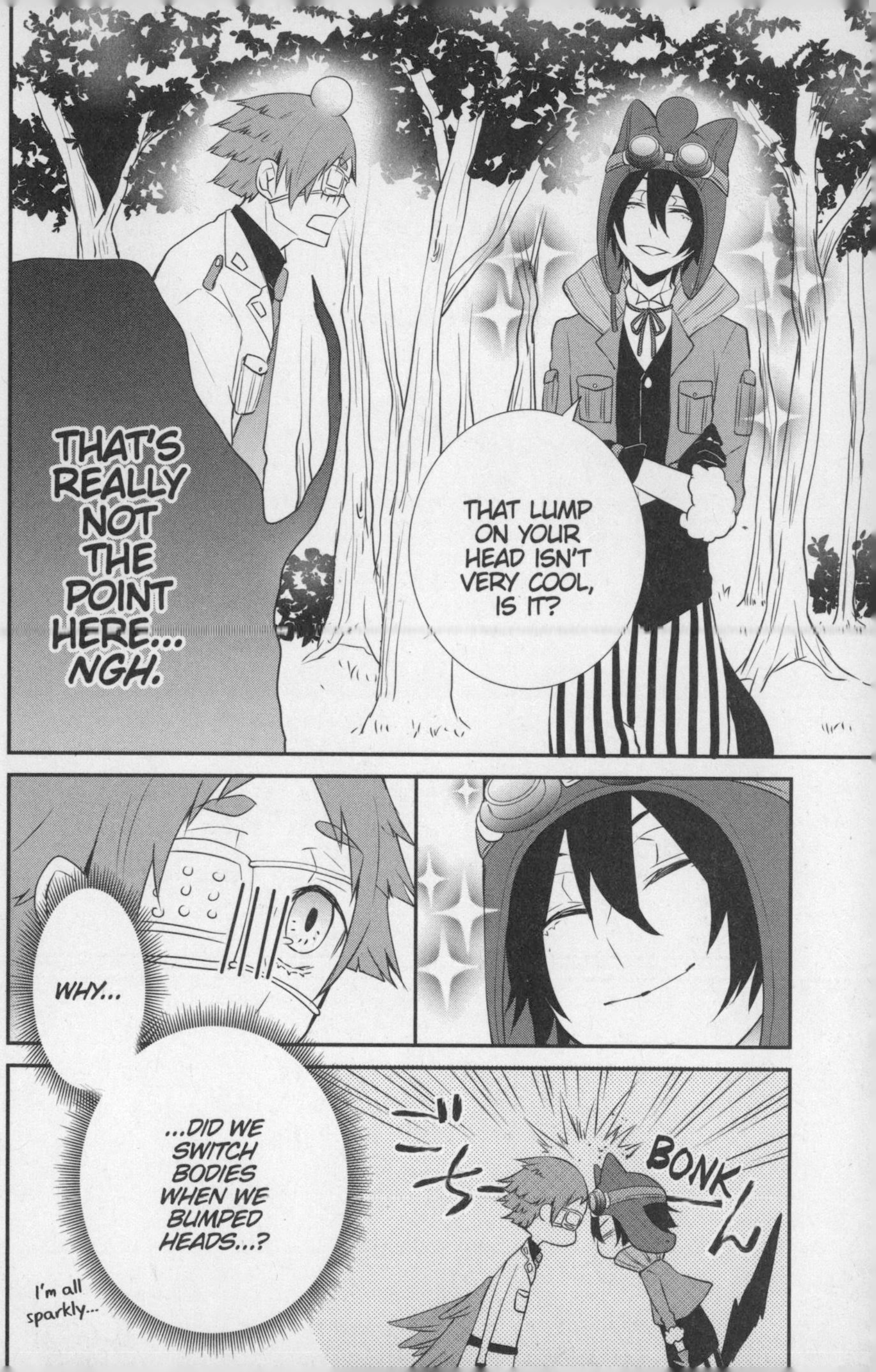
THAT LUMP ON YOUR HEAD ISN'T VERY COOL, IS IT?
THAT'S REALLY NOT THE POINT HERE... NGH.
WHY...
BONK
...DID WE SWITCH BODIES WHEN WE BUMPED HEADS...?
I'm all sparkly...

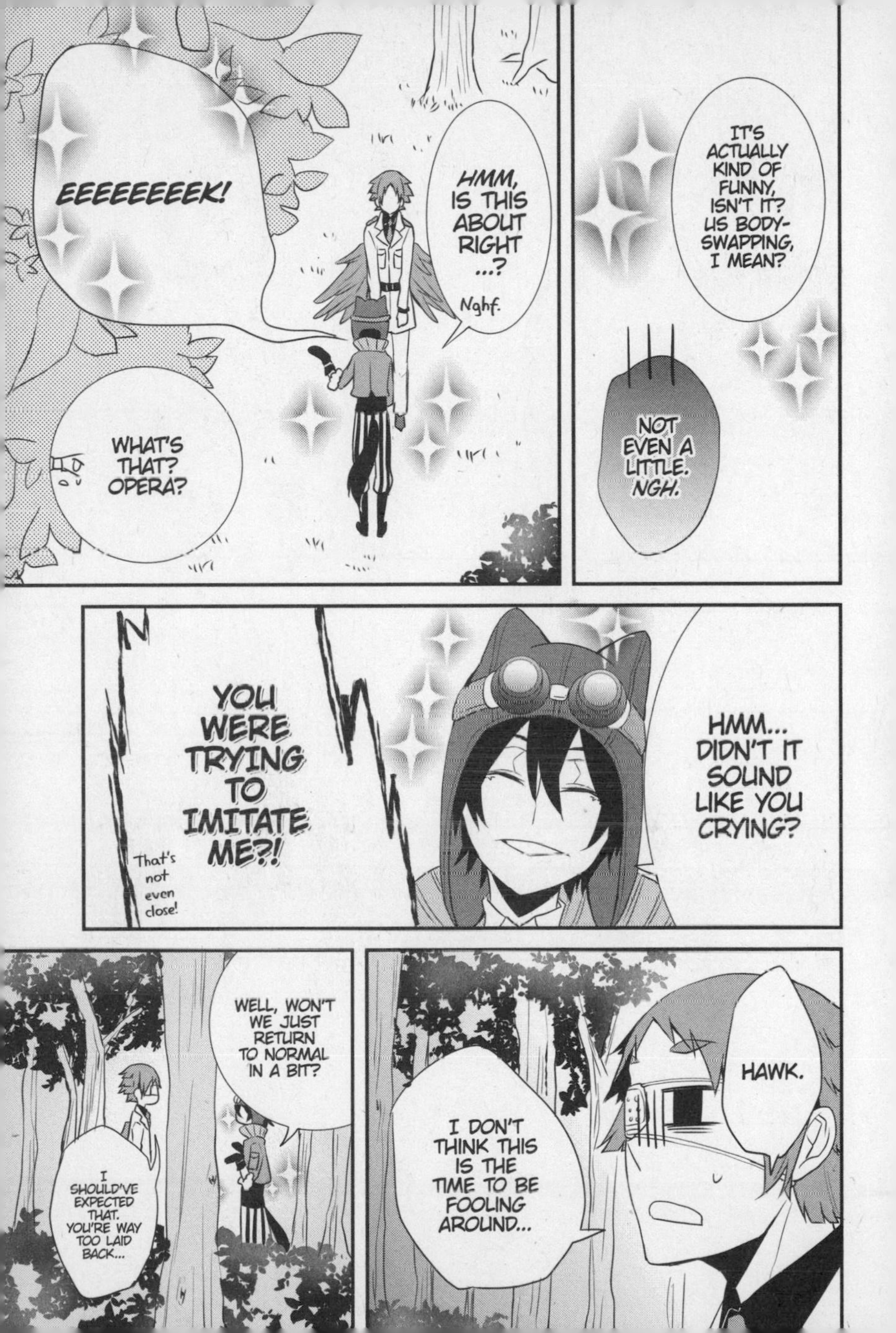
IT'S ACTUALLY KIND OF FUNNY, ISN'T IT? US BODY-SWAPPING, I MEAN?
NOT EVEN A LITTLE. NGH.
HMM, IS THIS ABOUT RIGHT ...?
Nghf.
EEEEEEEEK!
WHAT'S THAT? OPERA?
HMM... DIDN'T IT SOUND LIKE YOU CRYING?
YOU WERE TRYING TO IMITATE ME?!
That's not even close!
HAWK.
I DON'T THINK THIS IS THE TIME TO BE FOOLING AROUND...
WELL, WON'T WE JUST RETURN TO NORMAL IN A BIT?
I SHOULD'VE EXPECTED THAT. YOU'RE WAY TOO LAID BACK...

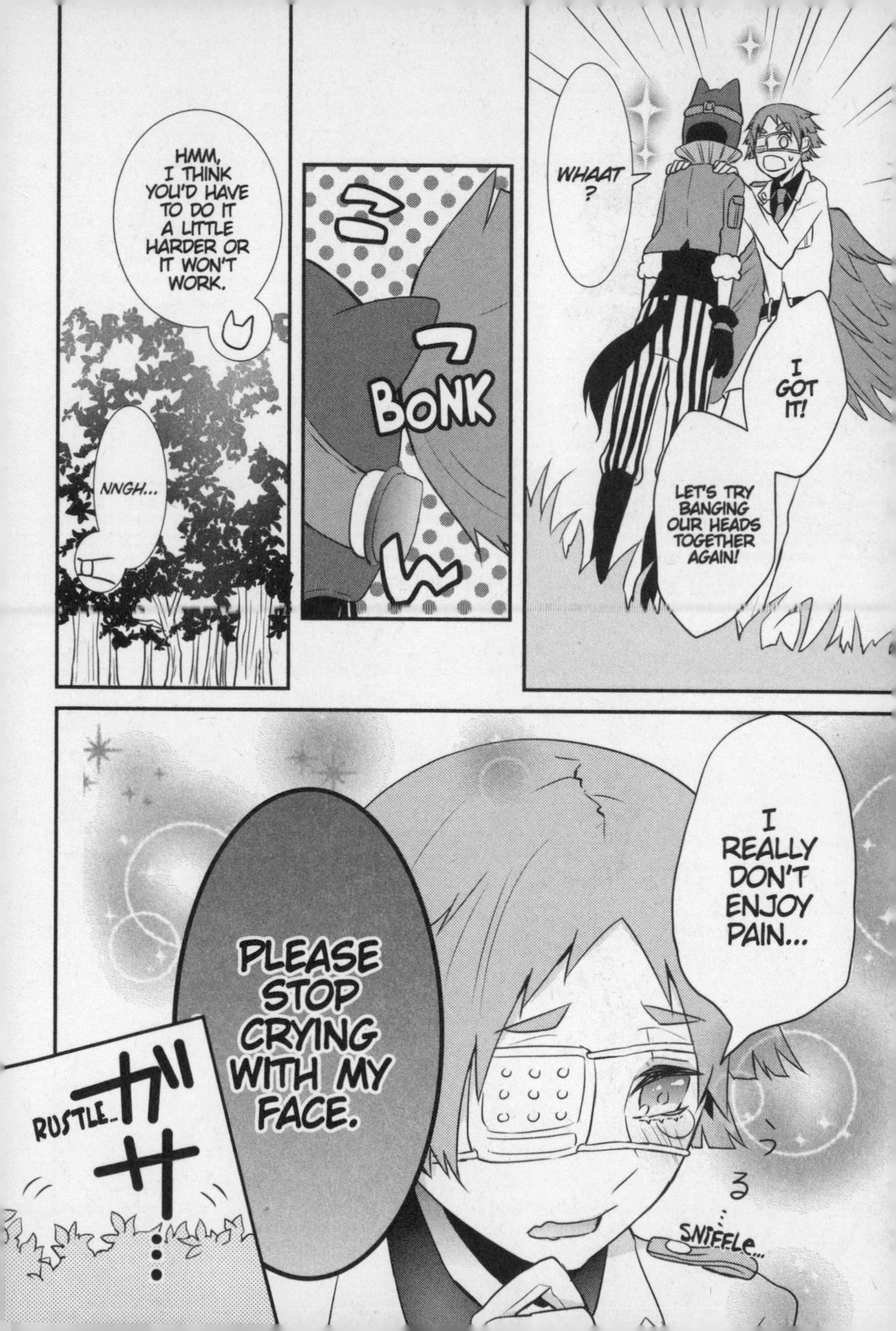
I GOT IT!
LET'S TRY BANGING OUR HEADS TOGETHER AGAIN!
WHAAT?
BONK
HMM, I THINK YOU'D HAVE TO DO IT A LITTLE HARDER OR IT WON'T WORK.
NNGH...
I REALLY DON'T ENJOY PAIN...
SNIFFLE...
PLEASE STOP CRYING WITH MY FACE.
RUSTLE...

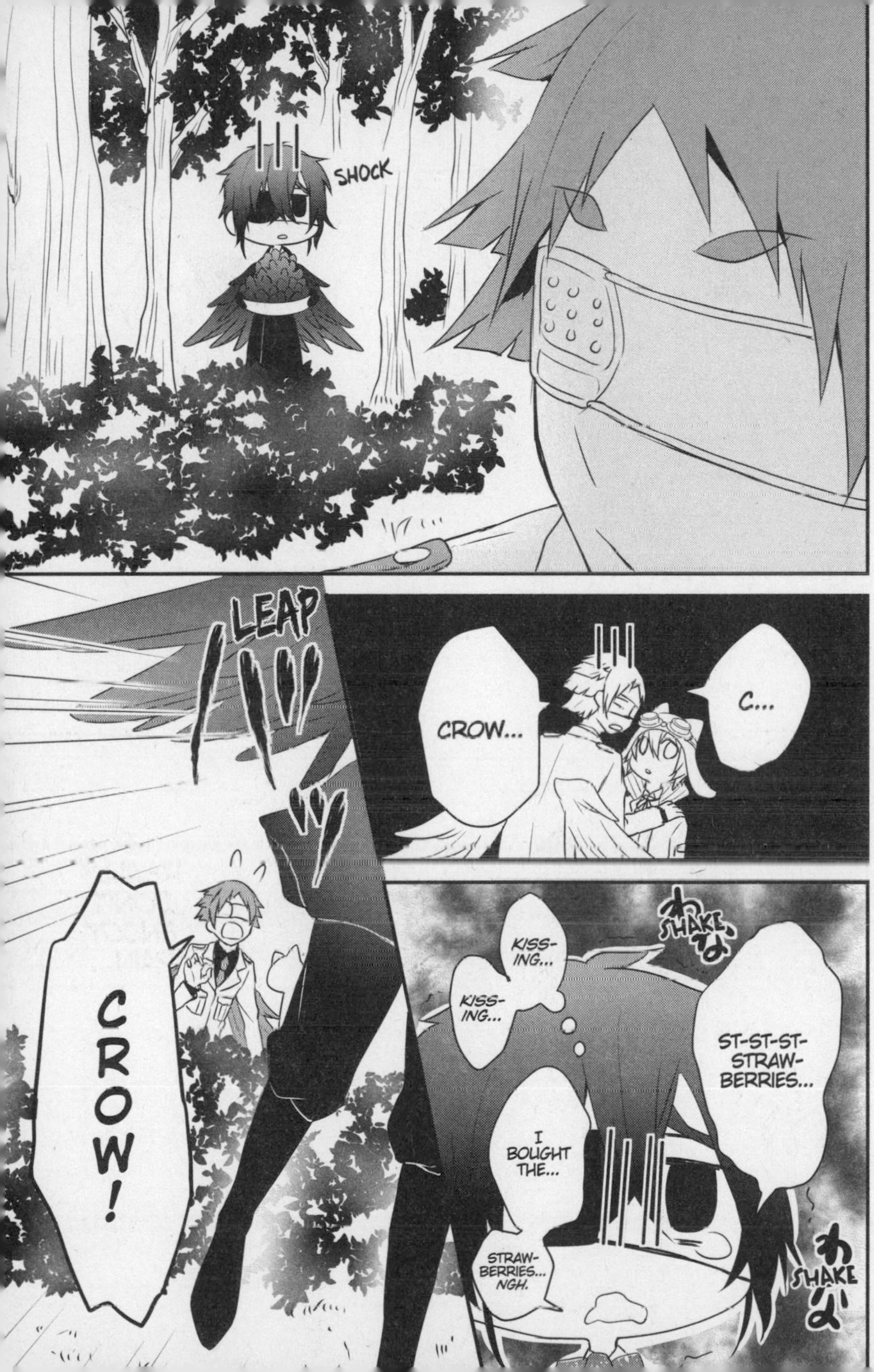
SHOCK
C...
CROW...
わ SHAKE な
ST-ST-ST-STRAW-BERRIES...
KISS-ING...
KISS-ING...
I BOUGHT THE...
STRAW-BERRIES... NGH.
わ SHAKE な
LEAP
CROW!

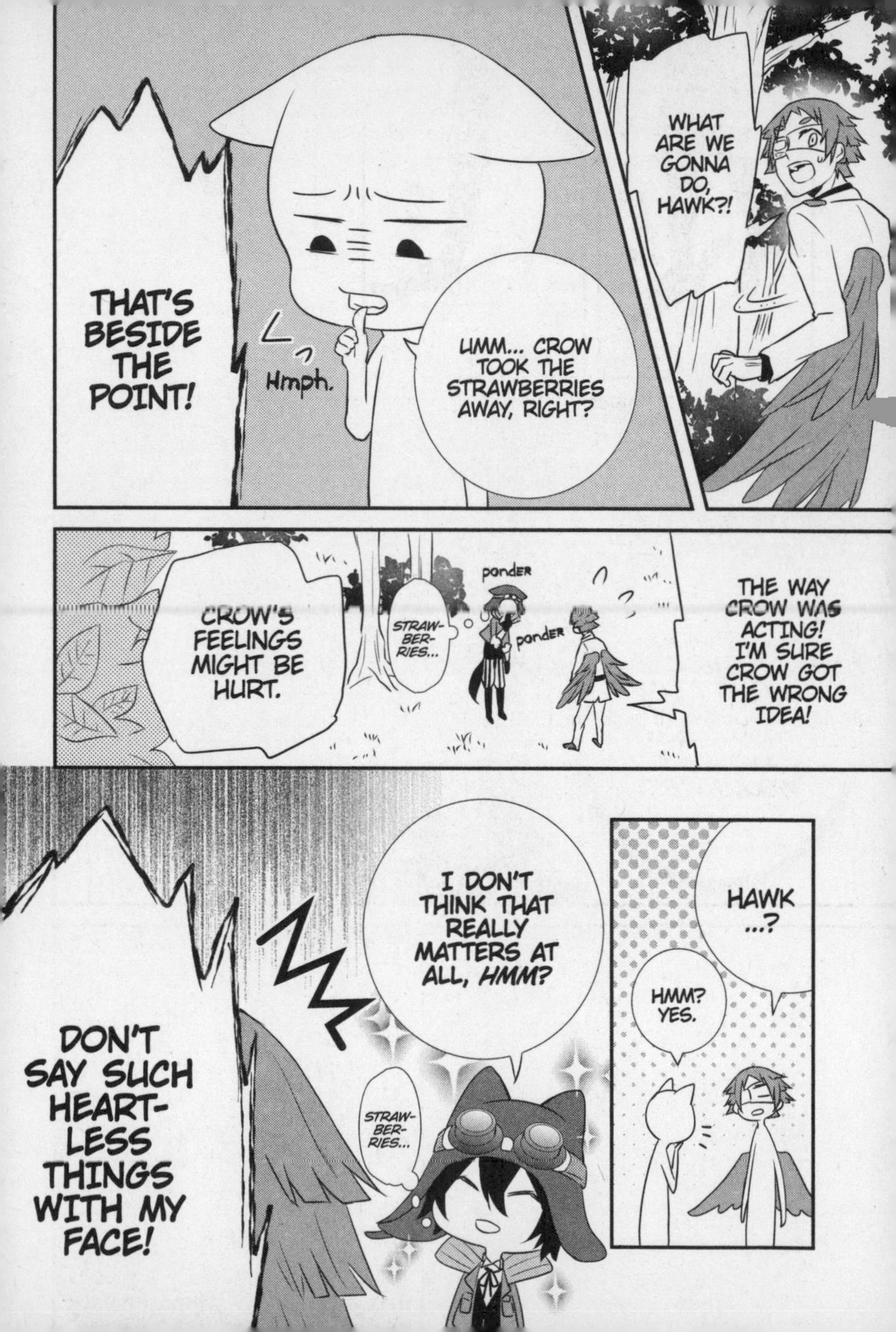
WHAT ARE WE GONNA DO, HAWK?!
UMM... CROW TOOK THE STRAWBERRIES AWAY, RIGHT?
Hmph.
THAT'S BESIDE THE POINT!
THE WAY CROW WAS ACTING! I'M SURE CROW GOT THE WRONG IDEA!
ponder
ponder
STRAW-BER-RIES...
CROW'S FEELINGS MIGHT BE HURT.
HAWK ...?
HMM? YES.
I DON'T THINK THAT REALLY MATTERS AT ALL, *HMM?*
STRAW-BER-RIES...
DON'T SAY SUCH HEART-LESS THINGS WITH MY FACE!

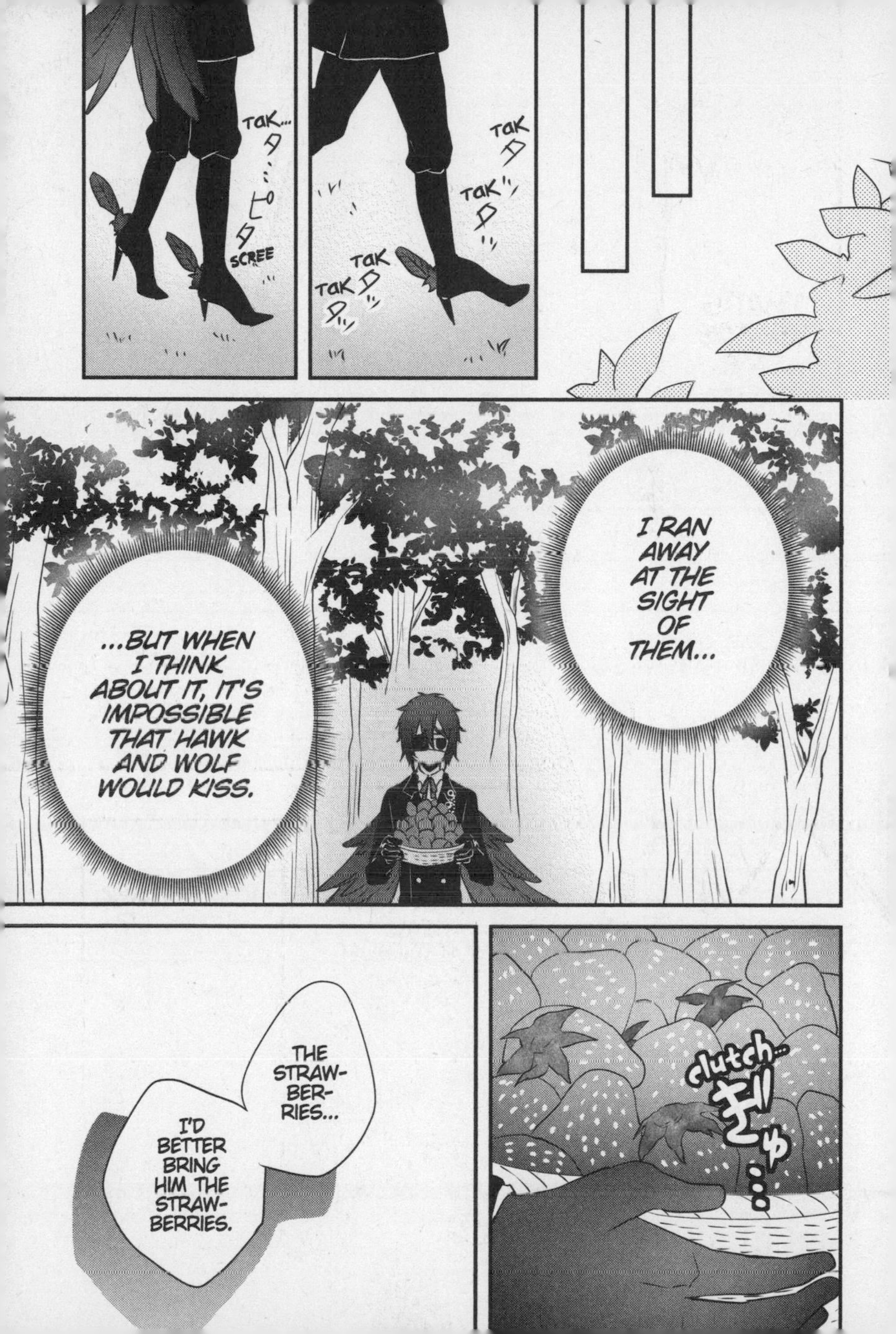
TAK
TAK
TAK
TAK
TAK...
SCREE
I RAN AWAY AT THE SIGHT OF THEM...
...BUT WHEN I THINK ABOUT IT, IT'S IMPOSSIBLE THAT HAWK AND WOLF WOULD KISS.
clutch...
THE STRAW-BER-RIES...
I'D BETTER BRING HIM THE STRAW-BERRIES.

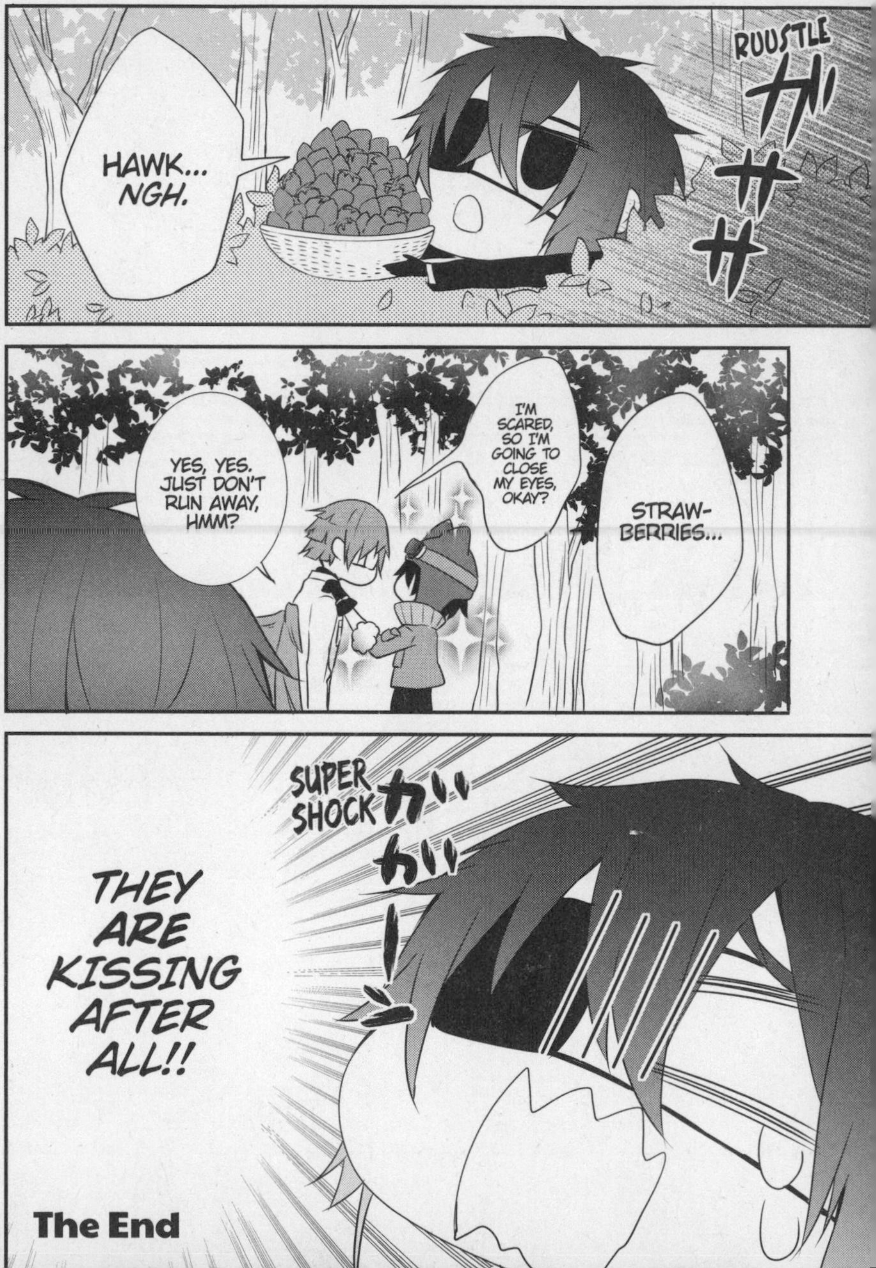
RUUSTLE
ガサササ
HAWK... NGH.
STRAW-BERRIES...
I'M SCARED, SO I'M GOING TO CLOSE MY EYES, OKAY?
YES, YES. JUST DON'T RUN AWAY, HMM?
SUPER SHOCK
THEY ARE KISSING AFTER ALL!!
The End

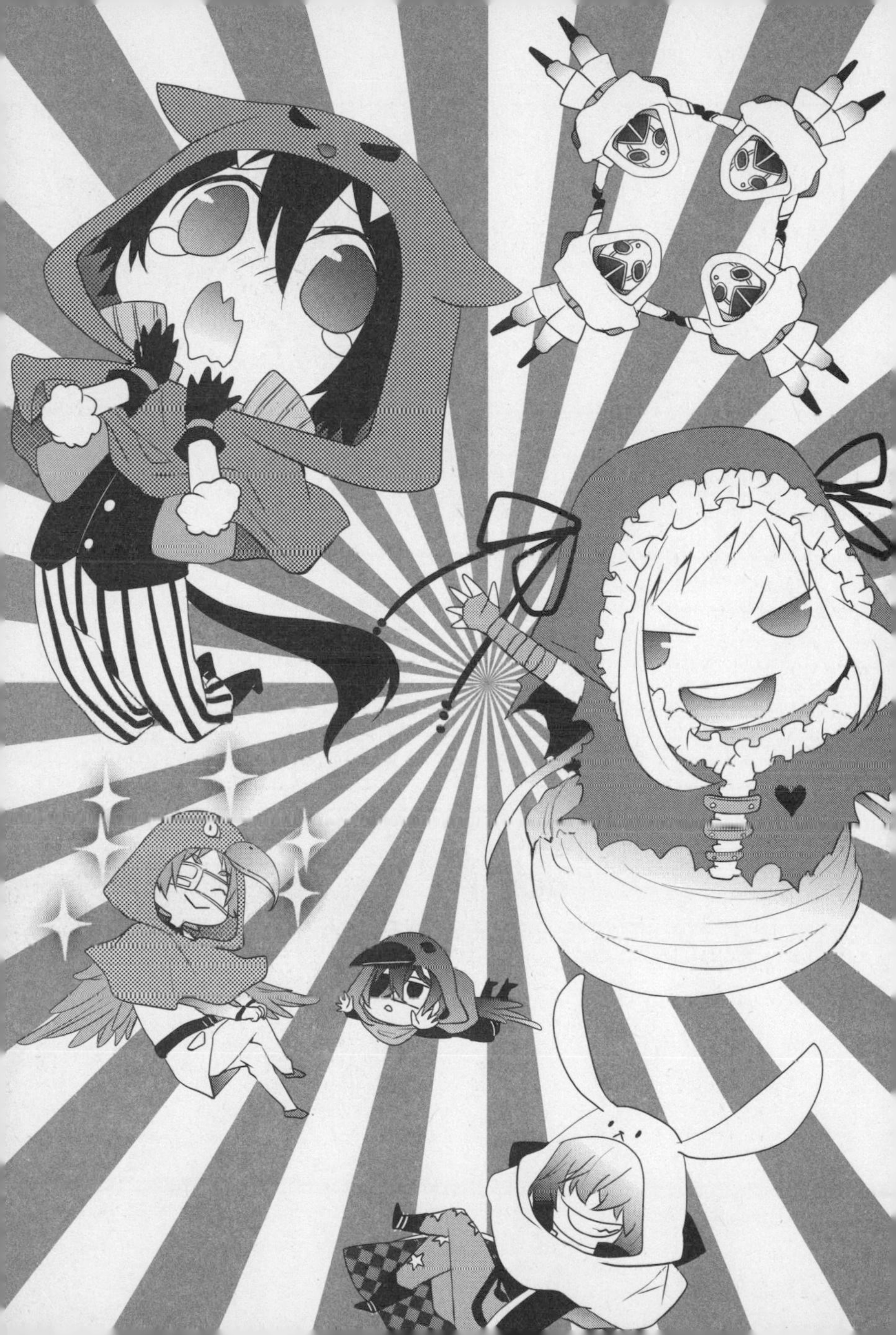

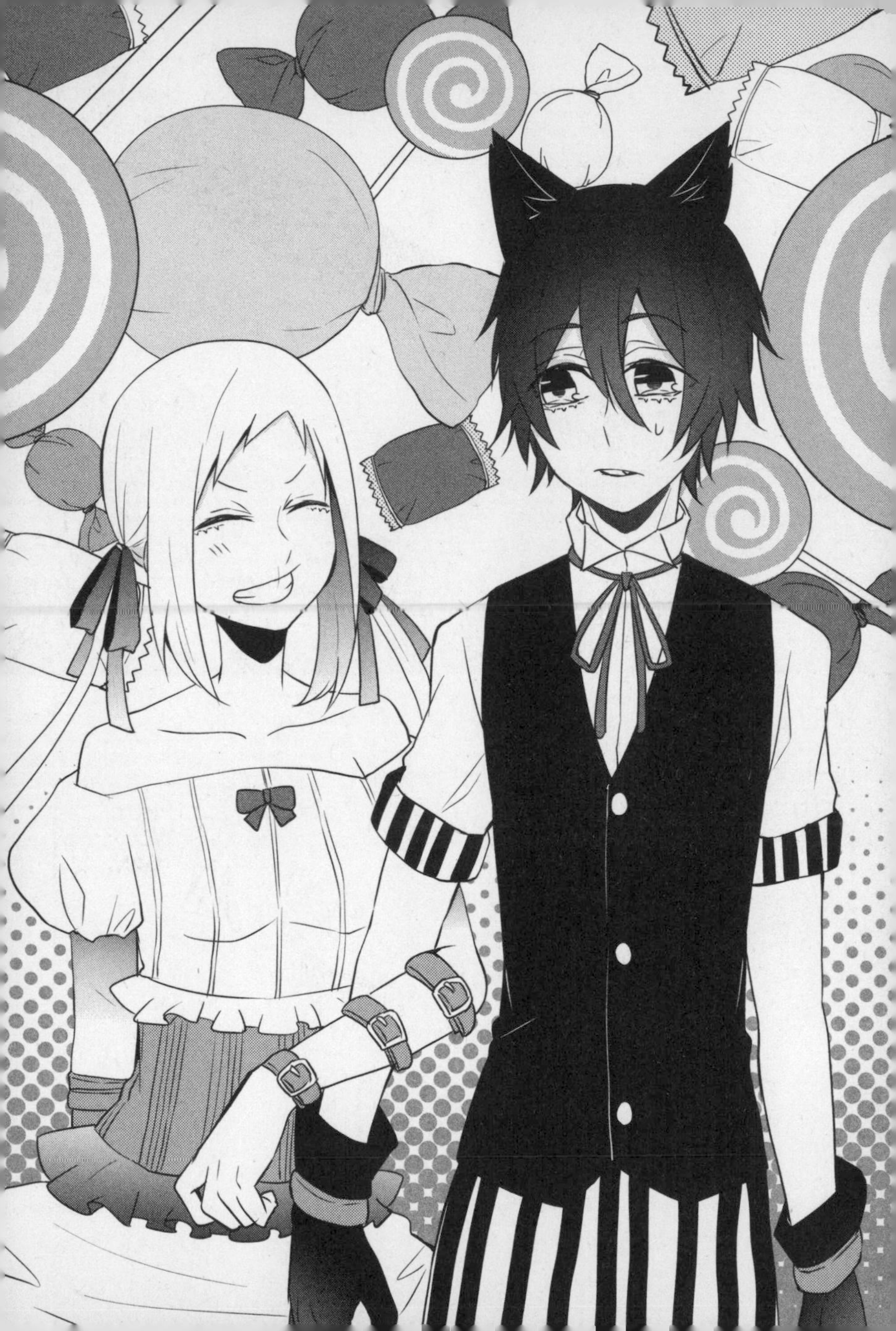

Extras Two

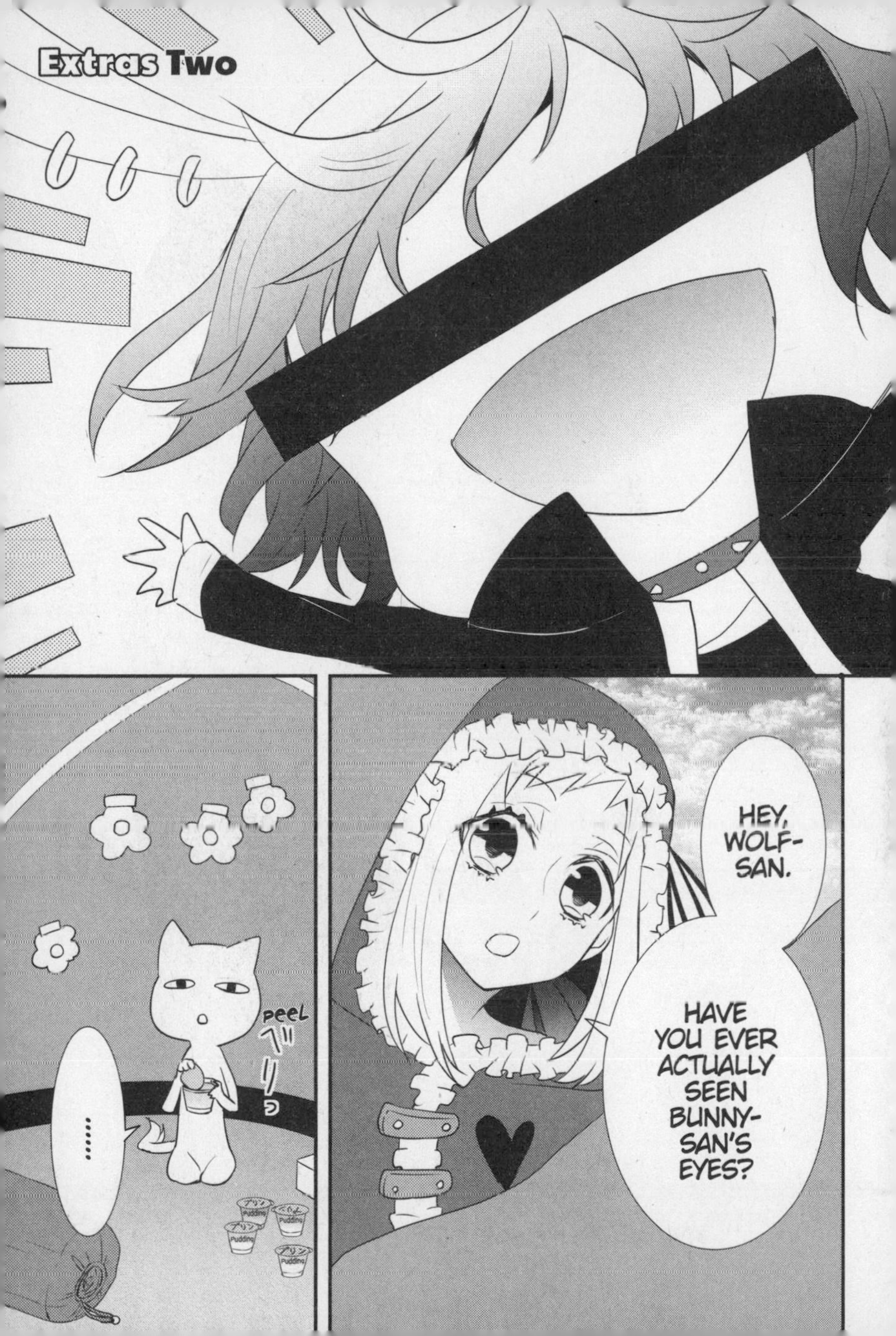

HEY, WOLF-SAN.
HAVE YOU EVER ACTUALLY SEEN BUNNY-SAN'S EYES?
PEEL
べりっ
......

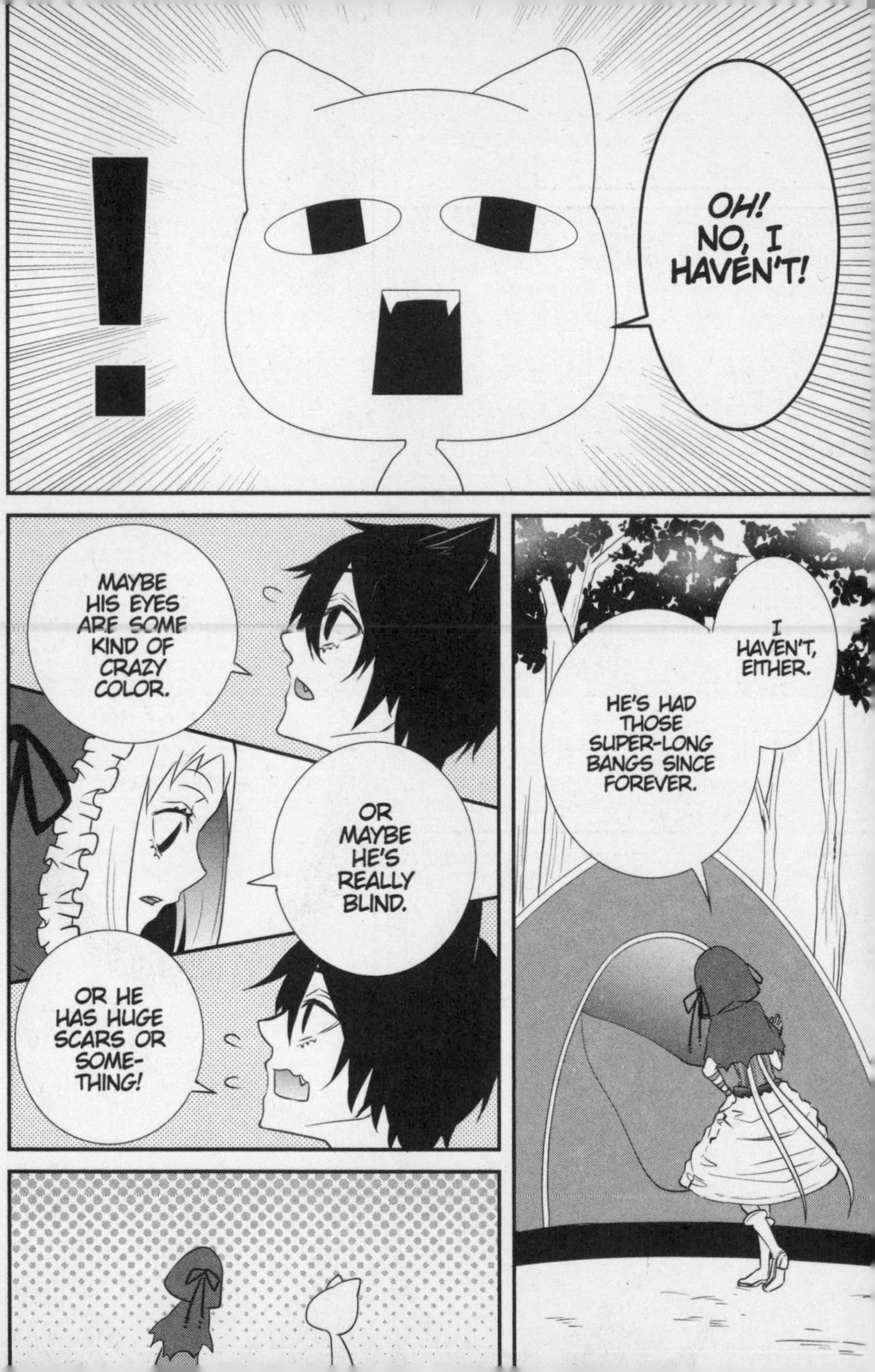
OH! NO, I HAVEN'T!
!
I HAVEN'T, EITHER.
HE'S HAD THOSE SUPER-LONG BANGS SINCE FOREVER.
MAYBE HIS EYES ARE SOME KIND OF CRAZY COLOR.
OR MAYBE HE'S REALLY BLIND.
OR HE HAS HUGE SCARS OR SOME-THING!

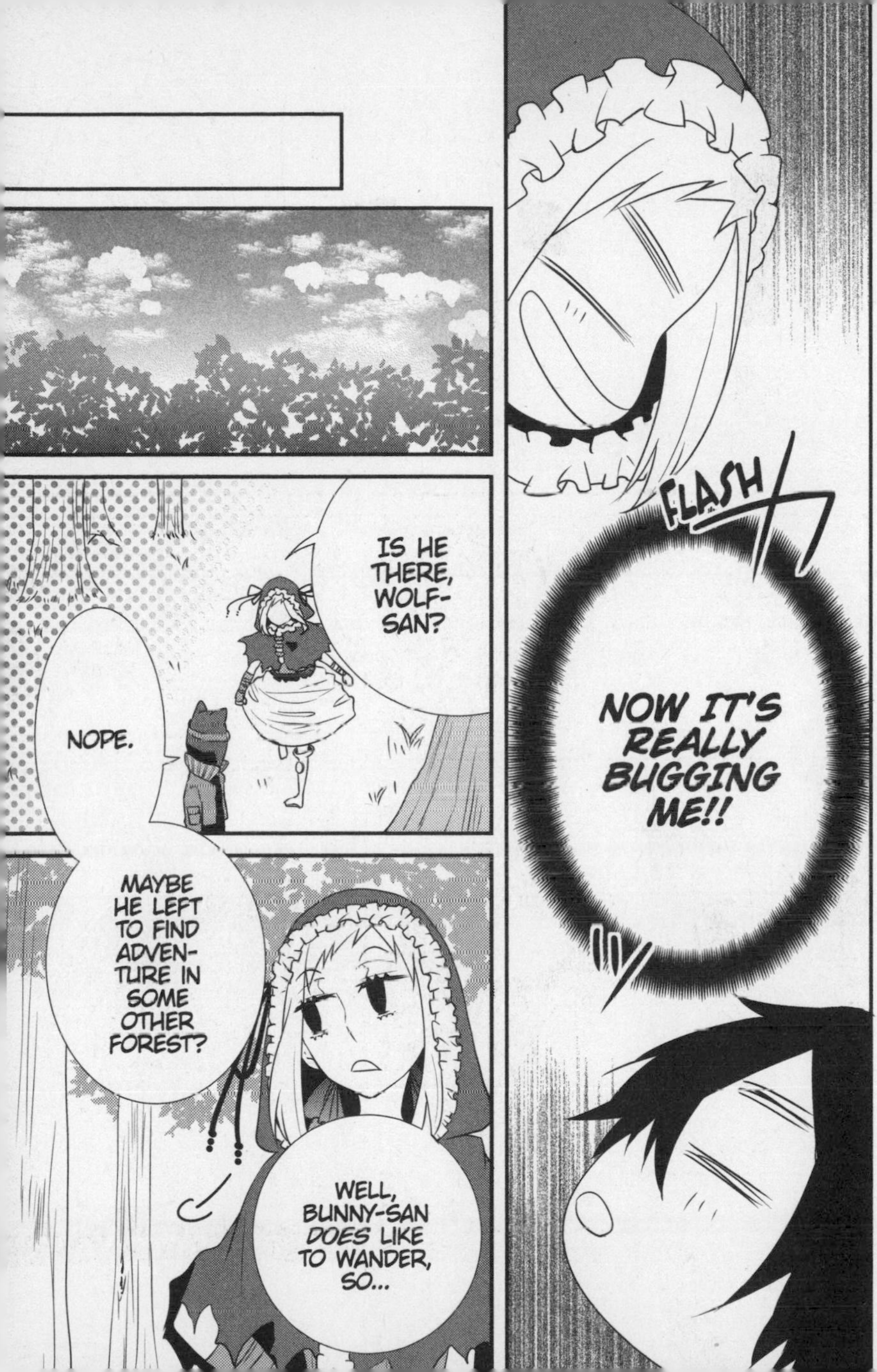
FLASH
NOW IT'S REALLY BUGGING ME!!
IS HE THERE, WOLF-SAN?
NOPE.
MAYBE HE LEFT TO FIND ADVENTURE IN SOME OTHER FOREST?
WELL, BUNNY-SAN DOES LIKE TO WANDER, SO...

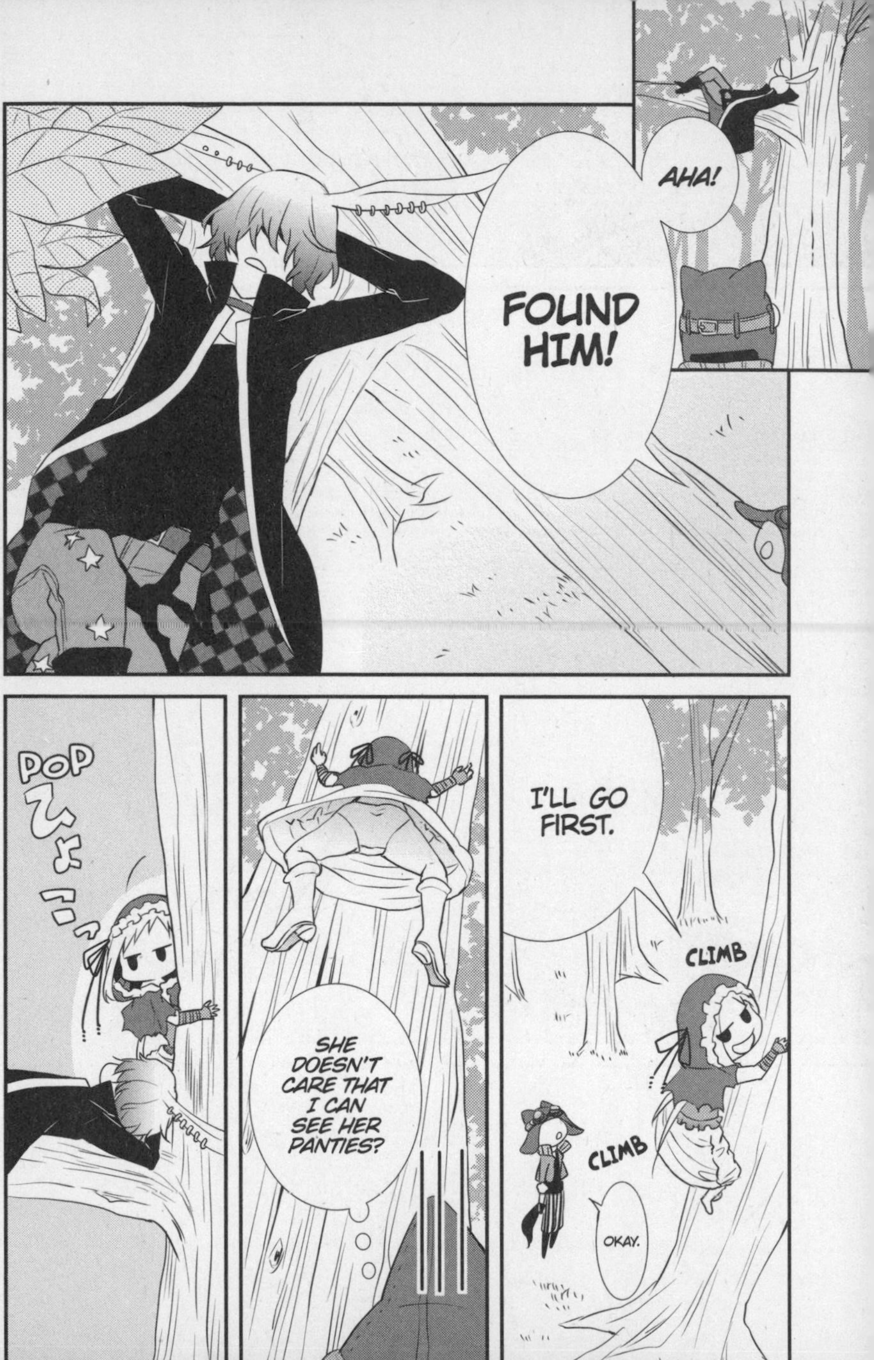
AHA!
FOUND HIM!
I'LL GO FIRST.
CLIMB
CLIMB
OKAY.
SHE DOESN'T CARE THAT I CAN SEE HER PANTIES?
POP

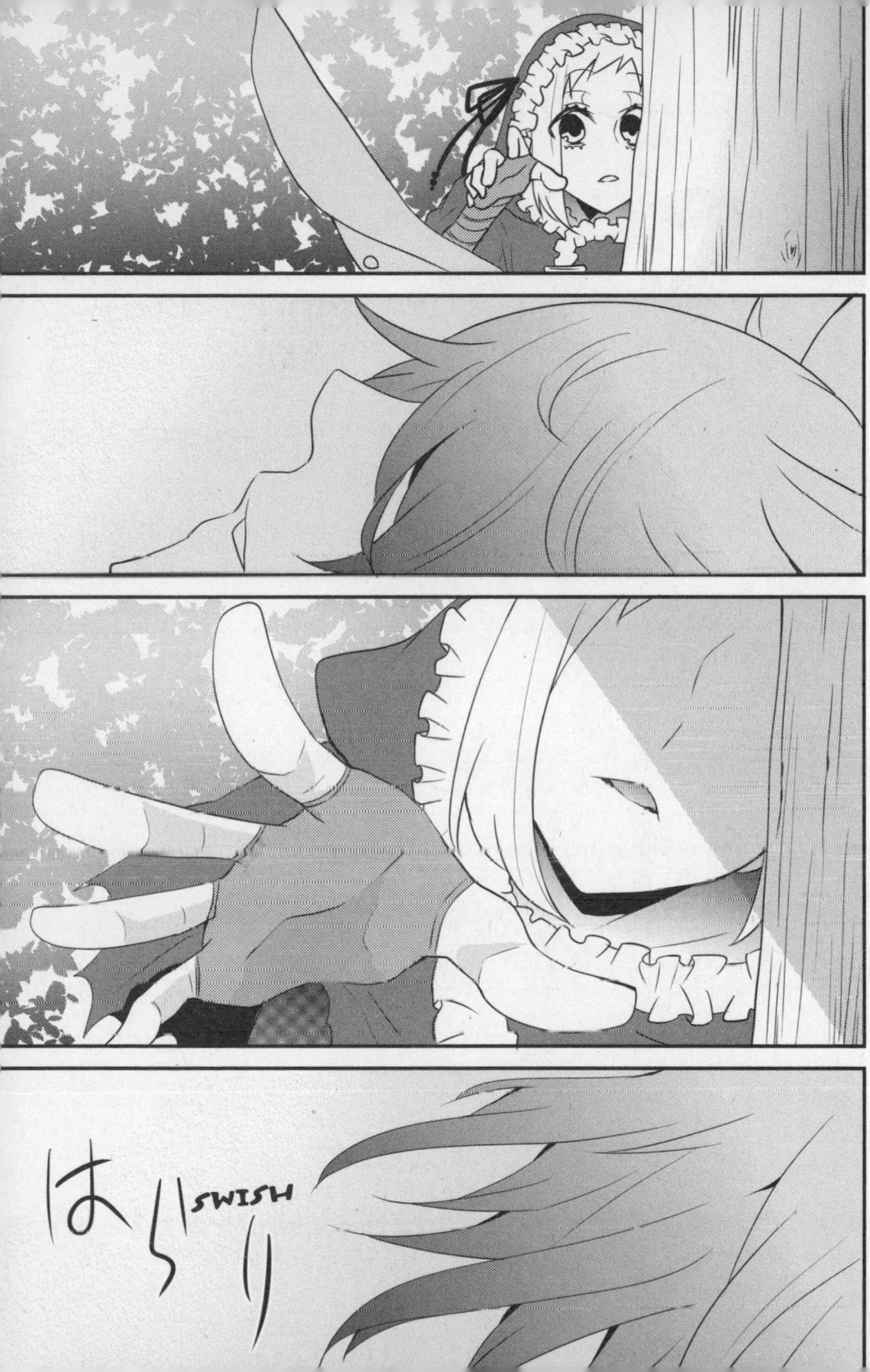
はらり
SWISH

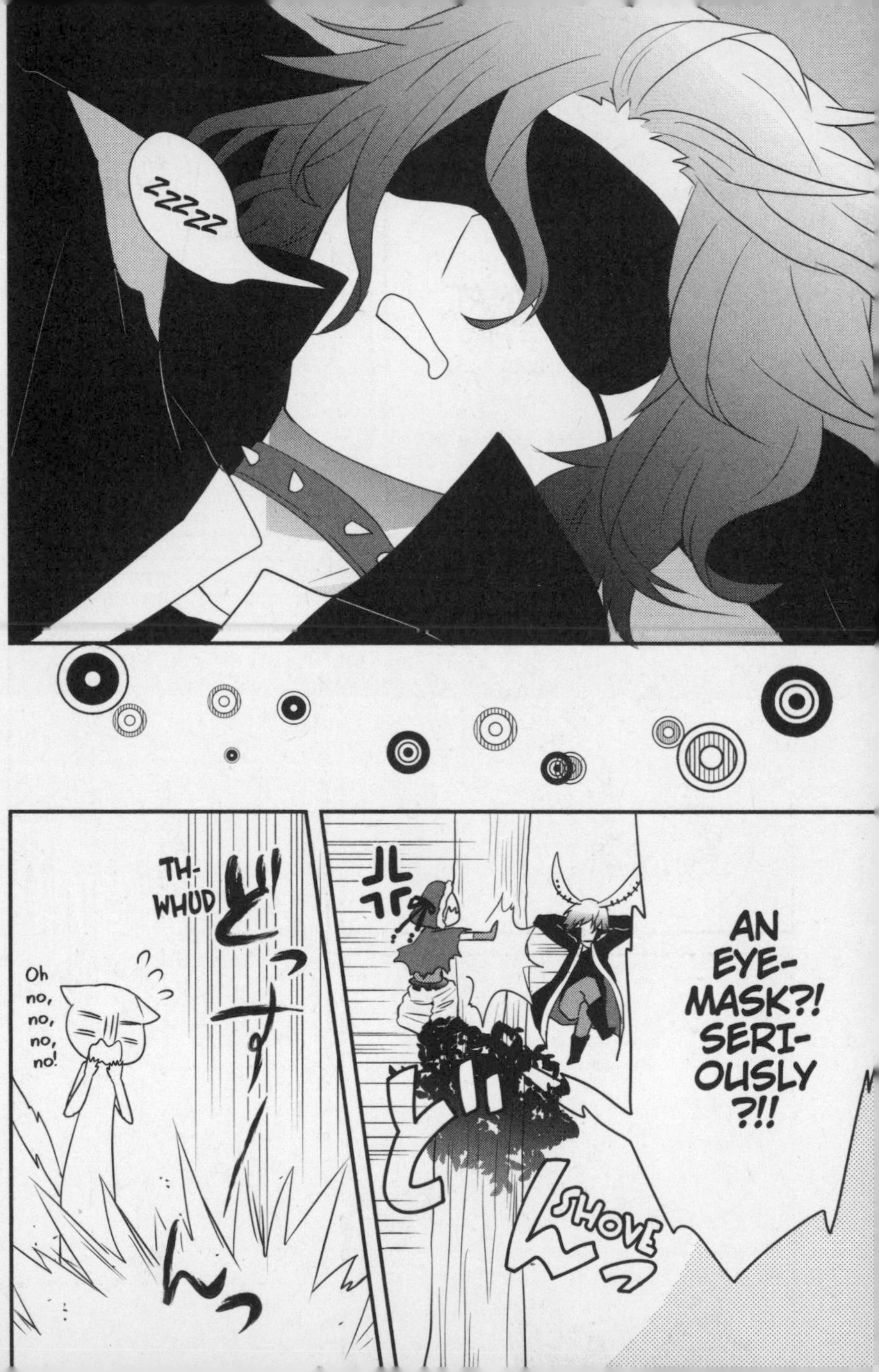
ZZZZZ
AN EYE-MASK?! SERIOUSLY?!!
SHOVE
TH-WHUD
Oh no, no, no, no!

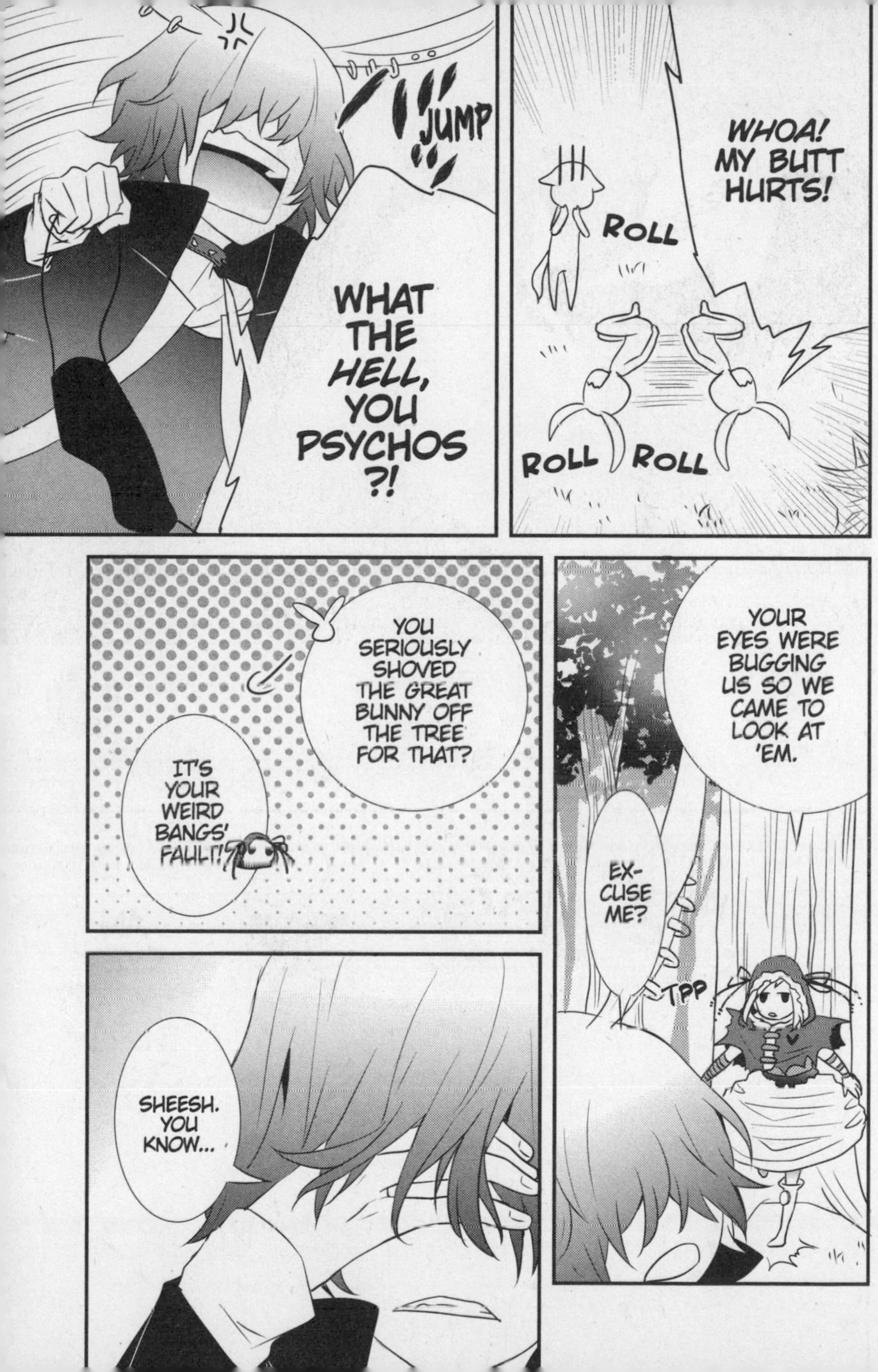
WHOA! MY BUTT HURTS!
ROLL
ROLL
ROLL
JUMP
WHAT THE HELL, YOU PSYCHOS?!
YOUR EYES WERE BUGGING US SO WE CAME TO LOOK AT 'EM.
EX-CUSE ME?
TPP
YOU SERIOUSLY SHOVED THE GREAT BUNNY OFF THE TREE FOR THAT?
IT'S YOUR WEIRD BANGS' FAULT!
SHEESH. YOU KNOW...

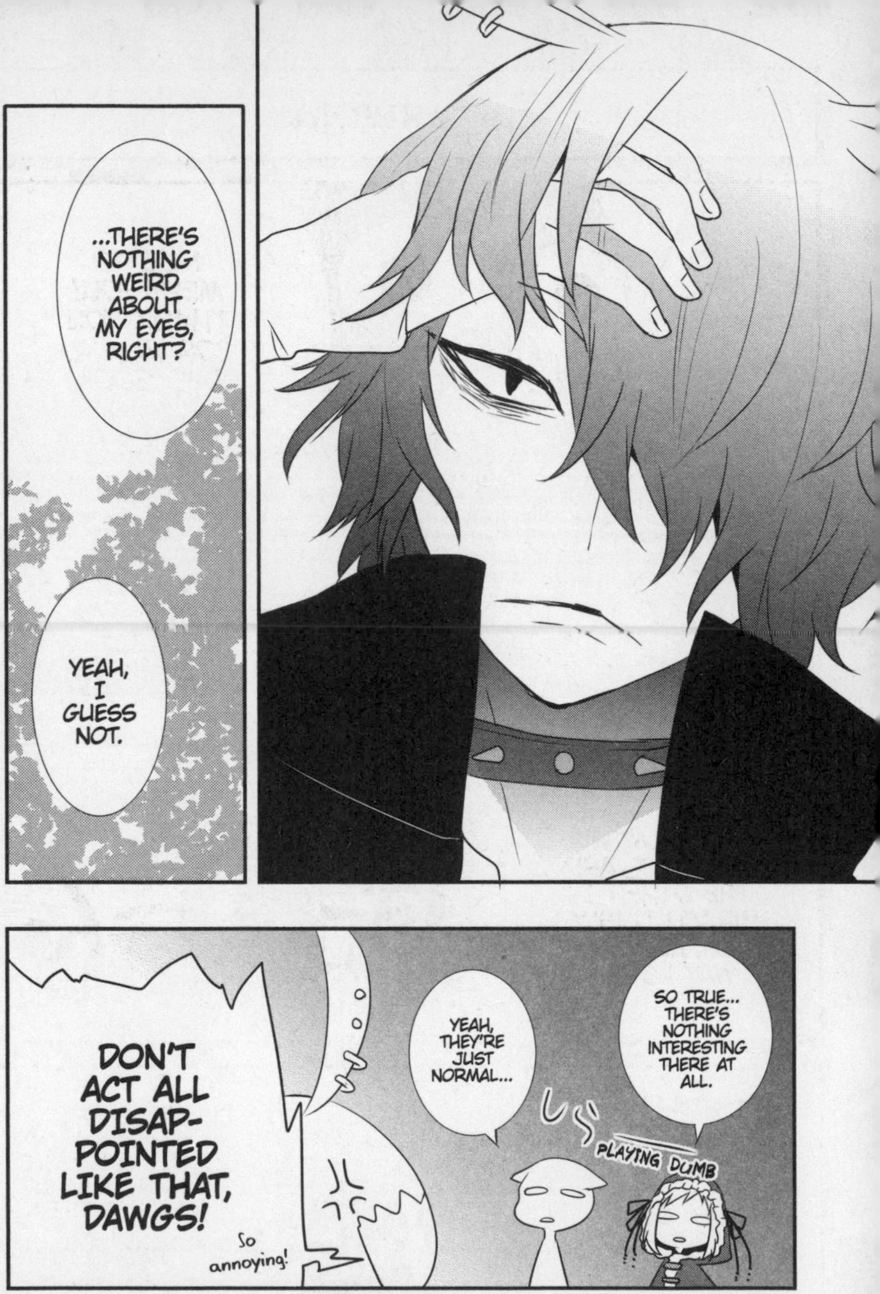
...THERE'S NOTHING WEIRD ABOUT MY EYES, RIGHT?
YEAH, I GUESS NOT.
SO TRUE... THERE'S NOTHING INTERESTING THERE AT ALL.
PLAYING DUMB
YEAH, THEY'RE JUST NORMAL...
DON'T ACT ALL DISAP-POINTED LIKE THAT, DAWGS!
So annoying!

The End

AFTERWORD

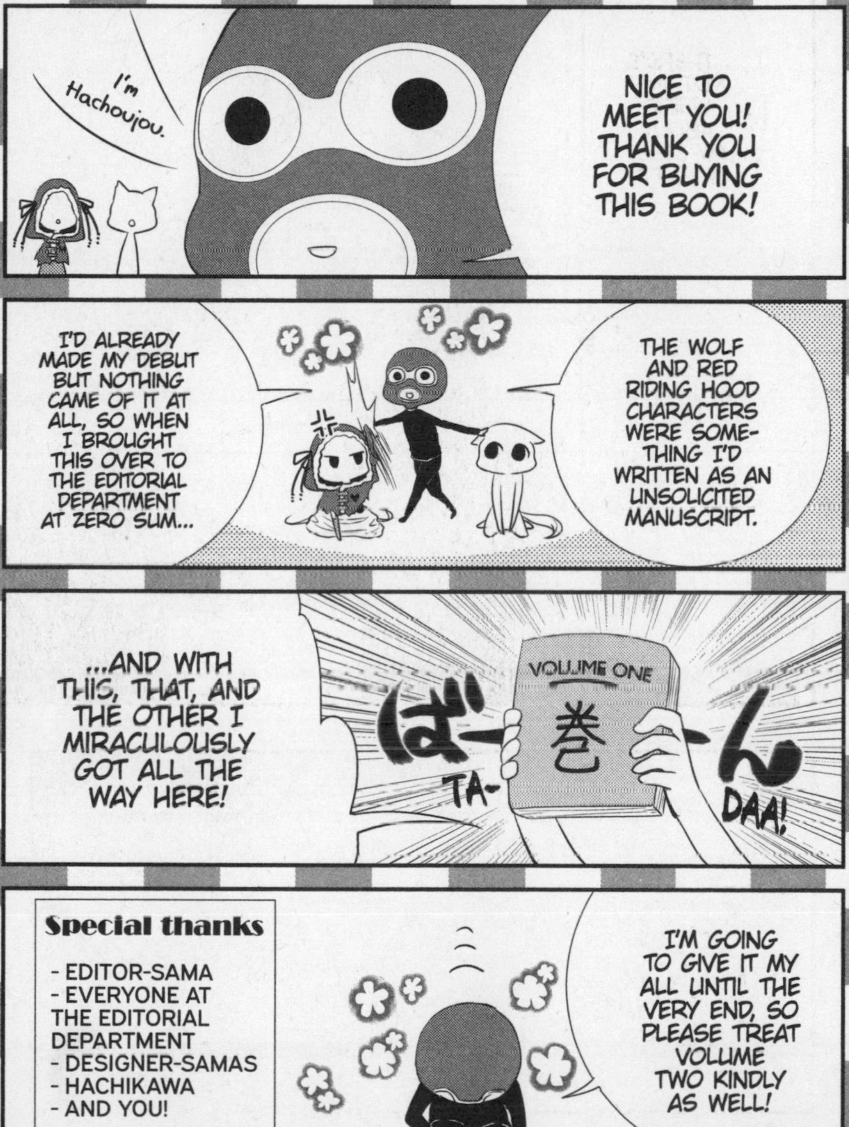
NICE TO MEET YOU! THANK YOU FOR BUYING THIS BOOK!
I'm Hachoujou.
THE WOLF AND RED RIDING HOOD CHARACTERS WERE SOME-THING I'D WRITTEN AS AN UNSOLICITED MANUSCRIPT.
I'D ALREADY MADE MY DEBUT BUT NOTHING CAME OF IT AT ALL, SO WHEN I BROUGHT THIS OVER TO THE EDITORIAL DEPARTMENT AT ZERO SUM...
VOLUME ONE
巻
...AND WITH THIS, THAT, AND THE OTHER I MIRACULOUSLY GOT ALL THE WAY HERE!
ばーーん
TA- DAA!
I'M GOING TO GIVE IT MY ALL UNTIL THE VERY END, SO PLEASE TREAT VOLUME TWO KINDLY AS WELL!
Special thanks
- EDITOR-SAMA
- EVERYONE AT THE EDITORIAL DEPARTMENT
- DESIGNER-SAMAS
- HACHIKAWA
- AND YOU!

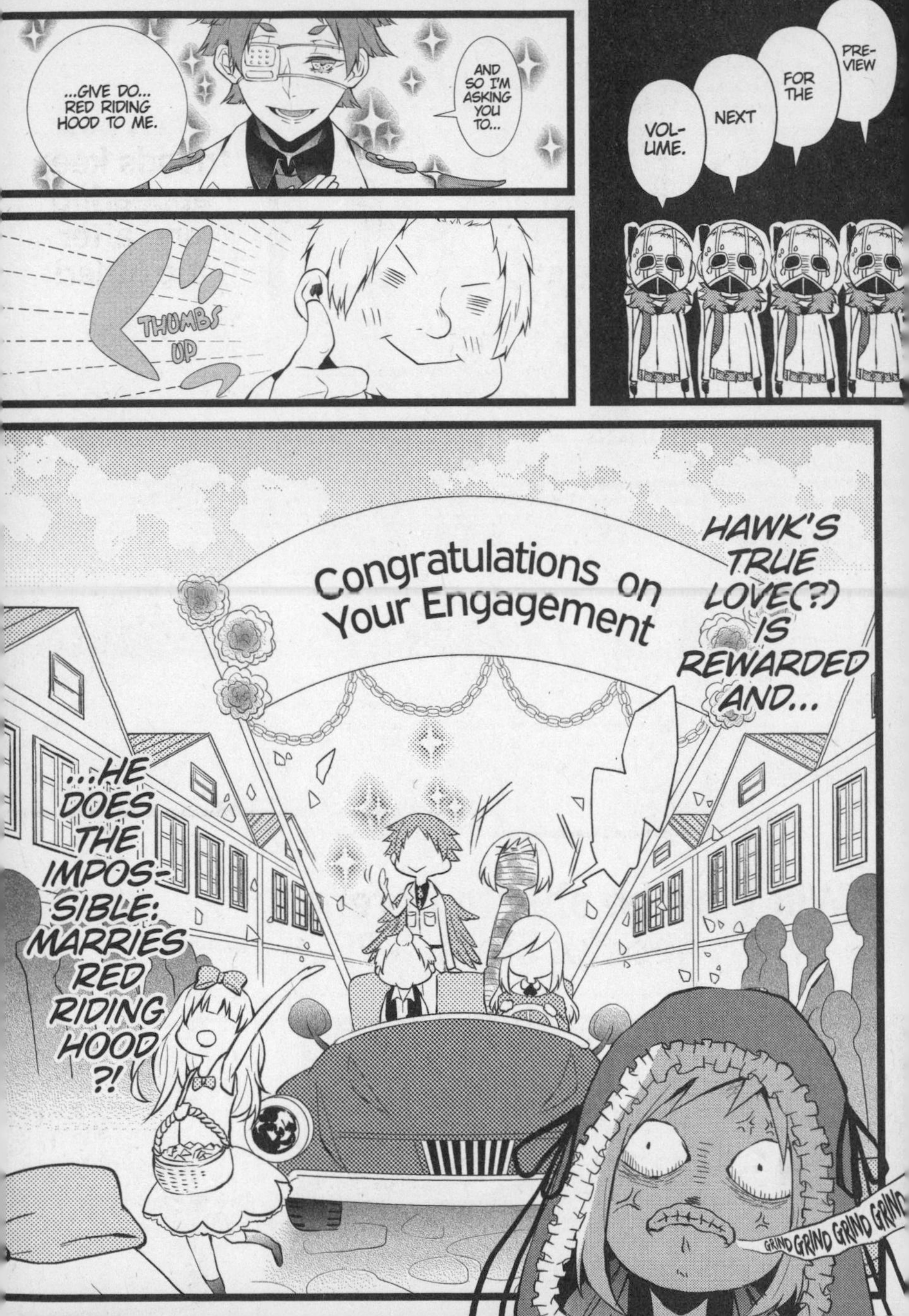
PRE-VIEW
FOR THE
NEXT
VOL-UME.
AND SO I'M ASKING YOU TO...
...GIVE DO... RED RIDING HOOD TO ME.
THUMBS UP
HAWK'S TRUE LOVE(?) IS REWARDED AND...
Congratulations on Your Engagement
...HE DOES THE IMPOS-SIBLE: MARRIES RED RIDING HOOD ?!
GRIND GRIND GRIND GRIND

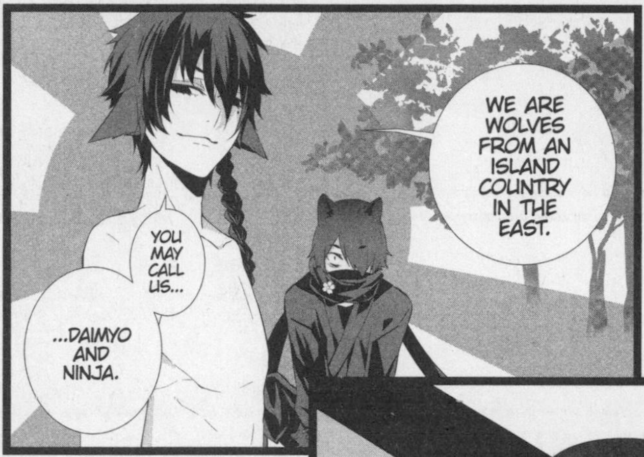
WE ARE WOLVES FROM AN ISLAND COUNTRY IN THE EAST.
YOU MAY CALL US...
...DAIMYO AND NINJA.

Then new friends keep appearing one after the other!

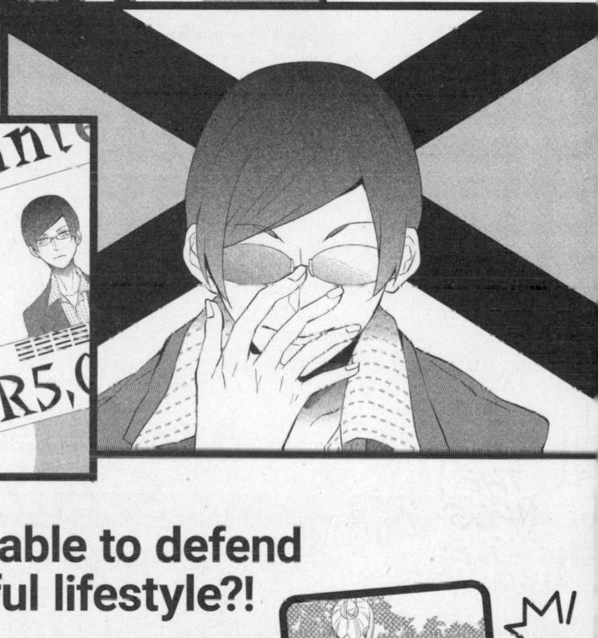

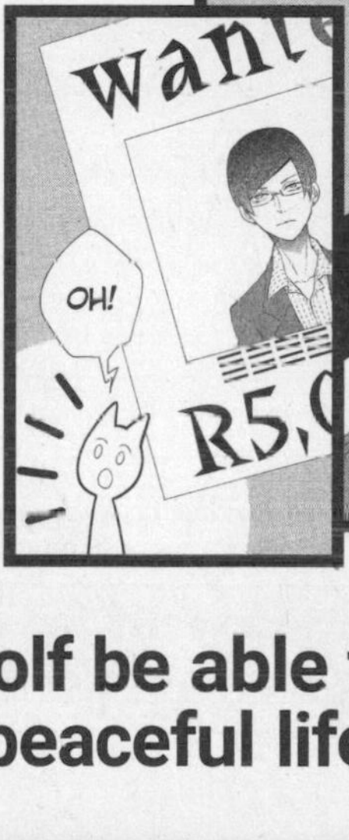
wan
R5,
OH!

More wolves, and a mysterious Wanted poster...

Will Wolf be able to defend his peaceful lifestyle?!

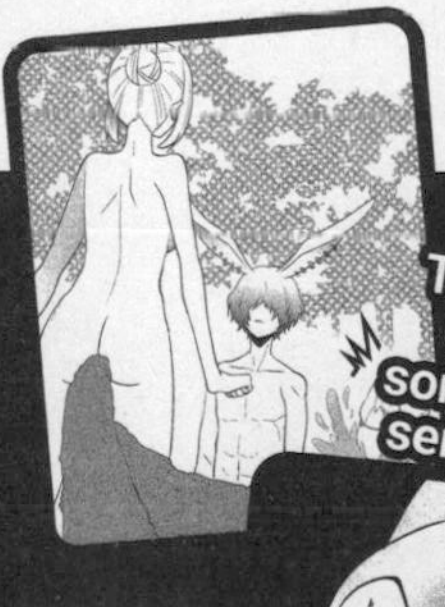

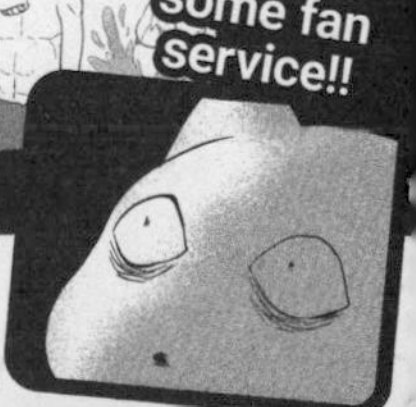

There's even some fan service!!

RED RIDING HOOD AND THE BIG SAD WOLF

Volume 2 Coming Soon!

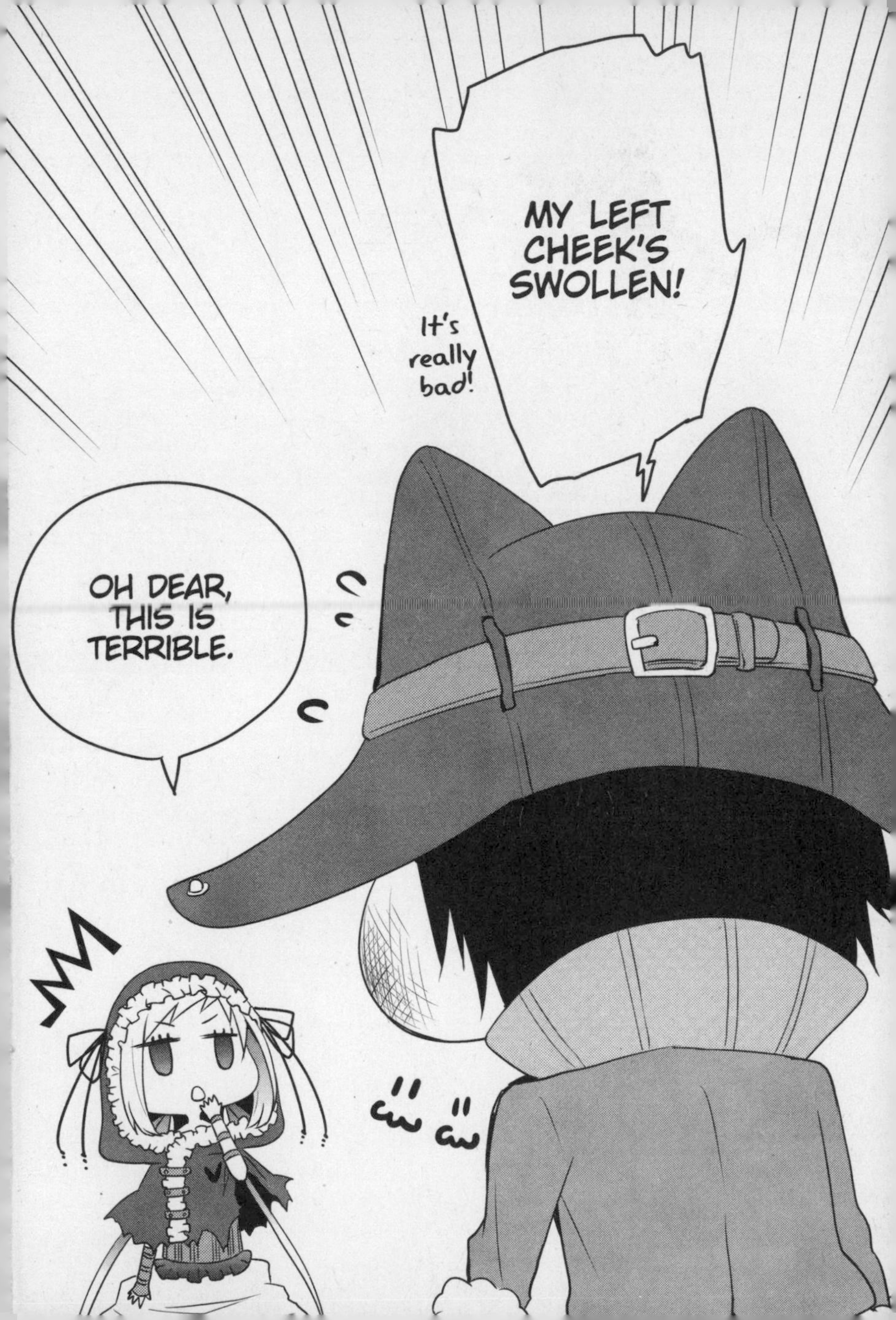
MY LEFT CHEEK'S SWOLLEN!
It's really bad!
OH DEAR, THIS IS TERRIBLE.